THE
CONSERVATIVE
BOOKSHELF

CONTENTS

THE CONSERVATIVE BOOKSHELF

Essential Works That Impact Today's Conservative Thinkers

CHILTON WILLIAMSON, JR.

CITADEL PRESS
Kensington Publishing Corp.
www.kensingtonbooks.com

CITADEL PRESS BOOKS are published by

Kensington Publishing Corp.
850 Third Avenue
New York, NY 10022

All Kensington titles, imprints, and distributed lines are available at special quantity discounts for bulk purchases for sales promotions, premiums, fund-raising, educational, or institutional use. Special book excerpts or customized printings can also be created to fit specific needs. For details, write or phone the office of the Kensington special sales manager: Kensington Publishing Corp., 850 Third Avenue, New York, NY 10022, attn: Special Sales Department; phone 1-800-221-2647.

First Printing: October 2004

10 9 8 7 6 5 4 3 2 1

Printed in the United States of America

Library of Congress Control Number: 2004106010
ISBN: 0-8065-2537-1

To the memory of my father-in-law,
Neil McCaffrey,
And to my mother-in-law,
Joan McCaffrey

V.
THE PROPHETIC ARTIST   209

VI.
THE PRESENT DAY   271

ACKNOWLEDGMENTS

The author wishes to thank Bob Shuman, Senior Editor at Kensington Corporation/Citadel Press, who conceived the idea for this book, and Tony Outhwaite, of JCA, for bringing us together.

Permission to reprint from the following sources is gratefully acknowledged:

Cicero: The Republic (Oxford World Classics), edited by Niall Rudd (translator). By permission of Oxford University Press.

Maistre: Considerations on France by Joseph de Maistre; Richard A. Lebrun (ed./trans.). Reprinted with the permission of Cambridge University Press.

Rationalism in Politics and Other Essays by Michael Oakeshott. Copyright 1962 by Michael Oakeshott. Reprinted by permission of Basic Books, a member of Perseus Books, L.L.C.

Ideas Have Consequences by Richard M. Weaver. ©1948 by the University of Chicago. Reprinted by permission of The University of Chicago Press.

Historical Consciousness: Or, the Remembered Past by John Lukacs. Published by Schocken Books, 1985.

The Road to Serfdom by F. A. Hayek. ©1956 by The University of Chicago. Reprinted by permission of The University of Chicago Press.

Reprinted by permission of Farrar, Straus and Giroux, LLC: Excerpts from *The Habit of Being,* edited by Sally Fitzgerald. Copyright ©1979 by Regina O'Connor. Excerpts from *The Cold War and the Income Tax: A Protest* by Edmund Wilson. Copyright ©1963 by Edmund Wilson. Copyright renewed 1991 by Helen Miranda Wilson.

INTRODUCTION

What is conservatism?

I would say: Conservatism, rightly understood, is man's willingness to discern for himself, and to accept from God, a fundamental, practical, just, human, and unchangeable plan for man—*and to stick with it*. Many necessarily will dissent from this definition, and it is perhaps tautological, as well as disingenuous, to suggest that genuine conservatives must concur. True, the conservative tradition as represented in this book is one man's attempt at a coherent vision of what he considers to be a very great and noble thing. It is untrue, however, that it is *only* one man's, since he has had company aplenty throughout the ages, while continuing to claim many brothers and comrades today—at the onset of the twenty-first century when it is easy for such people to conclude that the world, not as we know it only but as it was meant to be, is coming apart.

Clearly, therefore, the paramount difficulty in bringing together a conservative bookshelf (or library, for that matter) is that, among those people who call themselves conservatives, there is substantial disagreement as to what, exactly, the conservative tradition amounts to and even what "conservatism" actually *is*. This is because conservatism, like any other large historical thing, is not a linear phenomenon but a divergent one, consisting of numerous branches or subsets often in contradiction of each other. The primary distinction within the conservative tradition, almost by definition, is the most hoary one as well. It amounts to the difference between a conservatism founded uncompromisingly on eternal principles and the conservatism that appeals to historical context and the status quo, prudence, and pragmatism.

The term "Rightist" commonly designates conservatives of the first division, while "conservative" denotes those belonging to the second. Thus, a "conservative" seeks to conserve what exists in the present, while a "Rightist" is prepared to dismantle contemporary institutions in order to replace them with ancient ones resurrected from the past—monarchism, say, or the feudal system. In the culture of the modern West, Rightists are always the "extremists" (e.g., Patrick Buchanan), marginalized in public debate and practical politics alike in favor of "conservatives" who have so far discarded absolute principles while emphasizing pragmatist ones as to have become nearly indistinguishable from the relativistic liberals they claim to oppose. The Republican Party in the United States, the Tories in Britain, the Christian Democratic Union in Germany, and the Reassembly for the Republic in France are all exponents of a "practical" conservatism that differs from liberalism less in ideology than in schedule, always keeping a regular two or three paces behind the "opposition" vanguard.

Below the main categories of (a) Right and (b) conservative, we may set subcategories to the two headings. To the A column should be added the monarchists, the Catholic Rightists, the distributists, the agrarians, and the paleoconservatives; under B we may place the libertarian conservatives, the classical liberals, the free traders, the nationalists, and the neoconservatives. (Readers will become familiar with the various types or factions in the following text of this book.) Though some of these groups have at times made alliance with one another politically and borrowed from each other intellectually, in many respects they have little in common, besides their opposition to the common foes of communism, socialism, and corporate liberalism they (unequally) abhor. Environmentalism—a modern radical-liberal movement descended from conservationism and preservationism—has adherents on the Right (though not many among mainstream conservatives), which perceives a connection with both agrarian conservatism and the rugged individualism of the Old Believer (or "Don't Tread on Me" American) tradition. In all this, it is, indeed, difficult at times to discover anything like a coherent "conservative" tradition at all, but only a confused cacophony of opposing voices.

Yet, in the United States and in other Western societies, the meaning of conservatism is anything but an academic subject. Rather, it has become the billion-dollar question in which a great many people and institutions hold vested interests of a pecuniary as well as a career nature. And no wonder, since whoever defines conservatism defines liberalism as well, thus fixing the agenda for the dominant liberal program. If the conservative tradition and the movements claiming to represent it were better defined (also more honest in stating their beliefs and intentions), the dispute among the various claimants—Republican, neoconservative, paleoconservative—would scarcely have the intensity it in fact possesses. The reason, of course, is that a great deal less would hang on the conclusion of their argument. As it is, mainstream conservatism in the historic sense of the term has been almost entirely renovated and updated over the last century and today is in process of being hoisted inboard by the new postmodern progressivism. (Samuel Francis calls it "progressive conservatism.") For reasons that are not far to seek, both the renovation of conservativism and its appropriation by neoliberalism (i.e., neoconservativism) are far easier accomplished if the conservative tradition has first been redefined, reexplained, and reintroduced in terms acceptable to the political, economic, and ideological establishment.

High-powered, high-pressured modern society has largely succeeded in reducing conservatism from a broadly informed religious, intellectual, moral, and aesthetic tradition to a narrow and shallow party politics that often amounts to nothing more than a party line. The Republican Party is the present embodiment of this politics in the United States; yet it has not always been so. True, the GOP, in Abraham Lincoln's War Between the States, destroyed the original federal republic created by the founders; sold out the newly created nation-state to exploitive capitalism as represented by Andrew Johnson's Reconstructionists and to Ulysses S. Grant's robber barons and the industrialists of the Gilded Age; succumbed to imperial temptation in William McKinley's

Spanish-American War; and in 1917 collaborated with the Woodrow Wilson Democrats on the Progressive project of forming tangling alliances by concurring in an internationalist agendum to "make the world safe for democracy." The Republicans ineffectively and timorously opposed the New Deal in the 1930s and the Fair Deal after World War II; in the 1950s, the Dwight D. Eisenhower wing of the party permitted its leaders to accede to a new internationalist program justified by its advocates as necessary to national security in the Cold War. Unless we choose to equate conservatism with capitalism and imperialism, it is hard to make a case for the Republican Party being at any time in its history the party of conservatism.

Yet, for nearly five generations, it displayed many conservative impulses (including what today is demonized as isolationism) while taking on the coloration of much that was indeed conservative in America. The GOP, for one thing, was the party of Main Street, the party of the Midwest and much of the West, the party of the American heartland and small-town America that truly represented a conservative culture—though possibly not conservative in a sense that any sophisticated European observer would have recognized. It was, as we say today, culturally conservative; to a limited extent and by comparison with the multicultural Democratic Party, it still is. Culturally *and* politically speaking, the GOP at its best was represented by Robert A. Taft—"Mr. Republican"—the senator from Ohio, whose commitment to limited government as delineated by the U.S. Constitution and the anti-internationalist vision of the founders made him a lowercase republican as well as a party stalwart and the greatest congressional spokesman in his time for the conservative political tradition. But Taft, who should have received the presidential nomination instead of Eisenhower, died in 1953, and the liberal internationalist wing of his party moved to the fore. Yet, the Republican seachange occurred not in the 1950s but three decades later, as the direct result of an earlier transmutation in the conservative intellectual movement that began in the late 1960s: the rise of neoconservatism.

The radicalism called the New Left that defined and dominated the 1960s was intolerable not only to conservatives; it was too much for a certain kind of liberal as well. Or perhaps I should say "kinds," since the dissenting liberals in this period represented a wide background spectrum, including as they did former communists, socialists, Old Leftists, New Dealers, left liberals, and liberals of the garden variety. These were people who had abandoned, largely or entirely, doctrinaire socialism—without, however, having wholly sloughed off their revolutionary instincts and statist assumptions, and certainly without having replaced them with Rightist or traditionally conservative ones. They called themselves, and were soon called by everyone else, the neoconservatives, though the term "neoliberals" would have suited them just as well (as William Kristol, editor of the *Weekly Standard,* has recently admitted).

In the main, they were (and still are) northeastern academics, opinion journalists, and policy experts associated with various think-tanks and similar institutes, and well-regarded scholars and writers well placed to effect the fusion of responsible liberalism with conservatism to create what they regard as an updated and enlightened version of the traditional variety that would in time (as soon as possible, in fact) crowd out the old conservatism from the public square. How they accomplished this feat is too long and involved a story to be recounted here. The fact is that they did it, in a mere decade and a half and right on schedule for the inauguration of Ronald Reagan as president of the United States. Neoconservative scholars, "experts," and operatives were strongly represented in the two Reagan administrations and in foreign policy posts especially, where they found themselves positioned to develop and promote their program for "national greatness conservatism." This, to neoconservatives, amounted to an imperial prescription for extending, by force if necessary, American political, economic, and cultural institutions to every country and culture in the world, in the name of freedom and "global democracy." In this enterprise of national greatness, the neoconservatives' greatest triumph to date has been George W. Bush's Iraq War, predicted by Richard Perle (one of their leading strategists, formerly of the Defense Department's Defense Policy Board) to be a "cakewalk." (The "neoconservative cabal" and its role in promoting a dishonestly sold war are today a major media story that need not be emphasized here.)

Foreign adventurism, internationalist ambitions, and global crusades have never been conservative enthusiasms, with American conservatives especially. Nor has the old conservatism ever made its peace with big government, the replacement of federalism by centralism, the welfare state, and consumer capitalism. Neoconservatives, by contrast, accept—in fact, they embrace and seek to extend—all of these things, while adding a fervid commitment to multiculturalism and mass immigration from the Third World. No less a figure than Irving Kristol, the founding father of neoconservatism, has stated explicitly that he and his comrades set out to replace the old individualistic, federalistic, free-enterprise, and largely WASP conservatism with something better suited to the realties of a modern industrial welfare state and an increasingly multicultural society. Neoconservatives are distinguished from traditional conservatives not least by their determination to deny notions of peculiar national and cultural identities, which they seek to replace with the fantastical one of the First Universal Nation. Most important, neoconservatives have relentlessly promoted the secularization of government and of society to an extent that is wholly at odds with the explicitly Christian character of the Western tradition. (To our post-Christian age, this may seem a hard saying. Nevertheless, as Hilaire Belloc points out time and time again, it is simply an historical fact.) As, indeed, is the entire agendum of this shallow, arrogant, aggressive, and materialistic thing called neoconservatism; of which the best that can be said is that (as a percipient friend has remarked) it amounts to seven leaders and no followers.

Still, the triumph (however temporary) of neoconservatism is plain to see in the virtually total control the movement exercises over the Republican Party, the "conservative" press, and "conservative" discourse generally. The holdouts are pretty well confined to the "paleoconservatives," who persist in keeping the old conservative flame (Christian faith, national sovereignty and cultural identity, federalism, republicanism, restraint of capitalism, community, agrarianism, and homocentric environmentalism) alight and the conservative libertarians, who combine an inexhaustible enthusiasm for unfettered capitalist activity with respect for religion, traditional culture, national sovereignty, republican government, and anti-imperialism. But the paleoconservatives are few in number and in resources by comparison with the neoconservative intellectual majority; the conservative libertarians disadvantaged by their opposition to foreign adventurism and the New World Order, as well as by their mystical devotion to "free trade," which—as they never tire of pointing out to the embarrassment of almost everyone else—is not the heavily compromised version that goes by the same name today.

In compiling a bookshelf of fifty titles, I set out to select books representing, in the main, the traditional conservative canon. Necessarily, therefore, I have omitted such well-known neoconservative authors as Norman Podhoretz and his wife Midge Decter, Edward Banfield, George Gilder, Daniel Patrick Moynihan, Nathan Glazer, James Q. Wilson, Irving Kristol, and Jean-François Revel (to name a few in a long list of prominent writers) for the reason that, though they certainly hold certain ideas and beliefs in common with the old conservatives, they are not really of the breed. On the other hand, I have sneaked in a writer here and there to whom it would have come as news that he in any way represented the conservative tradition: for example, Edmund Wilson, the literary critic and historian, and Edward Abbey, the environmentalist author. My defense here is that these Old Believers shared more of the conservative tradition and outlook on life and the world than either one of them cared to recognize or admit. Individualists of a uniquely American type, they represented much of what was best in the Old American (the Old Believer) tradition.

With this book, I attempt to present a vision of conservatism having little or nothing to do with the caricature version signified by fat men in top hats and generals with swords that has seemed indelibly stamped on the popular mind since 1789. The conservative tradition has never been an apology for ignorance, superstition, despotism, war, power, wealth, or privilege; rather, it has been their scourge, their mortal enemy. Nor is the conservative tradition a narrow and restricted one; instead, it is as broad and varied as life, having all of life and of human experience in it though rooted in a specific culture, that is, Western culture. The reason for this seeming paradox is that Western culture has always been an eclectic affair created by bold borrowers—world ransackers in a constructive sense having nothing to do with imperialist exploitation and pillage—and creative synthesizers into the bargain. In this sense, Western culture may be understood as the West's giving-back to the cultures it colonized, prosyletized, and civilized, at whatever (admittedly often considerable) cost to themselves. Certainly, the fact of millions of formerly colonized peoples perennially seeking to migrate to the nations of the West suggests that they themselves preceive history that way.

All this by way of saying that what follows is an eclectic, maybe even an eccentric, compendium—because eclectic and eccentric are just what the tradition of the West is. *Conservatism, properly understood, is man's willingness to discern or accept a fundamental and unchangeable plan for man—and stick with it.* As such, it amounts to nothing less than the Western tradition at its deepest, and best.

Anyone with the temerity to select, from the vast literary canon from which the conservative and political intellectual movements of our time have been distilled, a list of fifty essential works is under a moral obligation to defend himself against the charge of presumption. *Fifty books!* From a tradition spanning three millennia and who knows how many thousands of volumes! As a book review editor and all-too-frequent reviewer myself, I had no trouble imagining the asperity with which reviewers were likely to attack so imprudent an exercise. Every conscientious writer is in the business of putting himself on the line daily, but no one is required to step up to the literary equivalent of the Maginot Line. Not only did Citadel Press limit me to fifty books, it requested me to *rank* those books in order of intellectual genius and historical influence!

I had a model before me in the form of Robert Wooster's *The Civil War Bookshelf,* a previous volume in Citadel Press's *Bookshelf* series. A learned, judicious, and beautifully written volume, Professor Wooster's book afforded me scant help nevertheless in designing the one I had been invited to write. The reason was simple: Wooster's job had been to select from a bibliography—a body of mainly academic work on a particular historical event. *I* faced the task of choosing from an intellectual *tradition*—two entirely different things. While it is, inherently, an arbitrary decision to declare any particular volume in a body of academic work on a given topic "number one" or "number fifty" in general importance, numerical designation becomes almost an absurdity when compiling a list of books that are not *about* history but amount, actually, to history itself.

My solution to the problem has been to devise a number of categories comprising the conservative canon, to rank the categories among themselves, and, finally, to order the various individual titles *within* those categories. The categorical ranking principle indicated that I should begin with the comprehensive and transcendental (theology) and conclude with the mundane (contemporary public affairs), having descended through the political, social, economic, and aesthetic levels of Western discourse. Hence, I have put the Bible at the head of the first category, on the indisputable ground that (with the obvious exception of the classical tradition) all of Western thought comes from it. The Bible is followed by the second, third, and forth most significant titles within the capital category, after which I step down to the second category, comprising works on government and politics and headed by Cicero's *The Republic,* which immediately precedes Edmund Burke's classic statement of conservative political thought, *Reflections on the Revolution in France.* Because this organizational plan will likely strike some readers as quixotic, I should point out that it adheres in some sense to the Catholic principle of subsidiarity, borrowed and adapted by generations of conservative thinkers from the Catholic Church; also that it seems (to me) to reflect the medieval concept of the Great Chain of Being, among the most venerable and beautiful concepts of all time.

Unlike Marxism or even liberalism, conservatism is both a way of life and of thinking about life, what the American novelist and story writer Flannery O'Connor calls a "habit of being"—not a plan, program, or even a programmatic way of thought. For this reason, and because conservatism is finally a cultural phenomenon and *all* culture is by definition conservative, I have not hesitated to include fiction, narrative nonfiction, and poetry in my version of the conservative canon; also a volume of letters (O'Connor's) and an autobiography (Whittaker Chambers's *Witness*—quite possibly the most explosive political memoir, after *Mein Kampf,* of the twentieth century). A novelist and story writer myself, I have been consistently tempted to include more of what is fatuously called "creative writing," but resisted the temptation. Though some of the greatest conservative writers have been novelists, poets, and playwrights, the fact remains that, as with all great artists, their message is their medium, not an articulated statement. Moreover, the present time is not only a narrowly politicized age, it is one from which conservative political, social, and economic ideas have largely been excluded, owing to liberalism's control of the terms of debate. In a time of pills and potions, soundbites and slogans, there is an enormous need for explicit encapsulated truths and insights, intellectual concepts taken neat or on the rocks. (When you are allowed just fifty of them to swallow, especially.)

I should add that, from the start, I took for granted the assumption that conservatism means Western conservatism, not the equivalent traditions of China, India, Byzantium, and so forth. Our subject here is restricted to Europe—Britain, France, Germany, Spain, and Russia—and the United States. It would be possible, I imagine, to apply the same principles to a compendium of world conservatism, if such a thing could be identified, but possibility is not the same thing as practicability. Or desirability. One way or another, the subject lies beyond the scope of this volume.

Laramie, Wyoming

Part I
RELIGION

1

THE BIBLE

The Bible—the Old and New Testaments—is the history of God's people under the Old Dispensation and the revelation of the New through His intervention on the history of the world. It is also the bedrock of Western civilization, as it was mysteriously anticipated by the greatest minds (Socrates, Plato) of the classical pagan civilization that preceded it.

"All culture," Russell Kirk writes, "arises out of religion." And culture, as I have said, is essentially a conservative project.

Europe, Hilaire Belloc says—he says it over and over—is the Faith, and the Faith is Europe. By "the Faith," Belloc as a Catholic means the Catholic Church: an historical view that Protestants must of course find wanting. Whether we are speaking of Catholicism or Protestantism, however, Christianity and the West (before the onset of the post-Christian era) were not only inseparable but unimaginable apart from one another, and never more so than when they appeared to be at odds—even at each other's throats. The West does have a rationalist anti-Christian tradition already six or seven centuries old, yet the basis of this tradition is, unshakably, Christian, and not just reactively but formatively and in essence. (In other words, anti-Christianism is often a Christian heresy, not a new religion, or an antireligion: scientism and humanism are examples.) The truth of Belloc's observation that the West and Christian culture are (were) identical is demonstrated by the fact that the anti-Western and anti-Christian forces in our time hold their ultimate enemy in common. All of these have identified the Christian religion as the principal object for destruction and the civilization associated with it a secondary target only, providing convenient cover for their agenda and a carefully arranged distraction from their ultimate aim.

"All culture arises out of religion."

Because the business of conservatives is the preservation of culture, that is reason enough for them to hold their religious belief and institutions in high regard. Another reason is their assurance not only in a Truth and a Power above anything man can supply of himself, but their faith in the demonstrable existence of *Absolute Truth* and *Absolute Power* forever unchanged and unchanging, communicating themselves to men by natural law supported and illuminated by Divine Revelation, and enjoining on them natural and supernatural responsibilities. This is not to ignore men and women who, though professing agnostics, secularists, and philosophical relativists, have displayed a cast of thought that is congruent with the conservative mind, in certain moods and on particular occasions, at least: taking "conservative" positions on social and political issues, entertaining "conservative" ideas and cultivating "conservative" sentiments, and writing books and creating works of art that express and embody the "conservative" understanding and appreciation of man and his place in the universe. Certain of these—for example, Michael Oakeshott, Friederich Hayek, Ernest Hemingway, Edmund Wilson, and Edward Abbey—are indeed included in this book. (Oakeshott, arguably the leading philosopher of conservatism in the twentieth century and a religious skeptic, argues that all that political conservatism requires is a belief in the desirability of limited government organized toward limited ends, for which a commitment to religious belief, notions of social hierarchy, tradition, and so forth are dispensable.) That said, however, piety (not necessarily of a formal kind) and an openness to the absolute remain the dominant, indestructible, inseparable component, and also the animating principle, of the generic conservative mind.

"All culture arises out of religion."

That is to say, specific cultures are grounded in specific religions. The cultures of Asian and Middle Eastern civilizations quite naturally are integrated with the lessons of Mohammed, Buddha, Confucius, Zoroaster, and the Dalai Lama. By contrast, Western civilization has internalized the teachings of Christ and of His Old Testament prefiguration, Moses; of St. Paul, St. John, and St. Peter. Books, the American novelist Cormac McCarthy observes, come from other books. And so it is not for Christian conservatives alone but Western conservatives generally that the Bible has been, for two millennia, the Book of Books, from which—however indirectly or confrontationally—all books since classical times have been made.

2

THE ABOLITION OF MAN

by C. S. Lewis

1947

Clive Staples Lewis (1898–1963), the Oxford and (later) Cambridge don who became the most famous literary apologist for Christianity in the twentieth century, was a novelist, poet, essayist, and literary critic with a particular talent for what is usually described as "children's literature." In fact, both the space trilogy (*Out of the Silent Planet, Perelandra*, and *That Hideous Strength)* and the fairy tales (e.g., the seven Narnia volumes beginning with *The Lion, the Witch, and the Wardrobe)* have delighted children of all ages—more accurately, perhaps, adults of every age. A native of Belfast, Ireland, who fought in World War I and was wounded in France, Lewis—like his Roman Catholic counterpart, G. K. Chesterton—took his own good time in confessing Christianity (the process is described in the recent book *The Most Reluctant Convert: C. S. Lewis's Conversion to Faith* by David C. Downing), in 1931 at the age of thirty-three. In *The Abolition of Man,* published in 1943, Lewis set forward in three lectures the critique of modern education he was shortly to dramatize in the space stories. A mere 120 pages long (with notes), this slim volume is central to the entire body of Lewis's work.

Its subject is the existential core of human existence, introduced by Lewis (borrowing from the Chinese tradition) as the *Tao,* or Way. "[This] is the reality beyond all predicates, the abyss that was before the Creator Himself. It is Nature, it is the Way, the Road. It is the Way in which the universe goes on, the Way in which things everlastingly emerge, stilly and tranquilly, into space and time. It is also the Way in which every man should tread in imitation of that cosmic and supercosmic progression, conforming all activities to that great exemplar." The *Tao,* Lewis explains, is not Christianity, or Judaism, or Platonism, or Aristotelianism, or Stoicism, or Orientalism. It is, rather, all of these—the expression of mankind's immemorial commitment to the concept of objective truth and moral value, which only in modern times has been challenged by the subjectivist, the relativist, the explainer-away: those persons familiar to us moderns as the Intellectual, the Innovator, the Conditioner who, stepping outside of the *Tao,* propose to create a superior Way constructed from materials wholly extraneous to it.

There are, Lewis emphasizes, but two stances to be taken in relation to the *Tao:* either inside it or outside it. Even this choice is more limited than it might appear, since those without the *Tao* are utterly unable to comprehend it from that vantage—and thus to make intelligent criticism of it. The outsider demands to know *Why?* and *Who said?* and *How do you know?*—impertinent questions that quite literally have no answers, since the *Tao* cannot justify itself—or be justified—on any grounds other than its own, for reasons theoretical and logical as well as ontological. Even if that were possible, however, the Innovator's position is futile, as well as impious. ("You must not hold a pistol to the head of the *Tao.*") "Let us suppose for a moment that the harder virtues could really be theoretically justified with no appeal to objective value. It still remains true that no justification of virtue will enable a man to be virtuous."

Of course, the Innovator recognizes values (incompatible with the traditionalist ones he debunks) about which he is not in the least subjective, since he regards them as essential to the nontraditionalist society he considers desirable. ("[His] skepticism about values is on the surface: it is for use on other people's values: about the values current in [his] own set [he is] not nearly sceptical enough.") The problem, wholly insoluble, for him is that the only way for him to justify *any* value, and any concept of value, is by reference to the rational core based on the practical principles men call Reason, as embodied in the *Tao* and that he is out to deny on "basic" or "realistic" grounds. "All the practical principles behind the Innovator's case for [innovation] are there from time immemorial in the *Tao*. But they are nowhere else. Unless you accept these without question as being to the world of action what axioms are to the world of theory, you can have no practical principles whatever. You cannot reach them as conclusions; they are premises."

If the *Tao* is only to be understood on its own terms, so, it seems, is everything else. "The Innovator attacks traditional values (the *Tao*) in defence of what he at first supposes to be (in some special sense) 'rational' or 'biological' values. But . . . all the values which he uses in attacking the *Tao*, and even claims to be substituting for it, are themselves derived from the *Tao*. . . . The rebellion of new ideologies against the *Tao* is a rebellion of the branches against the tree: if the rebels could succeed they would find that they had destroyed themselves." Finally, "[t]he human mind has no more power of inventing a new value than of imagining a new primary colour, or, indeed, of creating a new sun and a new sky for it to move in."

The great problem is the extreme difficulty the modern mind experiences in comprehending the *Tao* and accepting its authority. For moderns, the *Tao* is not an absolute, but a phenomenon like any other phenomenon, whether of nature or the mind of man. "Of course, while we did not know how minds were made, we accepted this mental furniture as a datum, even as a master. But many things in nature which were once our masters have become our servants. Why not this? Why must our conquest of nature stop short, in stupid reverence, before this final and toughest bit of 'nature' which has hitherto been called the conscience of man?"

Man, having mastered (to a certain extent: a lesser one, actually, than he imagines) his environment, would be free to choose his own destiny, thus mastering himself. This project would be accomplished in the name of "conquering nature"; the final battle with nature would then have been won. Yet who, in the context, *is* this "Man"? The conquest of nature would amount, really, to the acquisition of power by certain men to make other men what they decide they should be; to the rule of some hundreds of men over many billions of them, present and future. In order to accomplish this renovational program, the Conditioners must first select an artificial *Tao* to serve as a template in the production of the new Man. Thus they will be the motivators, and the creators of the new motives. "But how are they going to be motivated themselves?" Only by moving beyond the original *Tao*, by sacrificing, in effect, their share in traditional humanity for the purpose of deciding what the new, artificial humanity will look like. In doing so, they must eschew every notion of value, for which the satisfaction of irrational impulse must substitute. For "[e]very motive they try to act on becomes at once a *petitio*. It is not that they are bad men. They are not men at all. Stepping outside the *Tao*, they have stepped into the void. Nor are their subjects necessarily unhappy men. They are not men at all; they are artifacts. Man's final conquest has proved to be the abolition of Man." In this way, the "end of history" (imagined by one prominent neoconservative historian, Francis Fukuyama, as the establishment of a *Tao* designed for the production of a race of secular social-democratic-capitalist consumers) would be achieved.

In 120 pages, C. S. Lewis describes the core of the Left's historic agendum—the dehumanization of man and the invention of a humanoid alternative—and identifies conservatism's essential task: the determined and effective resistance of both.

3

CITY OF GOD

by St. Augustine

A.D. 413–426

City of God by Aurelius Augustinus (354–430)—or Augustine of Hippo, or, more familiarly, St. Augustine—is one of the towering works of the human intellect: a book to be studied, not read. Together with his contemporaries, St. Ambrose and St. Jerome, among the fathers of the Christian Church, Augustine is also the foundation block of Western thought in the postclassical Christian era. The importance of *City of God* has to do with its reconciliation of ancient paganism, pre-Christian Hebraicism, imperial Roman paganism, and early Christianity in making sense, for Christian minds, of Western history in all its confusing, paradoxical, and contradictory elements. Augustine's book accomplishes this feat by explaining history as a reciprocating process of the divine and the profane, the supernatural and the natural, the elect and the unredeemed, operating through the medium of time across the ages. It is fair to say that the intellectual tradition of the Christian West, with all its fundamental and distinctive components brought together at last, begins with the "publication" of

City of God, whose twenty-two books were written over a period of thirteen years, between 413 and 426.

Augustine, Bishop of Hippo Regius (after Carthage the second largest town in North Africa) where he had settled four years after his baptism in Milan in 387 to live as a monk in his native land, had lesser ambitions and a narrower end in mind as he began his book. Three years earlier, in 410, Alaric and his army had sacked Rome, a disaster for which the city's senatorial families and others of the pagan upper class blamed the Christians, whom they accused of bringing down on all Romans, impartially and without distinction, the wrath of the flouted gods of Rome, against whom even their own God of the Cross had been helpless or unwilling to save His people. Numerous wealthy and powerful citizens fled across the Mediterranean to Africa, where they continued to inveigh against the impious Christians. "This," Augustine later explains, "fired me with zeal for the house of God and I began to write the *City of God* to confute their blasphemies and falsehood."

City of God, composed over a period of many years and amid frequent interruptions, is neither a well-formed book nor, for the most part, a stylistically distinguished one. Owing to the intellectual decadence of the times, Augustine's education was largely in rhetoric, of which he had been a professor in Milan; ignorant of Greek history, thought, and literature, he knew almost nothing of Plato and nothing at all of Aristotle. As David Knowles observes, "It is a measure of the capacity and power of Augustine's mind that one who had never been trained in philosophical method . . . could himself join the select company of the world's greatest thinkers and be a prime agency in weaving Greek thought into Christian theology." Augustine's intellectual triumph was made possible to a considerable extent by a familiarity with the Neoplatonists. Yet, his book is shapeless, discursive, and self-distracted. Hardly a model of classic literary form, it fails to present its author as a systematic social or political thinker. *City of God* is among those works of genius that succeed against the odds, and against themselves.

Augustine's main preoccupation in this sprawling book of over

a thousand pages is to present the human world as divided between
two cities, the City of God and the City of Man, existing side by
side throughout history but overlapping also and intermingling,
institutionally as well as in terms of individual souls. The first is
comprised of God's people (the Pilgrim Church on Earth), the
second of those self-dedicated to the ways of man rather than to
the ways of God. Each city progresses toward its own separate
destiny awaiting it at the end of the world; until then, the two remain yoked together in a perplexing, sometimes tragic, and often
frustrating symbiosis in which, however, men with the aid of
Scripture and the Church may discern God's scheme for the salvation of man.

"God's City," Augustine explains, "lives in this world's city, as
far as its human element is concerned; but it lives there as an
alien sojourner." In his view, the City—or People—of God has always existed, at times in families or as a tribe. Thus, having re-
futed the enemies of God at the beginning of his book, he "write[s]
about the origin, the development, and the destined ends of the
two cities." Augustine traces humanity's twin lines of descent as
we read of them in the Old Testament, starting with the offspring
of Adam and Eve and proceeding on their separate ways: "Of
these two first parents of the human race, then, Cain was the first-
born, and he belonged to the city of men; after him was born
Abel, who belonged to the city of God. . . . [It] is recorded of
Cain that he built a city, but Abel, being a sojourner, built none.
For the city of the saints is above, although here below it begets
citizens, in whom it sojourns till the time of its reign arrives . . ."
Augustine next recounts the history of the earthly kingdom (the
Egyptians, the Greeks, the Assyrians, the Romans) in parallel
with the history of the Jews, from the birth of Abraham down to
the coming of Christ, and to the Jewish prophets' foretelling the
event of Christ's birth. In conclusion to book 18, immediately before his speculations on the last persecutions and the coming of
the Antichrist, Augustine makes the famous assertion that, just as
the Church contains the reprobate, or damned, in addition to the
elect, so the earthly city and the Jewish people both number many
godly persons, whom God in His wisdom has ordained to dwell

apart, physically or institutionally, from the People of God. Plainly, Augustine fails to draw clear distinctions between God's People as a leaven within pagan society, God's People as the Church (the mystical Body of Christ), and God's People ordered as a nation— a failing, if such it is, that has been noted by innumerable readers.

It has been observed, fairly, that *City of God* is less a discrete book than it is a succession of commentaries on various aspects of a single loosely defined subject. Only the first few books, for instance, directly address the author's stated purpose in writing this work, which was to confound the pagan Romans who asserted that the sack of Rome amounted to the revenge of the city's gods for having been denied and insulted by the Christian minority. (Rather, Augustine argues, those Romans "should give credit to this Christian era for the fact that these savage barbarians showed mercy beyond the custom of war—whether they so acted in general in honor of the name of Christ, or in places specially dedicated to Christ's name, buildings of such size and capacity as to give mercy a wider range.") The gods failed to save Ilium, as well as Rome, who owed her success not to the gods—who delight in, and even demand, obscenity both on stage and in their own religious ceremonies—but to her own virtue. These gods, if they exist at all, are rather demons, who can bless men neither with worldly happiness nor with eternal life.

Having dealt to his satisfaction with the denigrators of Christianity, Augustine proceeds to ridicule the "select" gods of Rome and to praise by contrast the Platonists as being near-Christians. He defends the truth of Scripture, discussing the scriptural understanding of creation, time, and angels, and also the nature of evil, which he calls nonexistent of itself, and causeless. ("Evil is contrary to nature; in fact it can only do harm to nature; and it would not be a fault to withdraw from God were it not that it is more natural to adhere to him. It is that fact which makes the withdrawal a fault. That is why the *choice* of evil is an impressive proof that the *nature* is good.") He confronts apparent scriptural "problems" such as man's creation, the existence of human monsters, unnatural longevity, and so forth, and suggests explanations for these mysteries. After this, he fixes the histories of the People of God and their earthly nemesis in relation to one another. Finally, in the last four books, Augustine deals with the nature of mankind's supreme good (which he identifies as peace), with the Last Judgment, the nature of eternal punishment, the Creation and Resurrection, and the Vision of God. Also, he returns to the subject of Scipio Aemilianus's understanding of the nature of the Republic, which he discussed earlier in the text. (Scipio, for having destroyed Carthage and Numantia, was one of the great heroes of the second century B.C.) And here Augustine appears to make a profound contribution to the modern understanding of the state, and of society itself.

G. K. Chesterton says that the problem with the modern world is not that it is wrong, but that it is crazed. Craze is a function of modernism's addiction to, and worship of, chaos: the satanic perversion of the divine order established by God. Augustine, in *City of God*, shows himself to have been keenly aware that the interests of the City of God are directly advanced by the encouragement of worldly peace and order in the City of Man. (That is why St. Paul instructs us to pray for our rulers.) And peace and order in the City of Man are furthered by the recognition of distinctions among individual men and among the peoples of the earth. If these distinctions are not observed, the social order of the earthly city tends to break toward chaos; and chaos operates to the detriment of the heavenly one, whose tribulations on earth are only deepened by social (and political) turmoil and confusion.

Augustine seems to have recognized the difficulties socially complicated societies face in maintaining order and holding chaos at bay, thus securing the ultimate salvation of the City of God. A degree of social complexity is, of course, not just inevitable but a part of God's plan for humanity as long as the present world shall last. On the other hand, complexity needs to be minimized wherever possible, to ensure the social order, intellectual coherence, and religious orthodoxy the Christian faith requires to accomplish its task of saving the greatest number of souls, while preparing the world as a final offering to be laid at the feet of Christ at the Second Coming.

"This heavenly city, then," Augustine writes,

> while it sojourns on earth, calls citizens out of all nations, and
> gathers together a society of pilgrims of all languages, not scru-
> pling about diversities in the manners, laws, and institutions,
> whereby earthly peace is secured and maintained, but recogniz-
> ing that, however various these are, they all tend to one and the
> same end of earthly peace. It therefore is so far from rescinding
> and abolishing these diversities, that it even preserves and
> adapts them, so long only as no hindrance to the worship of the
> one supreme and true God is thus introduced.

At first glance, this passage might easily be construed as advocating the creation of what a contemporary journalist has adver-
tised as the First Universal Nation, comprising "a society of
pilgrims of all languages." A closer reading shows that the "citizens" are called "out" in a spiritual way, rather than in a physical
sense: not from within the boundaries of their earthly nations to create a supernation in some other part of the world (such as America), but from the confinements of their spiritual ignorance and
sin, to bear witness to the God Who is Truth in their own lands.

And so today's shibboleth—multiculturalism—for St. Augustine would not be the outrageous contradiction in terms as we
know it, but the genuine thing: what used to be called the international community, its international components leavened to a
greater or lesser extent by centers or outposts of the heavenly one.

4

MEDITATIONS

by Marcus Aurelius

A.D. 167

The earliest English translations of Marcus Aurelius's *Meditations* appeared in 1634 and 1701. They remained scarcely known to the English-speaking public, however, before a widely popular one was made in 1862. Marcus's book (titled by the author "To Himself") illustrates how closely classical paganism at its best anticipated the Christian religion that, following immediately after it, animated Western civilization for nearly two thousand years. Of all the ancients, none better than Marcus Aurelius (121–180) deserves to be remembered as the Saintly Pagan. (Henry James, after viewing Marcus's equestrian statue in the Campidoglio in Rome, reflects that "in the capital of Christendom, the portrait most suggestive of a Christian conscience is that of a pagan emperor.")

In point of fact, Marcus's birthdate *was* A.D. 121—not 121 B.C. Educated in the Stoic tradition, he is counted among the last of the Stoics, whose teachings the early doctors of the Church considered in formulating an explicitly Christian philosophy from pagan antecedents.

16

The Stoics, in their conception of Reason, anticipated the Word ("Logos"), as in John I:1 ("In the beginning was the Word, and the Word was with God, and the Word was God."), while their trinity of God, Wisdom, and holy Spirit clearly anticipates the Christian Trinity of Father, Son, and Holy Ghost. As pantheists, they believed the universe to comprise an articulated society; Marcus himself expresses the idea when he writes that "the world is a single city" and refers to the "dear city of God" and "the primordial City and Commonwealth." As thorough-going materialists, the Stoics were hardly susceptible to the Gnostic view that the universe is divided between the material and the immaterial, Darkness and Light, Evil and Good. On the other hand, deprived of the concept of the Incarnation, Marcus saw one City embracing God and men—the good and the bad alike, united as brothers—where St. Augustine, three centuries later, was to perceive two, inhabited by the regenerate and the unregenerate living side by side. Christian believers may easily discover in this partial prefiguration of Christian understanding supporting evidence of G. K. Chesterton's assertion (in *Everlasting Man*) that Christ entered history at that precise moment when history had at last been prepared to receive Him.

Non-Christians as well as Christians, however, will not fail to perceive the striking and often-noted similarities between Marcus's *Meditations* and Thomas à Kempis's great devotional work *The Imitation of Christ*. The *Meditations* anticipate also the late medieval model and ideal of the Christian ruler, whose faith is expressed by his fairness, liberality, humanity, Christian wisdom and judgment, and self-control. Maxwell Staniforth (a Catholic priest as well as a classicist and translator) explains how Marcus should be read as a transitional figure in Stoic history, owing to his substitution of something approaching Christian humility for Stoicism's signature virtue of pride. Certainly, the following passage might have been written by any sincere and devout Christian:

Begin the morning by saying to yourself, I shall meet with the busybody, the ungrateful, arrogant, deceitful, envious, unsocial.

All these things happen to them by reason of their ignorance of what is good and evil. But I who have seen the nature of the good that it is beautiful, and of the bad that it is ugly, and the nature of him who does wrong, that it is akin to me, not [only] of the same blood or seed, but that it participates in [the same] intelligence and [the same] portion of the divinity, I can neither be injured by any of them, for no one can fix on me what is ugly, nor can I be angry with my kinsman, nor hate him. For we are made for co-operation, like feet, like hands, like eyelids, like the rows of the upper and lower teeth. To act against one another then is contrary to nature; and it is acting against one another to be vexed and to turn away.

This paragraph is the more telling when one reflects that the interference, ingratitude, arrogance, deceit, envy, and selfishness referred to were the daily lot of a Roman emperor, who ruled jointly with Lucius Verus (whom Marcus invited to share the throne with him) from 161 to 169 and, after the co-emperor's death, singly until his own death eleven years later.

Marcus's reign was marked from its inception by famine, plague, military rebellion in Asia, and barbarian invasion. In 167, the emperor traveled from Rome to the Danube, where he assumed personal command of his legions and where he composed the *Meditations*. ("To Himself" is really the superior title if only for the reason that it encourages the reader to recall that this small volume of maxims, aphorisms, and exhortations is addressed not to the reader but to the author, whose moral fervor is of the self-improving, rather than of the other-improving, sort.) In his cold and damp military camp, Marcus was infected by contagion and died on March 17, 180, aged fifty-nine.

"Weep not for me," he told his surrounding officers, "think rather of the pestilence and deaths of so many others." "[I]t is the part of the intellectual faculty . . . [t]o observe too," he writes in "To Himself," "what death is, and the fact that, if a man looks at it in itself, and by the abstractive power of reflection resolves into their parts all things which present themselves to the imagination in it, he will then consider it to be nothing else than an operation of nature; and if any one is afraid of an operation of nature, he is a child. This, however, is not only an operation of nature, but it is also a thing which conduces to the purposes of nature. To observe too how man comes near the deity, and by what part of him, and when this part of man is so disposed." Furthermore, ". . . remember that no man loses any other life than this which he now lives, nor lives any other than this which he now loses. The longest and shortest are thus brought to the same. For the present is the same to all, though that which perishes is not the same; and so that which is lost appears to be a mere moment. For a man cannot lose either the past or the future; for what a man has not, how can any one take this from him?"

Thirteen hundred and forty-eight years after Marcus's death, the publication of Baldassare Castiglione's *The Book of the Courtier* (1528) established the Neoplatonic model for the ideal courtier—learned, cultivated, socially refined, adept with weapons, physically graceful, and, above all, artfully artless and nonchalant—from which in turn the ideal of the English gentleman developed. As if to anticipate Castiglione's courtier, the Stoic Marcus Aurelius had created—thirteen centuries earlier—an equally compelling model for the ideal ruler: humble, conscientious, considerate, pious, and self-controlled, as well as responsibly controlling. (It is worth noting here that Marcus brutally persecuted his Christian subjects, never hesitating to put women and children to the sword.) The *Meditations,* in addition to being a great work of literary art and of moral philosophy, stands as well as a compelling monument to the mental and moral continuity of the Western mind in transition between the pagan age, the Christian era, and the Renaissance.

Whether the greatness of his achievement and its longevity would have impressed the author himself is open to question. "Short then is the time," Marcus writes, "which every man lives, and small the nook of the earth where he lives; and short too the longest posthumous fame, and even this only continued by a succession of poor human beings, who will very soon die, and who know not even themselves, much less him who died long ago."

Part II
POLITICS

_____

5

THE REPUBLIC

by Cicero

54–52 B.C.

Marcus Tullius Cicero (106–43 B.C.) completed *De Republica* less than a decade before the Roman Republic he wrote to praise and to commend to posterity perished in the throes of civil warfare. Though no book, perhaps, has been more relentlessly studied and written about than *The Republic,* the book as we have it is scarcely less of a ruin than the Roman Forum, its historical embodiment. The largest part has survived as a palimpsest in the Vatican Library, the superscribed text being a copy of St. Augustine's commentary of the Psalms made in the eighth century. Vast portions of the work are simply lost to history; in other instances, fragments exist as reflected images and embedded particles included as quotations in works by later writers (Augustine, Lactantius, and Nonius Marcellus), while the concluding "Dream of Scipio" has been preserved by separate tradition. Courtesy of Augustine's *City of God,* we have an explicit statement of the author's purpose in writing *The Republic.* In book 5, Cicero in his introduction quotes from Ennius, where the Roman poet writes,

On ancient customs and old-fashioned men
The state of Rome stands firm.

Cicero continues:

The compactness and truth of that line are such that the poet
who uttered it must, I think, have been prompted by an oracle.
For neither the men on their own (in a state which lacked such
a moral tradition) nor the state on its own (without such men in
charge) could have founded or long maintained so great and
wide-ranging an empire. Long before living memory our ances-
tral way of life produced outstanding men, and those excellent
men preserved the old way of life and the institutions of their
forefathers. Our generation, however, after inheriting our political organization like a magnificent picture now fading with
age, not only neglected to restore its original colours but did
not even bother to ensure that it retained its basic form and, as
it were, its faintest outlines. What remains of those ancient customs on which he said the state of Rome stood firm? We see
them so ruined by neglect that not only do they go unobserved,
they are no longer known. And what shall I say of the men? It is
the lack of such men that has led to the disappearance of those
customs. Of this great tragedy we are not only bound to give a
description; we must somehow defend ourselves as if we were
arraigned on a capital charge. For it is not by accident—no, it is
because of our moral failings—that we are left with the name of
the Republic, having lost since lost its substance.

When he wrote these words, Cicero, returned home from exile
into which the tribune Clodius had forced him, had maneuvered
himself into an impossible position between Pompey, Caesar, and
Crassus on the one hand and the optimates (aristocratical sena-
tors) on the other. Ensconced in his villa in Cumae in prudent re-
tirement from politics, Cicero determined to devote himself to
writing and to philosophy. *The Republic,* though described by the
author himself as a political treatise, is so only in the sense that
politics in the Roman world was regarded as a branch of philosophy, itself an aspect of the study of ethics. Certainly, Cicero wrote

with no narrow or immediate political purpose in mind, as his cautious decision to set his imaginary dialogue between Scipio Aemilianus (the Roman general who razed Carthage and Numantia) and his friends in the second century B.C. suggests. His models, therefore, were Plato and Aristotle—and not the statesman (himself) who, in better days and by one of the most famous orations in history, had destroyed the conspirator Cataline.

It is true that the Roman Republic was in crisis as Cicero labored at Cumae; yet politics, for him as for the tradition he represented both as an active politician and a philosopher, was more than a vocation, it was a form of substantive knowledge, like rhetoric or geometry. Thus, one of Cicero's principal concerns (so far as we can tell) in his book was to consider the three basic forms of government—monarchy, aristocracy, and democracy—from the point of view of justice, stability, and longevity; to show how one form tends to evolve into another; to suggest the preferability of a mixed government, embodying the other three in proportion, to one of the unmixed type; and finally, to establish the superiority of the Roman constitution, as it evolved across centuries, over every other. "[A] state should be organized in such a way," Cicero has Laelius say, "as to last forever. And so the death of a state is never natural, as it is with a person, for whom death is not only inevitable but also frequently desirable. Again, when a state is destroyed, eliminated, and blotted out, it is rather as if (to compare small with great) this whole world were to collapse and pass away." In fact, the Roman constitution praised by Cicero was even at that moment passing away, though the Roman state itself had centuries yet to live.

Unlike republicans of a later age—most notably the architects of the American Articles of Confederation as well as, in a lesser degree, the framers of the U.S. Constitution—the Romans of the Republican era saw the state as the creator (rather than the creation, expression, or preserver of) the good society. "The good life," Cicero thought, "is impossible without a good state; and [so] there is no greater blessing than a well-ordered state." This state, the republic, is the property of the public, but not of "any kind of human gathering, congregating in any manner, but a numerous gathering brought together by legal consent and community of interest." (The voguish concept of the twenty-first-century United States as the world's "first universal republic" would not have been convincing to Cicero.) "So the aim of our ideal statesman is the citizen's happy life—that is, a life secure in wealth, rich in resources, abundant in renown, and honourable in its moral character. That is the task which I wish him to accomplish—the greatest and best that any man can have."

For Cicero—the quintessential Roman, dedicated to the concept of the nobility of the law and the practical ideal—the highest ambition and calling was that of the statesman, who combined the speculative with the active ideal in his role as practical philosopher. For this reason, Cicero included in *The Republic* books devoted to the subjects of justice, education and morals, and the character of the ideal statesmen—only fragments of which survive by comparison with what we have regarding Roman history and the development of the Roman constitution. Book 3, finally, looks forward to *The Laws* (which Cicero wrote as a sequel to *The Republic*) in Laelius's disquisition on justice and natural law, defined here as "right reason in harmony with nature." The natural law, Laelius continues,

is spread through the whole human community, unchanging and eternal, calling people to their duty by its commands and deterring them from wrong-doing by its prohibitions. . . . This law cannot be countermanded, nor can it be in any way amended, nor can it be totally rescinded. We cannot be exempted from this law by any degree of the Senate or the people; nor do we need anyone else to expound or explain it. There will not be one such law in Rome, and another in Athens, one now and another in the future, but all peoples at all times will be embraced by a single and eternal and unchangeable law; and there will be, as it were, one lord and master of us all—the god who is the author, proposer, and interpreter of that law. Whoever refuses to obey it will be turning his back on himself.

The Republic can be understood as being to some extent an adaptation of Plato's *Republic* to the Roman political mind, concerned equally with matters of theory and practice; in a later age, it served as a model for republican theory and virtue, for British philosophers and statesmen in particular—and hence for their American counterparts in the founding era. As a practical politician himself, Cicero had his successes; also the defeats and failures that led to his proscription and assassination following the reconciliation of Octavian and Antony. Plutarch, in his "Life of Cicero," recounts how the emperor Augustus discovered a grandson of his trying to conceal the book he had been reading beneath his cloak, and took it from him. The volume was one by Cicero, in whose death Augustus had been complicit. As the boy watched in trepidation, his grandfather stood by him, carefully turning over the pages. "That was a master of words, my boy," Augustus said gravely. "A master of words and a lover of his country." And he gave the book back.

6

REFLECTIONS ON THE REVOLUTION IN FRANCE

by Edmund Burke

1790

Edmund Burke (1729–1797) is generally regarded as the father, or founder, of modern conservatism. Yet, being conservative, Burke was liberal—as Russell Kirk observes in *The Conservative Mind: From Burke to Eliot.* That is to say, as a lifelong defender of liberty and justice, which he believed to be inextricably linked both in nature and in fortune, he was liberal-*minded,* within the spacious framework of inherited tradition accumulated over the ages.

Burke, the son of a Dublin lawyer and a Protestant who served for some years as the Member from Bristol in the House of Commons, was associated most famously in his political career with the Rockingham Whigs in Parliament and with that party's sympathetic policies relating to the restive American colonies. Burke was as ready to admit the necessity of change as to insist on the indispensability of the tradition modified, so long as change was not transformative—or, in the rare instance in which transformation was necessary, it accomplished its ends through delicate, prudent, and nonrevolutionary means. The humane flexibility and patient tolerance of Burke's thought is directly attributable to its completely nonideological character. Burke despised what he derided as the closet philosophers of the Age of Reason who had devised rationalistic social and political systems based on the discovery of abstract human rights derived from an atheistic metaphysics. He put his faith in Providence, which he regarded as binding the dead, the living, and the unborn together in one vast providential scheme whose divinely ordained direction ought not necessarily to be conflated with what men call "progress." Though not as strongly as Alexis de Tocqueville after him, Burke nevertheless regarded an increase in the democratic element in politics and society to be inevitable in the coming era of European civilization. What alarmed and outraged him, intellectually as well as morally, was the spectacle—in France, in 1789—of the thoughtlessly deliberate and violent destruction of all the other harmonizing elements in society, in the interest of deifying one of them—equality—and sacrificing all else to this bloody and insatiable Moloch.

Reflections on the Revolution in France, published in 1790, is one of several great works—including *A Letter to a Noble Lord* and *Thoughts on a Regicide Peace*—Burke composed in the last seven years of his life. It is important to recall that the French Revolution at its outbreak created widespread enthusiasm in England, whose native variety of the French philosophes had accomplished much in the way of continentalizing Englishmen's understanding of politics, and of corrupting their sense of their country's political traditions. Burke himself was appalled by the storming of the Bastille and the events immediately following it. As a man, he felt for the French in their travail; as an English citizen, he kept himself "aloof" from them. On the other hand, as he was to explain in *Reflections,* "Whenever our neighbor's house is on fire, it cannot be amiss for the engines to play a little on our own."

On the lookout for dangerous sparks from across the channel, Burke imagined he perceived one in a sermon delivered by the Reverend Dr. Richard Price—a Dissenter who in November 1789 delivered a speech to the Revolutionary Society in London in which he praised the principles of the French Revolution, while presenting a wrongheaded and completely misinformed disquisition on the hereditary nature of the English monarchy and the relationship between the monarchs of England and their people. The book that Burke began to write after reading Price's speech takes the ostensible form of a letter written to a French correspondent across the channel, in which the author compares the English political tradition to the newly created French polity (greatly to the detriment of the second) and denies that his countrymen are seriously inclined to follow France's example. Word got about that Burke was at work on a treatise on the French situation, causing him to hasten its composition while dedicating himself to its perfection. It was published a year to the month after Dr. Price delivered his speech to the Revolutionary Society and sold out ten editions within twelve months' time. King George III called it a very good book; across the Channel another king, Louis XVI (soon to lose his head), made a translation into the French. *Reflections on the Revolution in France* turned the tide of public opinion in England against the events in France, and has been credited by modern historians with staying revolutionary sentiment in England for forty years.

In writing his book, Edmund Burke perhaps wrought better even than he knew. *Reflections on the Revolution in France* is one of the towering literary productions of European literature and one of English letters' finest ornaments: a work of philosophical, political, and literary genius that in its majestic periods calls to mind Samuel Johnson, and whose range of poetic imagination, expressive eloquence, rhetorical inventiveness, cogency of metaphor, and aphoristic wisdom and insight into human nature and the human condition repeatedly lifts the text to Shakespearean heights. The epistolary form (a favorite device employed by eighteenth-century writers) seems a particularly happy choice in this case, where it lends dramatic personal effect to the author's thunderous denunciations and heated turns of phrase: products of a fiery temperament that in a more formal intellectual presentation might seem overly emotional and unconvincing. Burke shared in the sensibility of late eighteenth- and early nineteenth-century Romanticism, fusing two fundamentally antithetical intellectual movements in a happy combination similar to that achieved by Sir

Walter Scott. Burke's Romantic side, expressed in his somewhat idealized view of British history and the institutions that shaped it, is apparent also in the passionate rhetoric that warms and directs his prose:

> It is now sixteen or seventeen years since I saw the queen of France, then the dauphiness, at Versailles, and surely never lighted on this orb, which she barely seemed to touch, a more delightful vision. . . . Oh! what a revolution! and what a heart must I have to contemplate without emotion that elevation and that fall! Little did I dream when she added titles of veneration to those of enthusiastic, distant, respectful love, that she should ever be obliged to carry the sharp antidote against disgrace concealed in that bosom, little did I dream that I should have lived to see such disasters fallen upon her in a nation of gallant men, in a nation of men of honor and of cavaliers. I thought ten thousand swords must have leaped from their scabbards to avenge even a look that threatened her with insult. But the age of chivalry is gone. That of sophisters, economists, and calculators has succeeded, and the glory of Europe is extinguished forever. Never, never more shall we behold that generous loyalty to rank and sex, that proud submission, that dignified obedience of the heart which kept alive, even in servitude itself, the spirit of an exalted freedom. The unbought grace of life, the cheap defense of nations, the nurse of manly sentiment and heroic enterprise, is gone! It is gone—that sensibility of principle, that charity of honor which felt a stain like a wound, which inspired courage whilst it mitigated ferocity, which ennobled whatever it touched, under which vice itself lost half its evil by losing all its grossness.

But now, Burke continues,

> all is to be changed. All the pleasing illusions which made power gentle and obedience liberal, which harmonised different shades of life, and which, by a bland assimilation, incorporated into politics the sentiments which beautify and soften private society, are to be dissolved by this new conquering empire of light and reason. All the decent drapery of life is to be

rudely torn off. All the superadded ideas, furnished from the wardrobe of a moral imagination, which the heart owns and the understanding ratifies as necessary to cover the defects of our naked, shivering nature, and to raise it to dignity in our own estimation, are to be exploded as a ridiculous, absurd, and antiquated fashion.

By contrast, the Roman aspect of Burke's mind is typically reflected in a fluid and ceaseless stream of brilliant political and philosophical aphorisms: "Laws are commanded to hold their tongues amongst arms, and tribunals fall to the ground with the peace they are no longer able to uphold." "People will not look forward to posterity, who never look backward to their ancestors." "Thus, by preserving the [organic] method of nature in the conduct of the state, in what we improve we are never wholly new; in what we retain we are never wholly obsolete." "Turbulent, discontented men of quality, in proportion as they are puffed up with personal pride and arrogance, generally despise their own order." "Let those large properties be what they will—and they have their chance of being among the best—they are, at the very worst, the ballast in the vessel of the commonwealth." "It is said that twenty-four millions ought to prevail over two hundred thousand. True, if the constitution of a kingdom be a problem of arithmetic." "[T]he restraints on men, as well as their liberties, are to be reckoned among their rights. But as the liberties and the restrictions vary with times and circumstances and admit to infinite modifications, they cannot be settled upon any abstract rule; and nothing is so foolish as to discuss them upon that principle." "The pretended rights of these theorists are all extremes; and in proportion as they are metaphysically true, they are morally and politically false." "This sort of people are so taken up with their theories about the rights of man that they have totally forgotten his nature." "Prejudice renders a man's virtue his habit, and not a series of unconnected acts. Through just prejudice, his duty becomes a part of his nature." "A perfect democracy is . . . the most shameless thing in the world. As it is the most shameless, it is also the most fearless." "Of all things, wisdom is the most terrified with epidemical fanaticism, because of all enemies it is that against which she is the least able to furnish any kind of resource." Little wonder that *Reflections on the Revolution in France* swung British public opinion round like a man-o'-war in the roadstead; while those chirping grasshoppers hiding beneath their leaves (whom Burke compared to the disadvantage of the British people grazing like great cattle beneath their ancient oaks) redoubled and trebled their efforts by a barrage of pamphlets—chief among them Tom Paine's *The Rights of Man*—to subvert the minds and corrupt the souls of their countrymen. Burke himself replied to the onslaught with his own counter-counterattack, including *A Letter to a Member of the National Assembly, Thoughts on French Affairs,* and *An Appeal to the Old Whigs.*

Burke's original plan for the book included sections on the Church of England, the monarchy, the aristocracy, and democracy. The finished manuscript dealt at length with the first institution, while omitting any discussion of democracy, in place of which the author substituted a thoroughgoing criticism of the actions of the French National Assembly, whose legitimacy as legislators he denied. In the course of the work, he attacks the British friends of the Revolution in France and the gross errors and evils of the revolutionists; elucidates and defends the constitutional principles of the British monarchy; explains what is truly meant by the canting phrase "the rights of man"; compares the French Enlightenment unfavorably to British traditionalism; explains the relationship of the Church of England to the British state and society and defends religious establishment, which "solemnly and forever consecrate[s] the commonwealth and all that officiate in it"; condemns the confiscatory acts of the National Assembly in Paris; offers a defense of the monarchy and the aristocracy under the ancien régime; deplores the treatment of the Gallican Church by the revolutionary government; criticizes the Assembly for its fiscal, legislative, and constitutional policies and actions; and concludes with an appeal to the people of Great Britain:

I wish my countrymen rather to recommend to our neighbors the example of the British constitution than to take models from them for the improvement of our own. In the former, they have got an invaluable treasure. They are not, I think, without some causes of apprehension and complaint, but these they do not owe to their constitution but to their conduct. I think our happy situation owing to our constitution, but owing to the whole of it, and not to any part singly, owing in great measure to what we have left standing in our several reviews and reformations as well as to what we have altered or superadded.

Reflections on the Revolution in France is a counterrevolutionary cannonball, projected by an almost superhuman compression of the foundational principles and sustaining thought of Western civilization over three millennia and carrying far into the revolutionary nineteenth century—and beyond. Wherever and whenever conservatives worthy of the name gather, and in whatever number, they will think and talk of Burke, as in their minds' ear they listen to the thunder of his magnificent artillery. *Reflections* indeed amounts to an entire intellectual military campaign, waged with the flair, gusto, and aplomb of conservatism's nemesis—the Emperor Napoléon, called by Lord Byron "Gaul's Vulture." Yet, mixing with the smoke and flash of battle is a milky aura, produced by a mild calmness and analgesic certainty of thought approaching to sweetness. It is Burke's Christian faith showing through.

"He who gave our nature to be perfected by our virtue willed also the necessary means of perfection. He willed therefore the State—He willed its connection with the source and original archetype of all perfection." As for society,

[I]t is indeed a contract . . . to be looked upon with other reverence; because it is not a partnership in things subservient only to a gross animal existence of a temporary and perishable nature. It is a partnership in all art; a partnership in every virtue and in all perfection. As the ends of such a partnership cannot be obtained in many generations, it becomes a partnership not only between those who are living, but between those who are dead, and those who are to be born. Each contract of each particular state is but a clause in the great primeval contract of eternal society, linking the lower with the higher natures, connecting the visible and invisible world, according to a fixed compact sanctioned by the inviolable oath which holds all physical and all moral natures, each in their appointed place.

Today, a twenty-first-century reader, well accustomed to the shallow vulgarity, ignorance, and mendacity of mass democratic politics, could be pardoned for doubting that a highly successful "politician"—not a theologian or an academic dreamer—was the author of these words.

7

CONSIDERATIONS ON FRANCE

by Joseph de Maistre

1797

Joseph de Maistre (1753–1821) has long enjoyed the reputation as *réactionnaire* par excellence. The historian Émile Faguet, in the nineteenth century, called him "a fierce absolutist, a furious theocrat, an intransigent legitimist, apostle of a monstrous trinity composed of Pope, King and Hangman, always and everywhere the champion of the hardest, narrowest and most inflexible dogmatism, a dark figure out of the Middle Ages, part learned doctor, part inquisitor, part executioner" whose "Christianity is terror, passive obedience and the religion of the State." M. Faguet was only trying (by comparison with other contemporary critics, that is) to be fair to Maistre, whose sole sin is that he not only accepted the doctrine of original sin as the foundation for his understanding of human history and human institutions, but embraced it with a kind of violent enthusiasm. "There is nothing," Maistre writes in *Considerations on France*, "but violence in the universe; but we are spoiled by a modern philosophy that tells us *all is good*, whereas evil has tainted everything, and in a very real sense, *all is evil,* since nothing is in its place. The keynote of the system of our creation has been lowered, and following the rules of harmony, all the others have been lowered proportionately. *All creation groans,* and tends with pain and effort towards another order of things." In result, "Unhappily, history proves that war is, in a certain sense, the habitual state of mankind, which is to say that human blood must flow without interruption somewhere or other on the globe, and that for every nation, peace is only a respite." Whatever man, by his reason, builds up, man, by his much deeper irrationality, must eventually destroy.

Maistre responded to the invasion of Savoy by the French revolutionary armies with a series of fierce pamphlets against the Revolution itself. For his indelicacy, he was dispatched to St. Petersburg as the king of Sardinia's minister and lived abroad in the Russian capital from 1803 to 1817, where he was summoned on occasion to advise the emperor, Alexander I. Following the restoration of the Sardinian king, Maistre was recalled to Turin, where he died four years later. Maistre, as he mentions in *Considerations on France,* never set foot in France and knew nothing of French intrigues; like Edmund Burke, he admits that the terrible events in that country are none of his business, save for the malign influence they threaten to extend throughout Europe. Maistre read and admired *Reflections on the Revolution in France.* His *Considerations,* published in 1797 (seven years after the *Reflections,* and in the same year as Burke's death), is the Continental equivalent of that work: Edmund Burke in a small space, with added ferocity and minus the peculiar affection, even sweetness, of Burke's magnum opus. In no respect was Maistre more influenced by his predecessor than in his conviction that (in Isaiah Berlin's gloss) "anything which goes back to the mists of antiquity was made by God and not by man."

Maistre considers revolution "the greatest calamity that can befall a people" and the French Revolution an example of what he calls "ordained revolution." In result, "the more one examines the apparently most active personages in the Revolution, the more one finds in them something passive and mechanical. We cannot repeat too often," he continues, "that men do not lead the Revolution; it is the Revolution that uses men. They are right when they say *it goes all alone.* This phrase means that never has the Divinity shown itself so clearly in any human event. If the vilest intruments are employed, punishment is for the sake of regeneration." France had abandoned the divine mission to Christianize Europe with which her magistracy—in its religious aspect particularly—had entrusted her, and in doing so she had demoralized all of Europe. Consequently, "It has been a long time since we have seen such frightful punishment inflicted on such a large number of guilty people"—among them the French aristocracy (whom Maistre judged harshly), now either dead or émigrés living abroad. Divine Will decreed that France should return to her mission once more—after paying the penalty for having abandoned it in the first place.

Maistre was quick to discern the hand of Providence where others saw God's indifference: In the delay of the counterrevolution he firmly expected. "Here again we may admire order in disorder, for it is evident . . . that the guiltiest revolutionaries could be felled only by the blows of their accomplices. If force alone had accomplished what they call the *counter-revolution* and restored the king to his throne, there would have been no way of rendering justice." That is to say, for justice to prevail, the revolution must devour its own. "All the monsters born of the Revolution have, apparently, laboured only for the monarchy." In the long run, Maistre was right. In the short run, there was still the Directorate, and after it Napoléon, for the Bourbons to wait through. (A little over a century after he wrote, moreover, the Bourbons were again gone, and France had become, constitutionally, a secular state.)

The French Republic, Maistre insists, will not last, and for two reasons. The first is that a large and free nation cannot exist under republican government. (This was classical politial doctrine; contradicted, apparently, by the phenomenon of the United States, which Maistre brusquely dismisses: "I know of nothing so provoking as the praises bestowed on this babe-in-arms. Let it grow.") The second is that the Revolution is "radically *bad,*" "pure impurity," and that evil, having nothing in common with life and being out of harmony with the Creator, can destroy but not create: "rottenness leads to nothing." "Look at history," Maistre urges, "and you will not see any institution of any strength or duration that does not rest on a divine idea." That idea, for France, is *"liberty through the monarchy."* Republican institutions have no roots; the monarchy is a planted and rooted thing. The suffering caused by the Revolution is the result of its having violated every custom, prejudice, and propriety. "This is what made the Revolution so painful, because it tramples underfoot all nobility of opinion. . . . [T]here is no dignity in France at the moment for the same reason that there is no sovereignty"—sovereignty, which is not tangible in a republic as it is in a monarchy: "the form of government that gives the most distinction to the greatest number of persons." This attribute had not prevented the rise of a "fraudulent nobility" anterior to the Revolution. Once, however, the French nobility recognizes its responsibility for the disasters that befell it, it will have done much to renovate itself and regenerate the country. When these things have been accomplished and Frenchmen have learned to suspect abstract reason and "believe history, which is experimental politics," the way will have been made straight for Restoration. "The king will bind up the wounds of the state with a gentle and paternal hand. In conclusion, this is the great truth with which the French cannot be too greatly impressed: the restoration of the monarchy, what they call the counter-revolution, will not be a *contrary revolution,* but the *contrary of revolution."*

Maistre believes that no nation has ever been free whose "natural constitution" did not contain "seeds of liberty as old as itself"; it follows that "[n]o nation can give itself liberty if it is not already free." If this insight was relevant to Maistre's time, it is equally—or even more—so to our own age, when "global democracy" has been set up as an idol and made the object of a vast secular crusade. "The Constitution of 1795," Maistre writes, "like its predecessors, was made for man. But there is no such thing as man in the world. In my lifetime I have seen Frenchmen, Italians, Russians, etc.; thanks to Montesquieu, I even know that *one can be Persian.* But as for *man,* I declare that I have never in my life met him; if he exists, he is unknown to me." And so, "a constitution that is made for all nations is made for none; it is a pure abstraction, an academic exercise made according to some hypothetical ideal, which should be addressed to man in his imaginary dwelling place. What is a constitution? Is it not merely the solution of the following problem? *Given the population, the mores, the religion, the geographic situation, the political circumstances, the wealth, the good and the bad qualities of a particular nation, to find the laws that suit it.*" As for the vaunted Constitution of 1795, it does not even attempt to find those laws; it is only *"a school composition."*

Government, then, is what we today would call "culturally specific." What goes in the United States does not necessarily go in China, the Sudan, or Iraq. Maistre's skepticism, however, is more radical still: He denies that *any* nation or government can be created *anywhere* as a conscious and deliberate act of will, whether individual or collective. "No mere assembly of men can form a nation, and the very attempt exceeds in folly the most absurd and extravagant things that all the Bedlams of the world might put forth." Thus, he likens the revolutionaries' attempt to "reinvent government" (as the modern cant phrase has it) to "mere children killing each other to build a house of cards." The French Republic is dead on the published page; it does not *live!* "What a multiplicity of springs and clockwork! What a fracas of pieces clanging away!" Great human institutions are not formed by committees; nor is constitution making on the order of shipbuilding or erecting a factory. "Modern philosophy is at the same time too materialistic and too presumptuous to perceive the real mainsprings of the political world."

But ancient and medieval philosophy were never up to the task, either; government being one of those massive mysterious forms darkly emergent from the mists of history whose origin is God, not man. For man to seek to re-create government out of a theory is as ignorant, impious, and disastrous an act as is his attempt to re-create man in a test tube. Joseph de Maistre would scarcely have been astonished to learn that, within less than two centuries, the one experiment led directly to the other. Maistre, we might say, was determined to refute and to discredit the intellectual and moral legacy of the Enlightenment, and in this way to destroy the benighted eighteenth century before it could engender the monstrous twentieth, and the twenty-first.

8

THE FEDERALIST

by Alexander Hamilton, James Madison, and John Jay

1787–1788

Professor Thomas Peardon, a member of the History Department at Barnard College half a century ago, was fond of remarking to students and colleagues that the United States reached its political and cultural apogee with the ratification of the U.S. Constitution in 1789—and has been going downhill ever since.

It is a usually forgotten or ignored fact that American history is divided almost evenly between its colonial and independent periods and that our colonial past, therefore, is at least as important to American history and the American identity as our national one is. The Constitution, drafted by the Constitutional Convention meeting in Philadelphia in 1787 and ratified two years later, created the "United States" as a political setup; it did not create "America," which had already existed for 183 years when George Washington took the oath of office in New York City as the nation's first president. By the time the independence movement arose in the second half of the eighteenth century, colonial America had matured into a refined, lettered, and socially balanced European American society, developed essentially to the

English pattern but modified by geography to a civilization unique in its own right and capable of producing men of the highest character, the broadest learning, and the greatest genius. The convention of delegates elected from the thirteen states associated under the Articles of Confederation and summoned to Philadelphia to devise an alternative plan of government was arguably the most intellectually distinguished gathering ever witnessed in American history, before or since.

The meticulously drafted, debated, and revised document it produced has been lately recognized as the universal model for "democratic" government, in whatever time or place. The framers, and those who advocated ratification, made no such universalist or ideological claims for their handiwork, arguing instead that the proposed Constitution was better suited than any other proposed scheme of government to the exigencies of the American situation and, more important, the American character. (It is true, they believed their own plan benefitted from modern improvements made in the "science of politics"; "The efficacy of various principles," as Alexander Hamilton (1755–1804) wrote in *The Federalist* No. 9, "[being] now well understood, which were either not known at all, or imperfectly known to the ancients.")

Modesty has proved to have been as becoming to the convention as it was realistic. As early as the 1820s, if not earlier, its vaunted Constitution was showing itself susceptible to the strains imposed on it by sectional tensions that resulted in one-half of the Union seceding from the other half in what the Southern states (quite accurately) insisted was a constitutional action on the part of the Confederacy. Five years later, after the United States had been forcibly reunited under one government, the stealthy process toward the discovery of what has come to be called the "living constitution" commenced, by which the nation's plan of government has been altered by judicial interpretation, rather than by amendment, to the point where the intent of the original document seems scarcely discernible. The plain fact is that the U.S. Constitution, world-famed as the best and most workable plan of government ever conceived, "worked" for several decades only, before provoking, first, a devastating national cataclysm and, later, a thoroughgoing political renovation as profound as it has been dishonest, subversive, and illegal.

The Federalist is therefore interesting, from the vantage of the twenty-first century, in three major respects: (1) for its explication of the U.S. Constitution specifically; (2) as a discourse on republican government in general; and (3) in the accuracy of its estimation of how completely and effectively the paper plan would realize itself as a workable *and* lasting system in practice. In regard to the third aspect, the eventualities, both immediate and distant, that "Publius" foresaw *would* result from ratification but *didn't,* as also those he believed *wouldn't* occur, but *did,* stand forth dramatically. This is not to impugn the wisdom and foresight of the men who wrote the Constitution and argued for it, given that the document as understood today bears little resemblance to the Constitution they knew by that name. It is simply to point out that, in order to ascertain the fullness of understanding and the justness of argument advanced by *The Federalist* on behalf of the Philadelphia plan, we need to work backward from the present, reading the authors' analysis in the light of our own time and of intervening periods.

The *Federalist* project was conceived by Alexander Hamilton, who saw the need for a series of essays defending the U.S. Constitution and explaining its various parts to the people of the state of New York, where ratification was widely opposed by the New York newspapers immediately following the Philadelphia Convention's release of their plan on September 17, 1787. According to James Madison (1751–1836), "the undertaking was proposed by . . . Hamilton to James Madison with a request to join him and and Mr. Jay in carrying it into effect." Little planning on the part of the three men seems to have gone into the scheme, which was begun without the authors having fixed on the total number of essays or their individual length, although they did agree on a division of labor in respect of subject matter. Publication of the first seventy-seven papers was staggered, each appearing first in a New York City journal, then republished after a delay of a day or two in another, and after that another, until the journalistic market had been saturated and exposure of the arguments made complete throughout the city. (The last eight appeared in the bound two-volume edition of 1788.) All of the essays appeared over the name "Publius," so that modern scholarship has been hard put to determine which of the authors in every case wrote which paper. It is now pretty well agreed that Hamilton was responsible for Nos. 1, 6–9, 11–13, 15–17, 21–36, 59–61, and 65–85; Madison for Nos. 10, 14, 37–48; and John Jay (1745–1829) Nos. 2–5 and 64, leaving Nos. 18–20, 49–58, and 62–63 a matter for speculation. Hamilton is thought to have written No. 1 in the cabin of a sloop descending the Hudson River to New York from Albany, where he had attended the fall session of the state supreme court. Throughout, the concern of "Publius" is to demonstrate the inadequacy of the existing Confederation, the thirteen states' need for a strong central government, and the care taken by the Constitutional Convention to prepare a document that embodied the highest principles of republican government acknowledged from ancient times down to the present. (New York state ratified the Constitution on July 26, 1788.)

The Constitution of the United States is, undoubtedly, among the great political and governmental achievements in history. Just as surely, *The Federalist* is one of the most important political treatises ever written; certainly, it stands as the most distinguished contribution by American letters. Though an "experiment," and to that extent a product of the theoretical thinking Edmund Burke deplored, the Constitution (unlike what the Jacobins produced in France) is nevertheless a "conservative" document in its reliance on the historical learning and precedent Burke insisted upon, and in its appeal to past practice and to the experience and wisdom of tradition, which its framers sought to distill into a single blueprint for government. Similarly, *The Federalist*, for its insight into the soundness of the constitutional plan for a solid, effective, and responsible government, is recognizably an expression of "conservative" political philosophy as well. Yet, the comparative innocence of eighteenth-century political thought on the eve of the Jacobin cataclysm shows through—more apparently in the passionate defense made by "Publius" on behalf of the U.S. Constitution than in the practical and unadorned text of the

Constitution itself. From the vantage point of the twenty-first century, *The Federalist* is only too easily read as the convincing and incisive explanation of why the design resulting from the framers' patient and painstakingly conscientious work ultimately broke down—not once, not twice, but many times—within less than a century and a half of its investiture as the plan of government for the United States of America.

The Constitution's designers and apologists enjoy a reputation for political realism, based on a soberly realistic understanding of human nature. Still, "Publius" regularly displays a more optimistic, at times almost sunny, character (partially assumed, no doubt, in the manner of the cheerful persuader). Both Hamilton and Madison—with some historical precedent—expected that attempted usurpation of power would occur, if it occurred at all, as an act by a state, or several states, against the federal government, rather than the reverse. Thus, in No. 17, Hamilton answers the charge that a powerful national government might be tempted to encroach on the states' authority in local affairs by confessing,

> I am at a loss to discover what temptation the persons entrusted with the administration of the general government could ever feel to divest the States of the authorities of that description. The regulation of the mere domestic police of a State appears to me to hold out slender allurements to ambition. Commerce, finance, negociation and war seem to comprehend all the objects, which have charms for minds governed by that passion. . . . [A]ll those things . . . which are proper to be provided for by local legislation, can never be desirable cares of a general jurisdiction. It is therefore improbable that there should exist a disposition in the Foederal councils to usurp the powers with which they are connected."

In the same essay, he notes approvingly that, whereas common men will interest themselves predominantly in more immediate, closer-to-hand matters that are entrusted to local and state governments, "[t]he operations of the national government on the other hand falling less immediately under the observation of the mass of the citizens the benefits derived from it will chiefly be perceived and attended to by speculative men." It is, of course, later generations of those "speculative men" known to modern society as "intellectuals"—and not ordinary citizens—who through pride and ambition have destroyed constitutional operations and "interpreted" the Constitution itself to the ends of their class. In a most un-Burkean passage, "Publius" (Hamilton, No. 22), writes that "[w]hen the concurrence of a large number is required by the constitution to the doing of any national act, we are apt to rest satisfied that all is safe, because nothing improper will be likely *to be done*; but we forget how much good may be prevented, and how much ill produced, by the power of hindering the doing what may be necessary, and of keeping affairs in the same unfavorable posture in which they may happen to stand at particular periods." In No. 23, which defends entrusting the federal government with the common defense, he argues that once the issue has been decided in favor of the government, "that government ought to be cloathed with all the powers requisite to the complete execution of its trust. And unless it can be shewn, that the circumstances which may affect the public safety are reducible within certain determinate limits . . . it must be admitted, as a necessary consequence, that there can be no limitation of that authority, which is to provide for the defence and protection of the community, in any matter essential to its efficacy; that is, in any matter essential to the *formation, direction,* or *support* of the NATIONAL FORCES."

The inclusion of the word "support" invites speculation as to whether Hamilton envisioned, or would have approved, the unconstitutional measures adopted by President Abraham Lincoln (suspension of habeas corpus, etc.) during the War Between the States; the suspension of civil liberties by the Wilson administration in World War I; and the patently illegal Patriot Act, among other constitutional subversions, achieved by President George W. Bush's government in the so-called War on Terror. The threat of usurpation of power, "Publius" believes, is more likely to arise from any or several of the state governments, than from the central one; but "Power being almost always the rival of power; the General Government will at all times stand ready to check the usurpations of the state governments; and these will have the same disposition towards the General Government. The people, by throwing themselves into either scale, will infallibly make it preponderate. If their rights are invaded by either, they can make use of the other, as the instrument of redress." Yet, "[i]t may safely be received as an axiom in our political system, that the state governments will in all possible contingencies afford complete security against invasions of the public liberty by the national authority." And in No. 33, Hamilton bids the reader consider what for him is nearly unthinkable: "Suppose by some forced constructions of its authority (which indeed cannot easily be imagined) the Foederal Legislature should attempt to vary the law of descent in any State; would it not be evident that in making such an attempt it had exceeded its jurisdiction and infringed upon that of the State?"

Certainly, the framers did their best to build a degree of elasticity into the Constitution, in accordance with the necessity Hamilton identifies (in No. 33) for "a CAPACITY to provide for future contingencies, as they may happen; and, as these are illimitable in their nature, it is impossible safely to limit that capacity." Here is a paramount reason why justices and legislators ought always to consider the intent of the authors of the Constitution, rather than interpret for themselves after consulting their own preferences and intentions. They were aware, also—as they had to be, and as Hamilton in the voice of "Publius" directly expressed it (No. 28)—that corruption and usurpations, by the states or by the central government, could only be defended against for so long as the citizens understood their rights under the Constitution *and remained prepared to defend those rights.*

All in all, however, *The Federalist*—perhaps reflecting the understanding of the Convention itself—either overestimates the ability of a federal government to control latent sectional tensions among the thirteen states, or, as is more likely, underestimates the force of those tensions. *The Federalist* papers advert repeatedly to the putative dangers of disunion, and, just as often, insist on the superiority a federal system would have over "a species of leagues" in avoiding the use of force to discipline rivalrous states. Disunionist tendencies in fact may have been an insurmountable problem for the framers; if so, they ought to have recognized it for what it was and included in the Constitution an explicit exit clause for disaffected states. On a closely related subject, Hamilton (No.22), having identified "the right of equal suffrage among the states" as "another exceptionable part of the confederation," condemns it for contradicting "that fundamental maxim of republican government which requires that the sense of the majority should prevail" and allowing for "the obvious impropriety of an equal vote between States of the most unequal dimensions and populousness."

Here, "Publius" touches on the dilemma for which, decades later, John C. Calhoun of South Carolina was to propound his theory of a "concurrent majority" as a means to reconcile the national political imbalance that produced the so-called Civil War— a dilemma *The Federalist* is unable (or unwilling) to recognize or foresee. Nor did war provide a lasting solution to that dilemma, as the political crisis surrounding the 2000 presidential election made clear. Scarcely had the Supreme Court found against the Democratic candidate who had already won the popular election by half a million votes but needed the electoral votes of the state to Florida to declare victory, when the cry was heard once more against the "undemocratic" nature of the electoral college that had favored a minority vote representing an entire continent over a majority one cast in geographically restricted areas of the country.

Alexander Hamilton, who wrote the bulk of *The Federalist,* in addition to being a brilliant and learned lawyer, statesman, and writer, was also an enthusiastic nationalist and statist, ardently committed to the proposed Constitution he regarded as the blueprint for a strong and active federal government. *The Federalist,* which he imagined, brought into being, and largely composed, is fairly considered to be America's greatest contribution to political philosophy. In both inspiration and purpose, it was frankly partisan, however; leading its authors—far more Hamilton than Madison and Jay—to overlook, underestimate, and understate latent or inherent weaknesses in a plan of government that was, still and all, a work of political genius.

The first of two resulting oversights was the failure to anticipate sectional tensions and urge a means for their constitutional

remedy. The second was an historically unimaginative acquiescence in the provision for judicial review, that within the past sev-
enty years has been misinterpreted to establish the nine justices of
the U.S. Supreme Court as judicial oligarchs or philosopher
kings, invested with the power to override the legislative branch of
government and to encroach on the executive as well. (Clyde N.
Wilson argues that the mistake of the framers was graver still, in
failing to overbalance the federal government in favor of Congress, the people's branch.) Astoundingly, from the standpoint of
the present time, Hamilton feared the legislative branch as a potential aggressor against the other two branches far more than he
feared the judicial one; the judiciary, he insisted, was the *least*
dangerous to the Constitution, being "least in a capacity to annoy
or injure" the "political rights of the constitution" and possessing
"neither Force nor Will, but merely judgment"! It was "rational,"
he thinks, "to suppose that the courts were designed to be an in-
termediate body between the people and the legislature, in order,
among other things, to keep the latter within the limits assigned
to their authority," the people themselves being superior to both
(Nos. 71 and 78.) Not quite two hundred years later, Justice
William Brennan of the U.S. Supreme Court opined that judges
"are not mere umpires but, in their own sphere, lawmakers."

Moreover, *The Federalist* evinces a notable predilection to distrust and disparage local units of government, and of society, in a
manner that must strike twenty-first-century readers dismayed by
relentless centralization, political gigantism, and mass democracy
as politically insensitive, and even ominous. The prejudice against
the small political unit and the local interest is explicit in *Federalist*
No. 11—Madison's famous disquisition on faction—when he
writes, "Hence it clearly appears, that the same advantage, which
a Republic has over a Democracy, in controling the effects of faction, is enjoyed by a large over a small Republic—is enjoyed by
the Union over the States composing it. Does this advantage consist in the substitution of Representatives, whose enlightened views
and virtuous sentiments render them superior to local prejudices,
and to schemes of injustice? It will not be denied, that the Representation of the Union will be most likely to possess these requi-

site endowments." So again in No. 15, where Hamilton warns against the likelihood of the "love of power" manifesting itself in the state governments against the general one and refers to "that strong predilection in favor of local objects," as if this were a sinister thing!

Withal *The Federalist,* both as an intellectual construct and a work of literary art, is worthy of its great subject (or object), in itself an imperfect wonder of a political golden age, now fallen into sad abuse—an historical possibility briefly contemplated by Hamilton. "[A]s to those mortal feuds," (he writes in No. 17),

> which in certain conjunctions spread a conflagration through a whole nation, or through a very large proportion of it, proceeding either from weighty causes of discontent given by the government, or from the contagion of some violent popular paroxysm, they do not fall within any ordinary rules of calculation. When they happen, they commonly amount to revolutions and dismemberments of empire. No form of government can always avoid or control them. It is in vain to hope to guard against events too mighty for human foresight or precaution, and it would be idle to object to a government because it could not perform impossibilities.

The United States in the last century (and now in this one) suffered a revolution in thought and understanding and a related one in morals and character, against which no constitution, vulnerable as well to the process of entropic corruption, is ever proof. After a century and a half of mass immigration from everywhere, the United States is no longer as Jay (No. 2) describes it: "one connected country [given by Providence] to one connected people, a people descended from the same ancestors, speaking the same language, professing the same religion, attached to the same principles of government, very similar in their manners and customs." A government, as both Hamilton and Madison recognized, is only as good as its administration; the administration only as good as its administrators; and the administrators no better than the citizens who elect and tolerate them. ("What is government itself," Madison demands in No. 51, "but the greatest of all reflections on human nature?") In Nos. 55 and 57, he states explicitly that the Constitution is tailored, not to the French or the Italian people, or to universal "Man," but to the "present genius of the people of America"—the American people, moreover, "in their present temper," on whom "the genius of the whole [proposed constitutional] system depends."

It is an expression of Madison's regard for the character of his compatriots that he can list, in a spirit of sweet reasonableness, the motives and interests binding the people's representatives to faithful and honest public service, and assure his readers that the federal government and those of the states may be trusted to observe the limits established for them by the Constitution. It can be no reproach to the framers of the U.S. Constitution, or to its defenders and advocates who wrote what they could not know was to become its classic exposition, that they failed to foresee the distant revolutions that in fact occurred, and anticipate their fatal effects.

9

RATIONALISM IN POLITICS, AND OTHER ESSAYS

by Michael Oakeshott

1962

Rationalism in Politics, and Other Essays is a good introduction to the work of the British philosopher Michael Oakeshott (1901–1990), for the reason that, in arguing against rationalism as the basis for political thought and activity, Oakeshott makes the case against rationalism as the basis for every other human activity as well, from cooking to poetry to designing women's sportswear. (By "rationalism," Oakeshott means not rationality itself, but the view that reason and experience are not only superior to sensory and nonrational perceptions, they are the necessary means both to knowledge of the highest kind and to the effective action that knowledge makes possible.) Another reason is the presence in this volume of Oakeshott's famous essay "On Being Conservative"— widely accepted as the classic portrait of the generic conservative temperament, though it disappoints traditionalists by arguing that the notion of limited government to which a limited sphere of activity is entrusted is sufficient to *political* conservatism, which is independent of a belief in metaphysical and spiritual truth, social hierarchy, tradition, and social custom for its basis. (It is interesting, in respect of Oakeshott's position, that he is not more read today by those secularist, capitalist-progressive enthusiasts, the neoconservatives.)

In the title essay, Oakeshott considers the problem of rationalism in its determinative relationship to politics and the political life; in "The Political Economy of Freedom," he discusses rationalist thought as it has been applied to the concept of liberty, in the political-economic sphere as elsewhere. "The Tower of Babel" discusses rationalism as the preponderant element in moral behavior. "Rational Conduct" provides a philosophical comprehension of the meaning of that distinctive human activity, and "Political Education" suggests an education appropriate to the statesmen and the thinkers who presume to counsel him; while "On Being Conservative" is concerned with conservatism in its personal aspect. Included also in this collection are essays on poetry and the conversation of mankind, historianship, Thomas Hobbes, and political education in the university. The philosophical core of the book, however, consisting in the aforementioned chapters, will serve to give the reader a strong purchase on the thought of one of the twentieth century's foremost, if underappreciated and understudied, philosophers. (Unable to lay hand on my own copy as I worked in the fall of 2003, I borrowed one from the University of Wyoming's Coe Library in Laramie. The volume, a 1983 edition, had been checked out by precisely one other borrower over a period of twenty years.)

Oakeshott begins "Rationalism in Politics" by noting that what he calls rationalism, while not the sole political fashion, has nevertheless spilled across party lines to infect every political persuasion represented in the political life of contemporary Europe (the essay was first printed in 1947); in consequence, almost all of modern politics, those of pseudo-conservative parties (e.g., the Tories and Republicans) and movements included, have become "Rationalist, or near-Rationalist."

"The general character and disposition of the Rationalist," Oakeshott continues, are, I think, not difficult to identify. At bottom he stands (he always *stands*) for independence of mind on all occasions, for thought free from obligation to any authority save that of "reason." His circumstances in the modern world have made him contentious: he is the *enemy* of authority, of prejudice, of the merely traditional, customary, or habitual. His mental attitude is at once sceptical and optimistic: sceptical, because there is no opinion, no habit, no belief, nothing so firmly rooted or widely held that he hesitates to question it and judge it by what he calls his "reason;" optimistic, because the rationalist never doubts the power of his "reason" (when properly applied) to determine the worth of a thing, the truth of an opinion or the propriety of an action. Moreover, he is fortified by a belief in a "reason" common to all mankind, a common power of rational consideration, which is the ground and inspiration of argument. . . . But besides this, which gives the Rationalist a touch of intellectual equalitarianism, he is something also of an individualist, finding it difficult to believe that anyone who can think honestly and clearly will think differently from himself.

It is more than possible that this last insight was the inspiration of William F. Buckley Jr.'s famous quip, back in the 1950s or thereabouts, to the effect that, while the liberal is willing to hear the opposite side in any argument, he is always surprised to learn that there *is* another side.

The Rationalist does *not* neglect experience. Only, the experience he heeds is always his *own*—never that of his forebears', or other peoples'. This trait deprives him of any sense of cumulative experience, and so the past is to him simply an encumbrance. His mind, which is of the Gnostic variety, is uninitiated to his cultural inheritance; at best, it is well trained rather than educated, a neutral, finely calibrated instrument. Indeed, he desires to owe nothing to inheritance, but prides himself on being independent of the past, a self-made man in point of view of history. "With an almost poetical fancy, he strives to live each day as if it were his first, and he believes that to form a habit is to fail." Most important, however, is the source of the Rationalist's inspiration, his guide to political understanding and activity. And this guide is ideology, neatly defined by Michael Oakeshott as "the formalized abridgment of the supposed substratum of rational truth contained in the tradition"—a kind of handbook or user's manual, devised by the Rationalist himself. By this handbook, he judges every institutional aspect of his inheritance. And finds it wanting.

For the Rationalist, politics amount to a set of problems related to immediate "felt needs," for which he proposes engineering solutions. History for him thus reduces to a series of crises, each to be resolved by "reason" applied to the realization of perfection and, therefore, of uniformity. The Rationalist is able to imagine a political problem to which he himself is unequal. "But what he cannot imagine is politics which do not consist in solving problems, or a political problem of which there is no 'rational' solution at all. Such a problem must be counterfeit." And so, for the Rationalist, "[p]olitical activity is . . . the imposition of a uniform condition of perfection upon human conduct."

Oakeshott divides knowledge into two sorts. The first is technical knowledge: knowledge of technique that, whether or not it is formulated, is nevertheless capable of formulation. The second is practical knowledge, which exists through its own use and is not susceptible of formulation in a set of rules. Both kinds of knowledge are necessary to any and every kind of action; yet, the Rationalist would assert that practical knowledge is no knowledge and that technical knowledge is not only the higher form of knowledge, it is the only kind of knowledge there is, beginning as it does with certainty and ending in it, having never departed from certainty along the way. The assurance of certainty has a long intellectual pedigree in Western intellectual history, sketched by Oakeshott in brief. In the past four centuries, the fortunes of Rationalism have ebbed in every human activity—except that of politics, where it is now more strongly entrenched than ever—including the *resistance* to Rationalism, which has itself been ideologized. ("This is," Oakeshott notes slyly, "the main significance of Hayek's *Road to Serfdom*—not the cogency of his doctrine, but the fact that it is a doctrine.") The possibilities Rationalism affords to ideology and to scientific technique are among its chief attractions for a certain type of politician: the postaristocratic, bourgeois type, which, not having been bred for politics and political activity, is grateful for the handbook with which ideology provides him. Hence, to the question, "What are the circumstances that promoted this state of affairs [i.e., the rule of Rationalism in modern times]?" Oakeshott responds, "the politics of Rationalism are the politics of the politically inexperienced." For Michael Oakeshott, Marxism is simply "the greatest of all political cribs," and the Declaration of Independence "a characteristic product of the *saeculum rationalisticum*. It represents the politics of the felt need interpreted with the aid of an ideology." (Recall that Oakeshott was an Englishman. It can be argued, of course, that the Declaration of Independence was simply an elaborate excuse for, and justification of, what the American colonists were bent on doing anyway.)

Echoing Edmund Burke (whom he did not overly admire), Oakeshott argues (in "The Political Economy of Freedom") that British society represents a "diffusion of authority between past, present, and future," the overbearance of any one of which would threaten tyranny. Unfortunately, "[w]ith eyes focused upon distant horizons and minds clouded with foreign clap-trap, the impatient and sophisticated generation now in the saddle has dissolved its partnership with its past and is careful of everything except its liberty." In Oakeshott's view, the aim of political education should therefore be "a knowledge, as profound as we can make it, of our tradition of political behavior. . . . Moreover, political education is is not merely coming to understand a tradition, it is learning how to participate in a conversation: it is at once an inititation into an inheritance in which we have a life interest, and the explorations of its intimations," in the careful assessment and development of which the art of politics (political change) consists. In a free country such as Great Britain, society has no preconceived "purpose," no prefabricated "program": only a commitment to continuity, which means the slow and careful realization of intimation. Politics is not therefore the science of "reconstructing" society or even ensuring its indestructibility; rather, as Oakeshott so gracefully puts it, "it is the art of knowing where to go next in the exploration of an already existing traditional kind of society."

For a rationalist, to act morally is to pursue self-consciously a set of moral precepts embodied in, and presented by, ideals. In "The Tower of Babel," Oakeshott considers the two basic forms of the moral life, the "habit of affection and behavior" and the "habit of reflective thought," and the kinds of society produced when one of these two forms dominates the other. The first of these forms is obviously suited to a traditional society, if only for the reason that it is the form of moral behavior to which traditional societies give rise. The second is, just as clearly, better suited to a mobilized, ideological society, which operates by a process of prethought and prereflection toward preconceived— and equally selfconscious—ends. The habit of affection promotes stability since, not being understood as a system, it can fail in part without collapsing as a whole. Moreover, and for the same reason, it is elastic and evolutionary in its unassertive and unselfconscious way. By contrast, the habit of reflection is determined, not by habit at all, but by *the reflective application of a moral criterion,*" involving *"the self-conscious pursuit of moral ideals"* and *"the reflective observance of moral rules."* Thus, life is reduced to a succession of problems, in response to which not concrete behavior but the realization of the rule toward a recognized end is paramount. "Indeed," Oakeshott insists, "it is not desired, in this form of the moral life, that tradition should carry us all the way; its distinctive virtue is to be subjecting behavior to a continuous corrective analysis and criticism." The reflective form demands that each citizen be at least something of a philosopher and that he hold a vision of perfection ahead of himself, always seeking virtue "as the crow flies." "In short," Oakeshott concludes, "this is a form of the moral life which is dangerous in individuals and disastrous in a society." It is, for one thing, a prolific generator of the modern moral hypocrite, who thrives on the useful (to him) dislocation between private and public morality that conspicuous social and political benevolence encourages. ("A man who fails to practice what he preaches does not greatly disturb us; we know that preaching is in terms of moral ideals and that no man can practice them perfectly. . . . But when a man preaches 'social justice' . . . and at the same time is obviously without a habit of ordinary decent behavior . . . tension . . . makes its appearance.")

The reflective also happens to be the dominant form of morality in the civilization of the West in modern times. It is a legacy of the decaying classical period, of the theoretization of early Christian teaching, and of a "corrupt consciousness" that allows us to regard the "moral ideology" we have inherited as a blessing, instead of as a curse:

> For the remarkable thing about contemporary European morality is not merely that its form is dominated by the self-conscious pursuit of ideals, but that this form is generally thought to be better and higher than any other. A morality of habit of behavior is dismissed as primitive and obsolete; the pursuit of moral ideals . . . is identified with moral enlightenment. And further, it is prized . . . because it appears to hold out the possibility of that most sought-after consummation—a "scientific" morality. It is to be feared, however, that in both these appearances we are sadly deceived. The pursuit of moral ideals has proved itself (as might be expected) as an untrustworthy form of morality, the spring neither of a practical nor of a "scientific" moral life.

The great essay "On Being Conservative," finally, is a descriptive—as opposed to a theoretical—masterpiece that only a positivist critic or academic would presume to dissect, explain, and expatiate on. It is more of a musical work than a literary one, in the sense of being almost beyond words, though of them; a thing of supreme truth and beauty that even graduate students have been known to appreciate. It is nothing to be read *about*, but only to be read, as a Bach partita is to be heard:

> To be conservative, then, is to prefer the familiar to the unknown, to prefer the tried to the untried, fact to mystery, the actual to the possible, the limited to the unbounded, the near to the distant, the sufficient to the superabundant, the convenient

to the perfect, present laughter to utopian bliss. Familiar relationships will be preferred to the allure of more profitable attachments; to acquire and enlarge will be less important than to keep, to cultivate, and enjoy; the grief of loss will be more acute than the excitement of novelty or promise. It is to be equal to one's fortune, to live at the level of one's own means, to be content with the want of greater perfection which belongs to itself and one's circumstances. With some people this is itself a choice; in others it is a disposition which appears, frequently or less frequently, in their preferences and aversions, and is not itself chosen or specifically cultivated.

If Edmund Burke is conservativism's Shakespeare, then Michael Oakeshott may be its Cicero, *and* its Johann Sebastian Bach.

10

THE CONSERVATIVE MIND: FROM BURKE TO ELIOT

by Russell Kirk

1953

Judged by its title, *The Conservative Mind: From Burke to Eliot* might be a companion volume to Kenneth R. Minogue's *The Liberal Mind* in a series devoted to social thought and political theory. In fact, the two books are as dissimilar as their titles are alike, Minogue's being the work of a philosopher, Russell Kirk's the product of an intellectual historian. Minogue is a concise but demanding writer, Kirk (1918–1994) a formal yet always accessible rhetorician. (His book runs to nearly five hundred pages, over twice the length of Minogue's slim two-hundred-page volume.) *The Liberal Mind,* appearing to no considerable fanfare, has sold steadily since its publication in 1963 and has for years been regarded as a classic in the curriculum of political theory. *The Conservative Mind,* published ten years earlier, was a best seller in 1953, when Peter Viereck and the "New Conservatives" of the 1950s were of interest even to the editors of *Time* magazine. Yet it seems little read today, beyond the paleoconservative circle of which Russell Kirk was a prominent member.

Born and raised in central Michigan, the grandson of a railroad engineer on his father's side and the descendant of local timber barons on his mother's, Kirk was a college professor as well as an author, journalist, and founding editor of *National Review*, to which he contributed a regular column, "The Ivory Tower." After inheriting the family home in the little town of Mecosta, Kirk made it his residence for the rest of his life, dividing his time between reading, writing his many books, essays, and reviews, and planting trees as a means to expiate the depredations his ancestors had wrought on the forests of primeval Michigan: a portly figure in a three-piece suit, wearing a watch chain and gripping a shovel as if it were an ax. When William Buckley, on a visit to Mecosta from New York, increduously asked Kirk what he did for company in the wilds of the Old Northwest, his host indicated the thousands of shelved volumes surrounding them with a sweep of his blunt hand.

"This study," Kirk begins, "is a prolonged essay in definition. What is the essence of British and American conservatism? What system of ideas, common to England and the United States, has sustained men of conservative instincts in their resistance against radical theories and social transformation ever since the beginning of the French Revolution?"

Kirk credits Edmund Burke with having originated conservatism in the modern sense with his *Reflections on the Revolution in France,* published in 1790: "In that year the prophetic powers of Burke defined in the public consciousness, for the first time, the opposing poles of conservation and innovation." Among possible earlier preceptors contending for the title of conservatism's founder, Kirk dismisses Henry St. John, the first viscount of Bolingbroke, for his skepticism in religion, Thomas Hobbes for his Machiavellianism, and Sir Robert Filmer for his absolutism, while the greatest of Burke's immediate successors—George Canning, Samuel Coleridge, Sir Walter Scott, Robert Southey, and William Wordsworth—are, in Kirk's estimation, derivative from him. After warning that "[c]onservatism is not a fixed and immutable body of dogma, and conservatives inherit from Burke a talent for reexpressing their convictions to fit the time," he states as a working premise that "the essence of social conservatism is preservation of the ancient moral traditions of humanity. Conservatives . . . think society is a spiritual reality, possessing an eternal life but a delicate constitution: it cannot be scrapped and recast as if it were a machine."

History, for the conservative, is "the unfolding of a Design," a process determined not by chance or by fate, but rather the operation of Divine Providence according to "a moral law of polarity." Somewhat in the spirit of Minogue, Kirk identifies (in "The Idea of Conservatism") "six canons of conservative thought," as the conservative tradition is generally understood: 1. "Belief that a divine intent rules society as well as conscience, forging an eternal chain of right and duty which links great and obscure, living and dead. Political problems, at bottom, are religious and moral problems." 2. "Affection for the proliferating variety and mystery of traditional life, as distinguished from narrowing uniformity and equalitarianism and utilitarian aims of most radical systems." 3. "Conviction that civilized society requires orders and classes." 4. "Persuasion that property and freedom are inseparably connected, and that economic leveling is not economic progress." 5. "Faith in prescription and distrust of 'sophisters and calculators.' " 6. "Recognition that change and reform are not identical, and that innovation is a devouring conflagration, more often than it is a torch of progress. . . . Providence is the proper instrument for change, and the test of a statesman is his cognizance of the real tendency of providential social forces."

The Conservative Mind begins with "Burke and the Politics of Prescription" and "John Adams and Liberty Under Law," which includes discussion of Alexander Hamilton and Fisher Ames, that dour New England Federalist. It goes on to consider "Romantics and Utitlitarians" (Jeremy Benthan, Scott, Canning, and Coleridge); "Southern Conservatism: Randolph and Calhoun"; "Liberal Conservatives: Cooper and Tocqueville"; "Traditional Conservatism: New England Sketches" (John Quincy Adams, Orestes Brownson, and Nathaniel Hawthorne); "Conservatism with Imagination" (Benjamin Disraeli and John Henry Newman); "Legal and Historical Conservatism" (James Fitzjames Stephen, Sir Henry Maine, and W. H. Lecky); "Conservatism

Frustrated: America, 1865–1918" (James Russell Lowell, E. L. God-
kin, Henry and Brooks Adams); "English Conservatism Adrift:
The Twentieth Century" (George Gissing, Arthur Balfour, and
W. H. Mallock); and "Critical Conservatism" (Irving Babbitt,
Paul Elmer More, and George Santayana). The themes, rather
than the theses, of the book overall are the preeminence of British
and American conservatism in preserving, substantially intact,
the European American conservative tradition over a period of
two centuries; the nonideological nature of conservative thought,
which amounts to a habit of mind rather than an intellectual system; and, more speculatively, the prospect for an American revival, postwar, of conservative instincts and ideas in reaction to
the catastrophic implosion of Europe's ideological totalitarian
regimes.

Conservatives are never the most hopeful—hopeful, that is, in
a worldly sense—of men; still, many American conservatives in
the 1950s allowed themselves an unwonted degree of optimism,
as they contemplated the discreditation of communism, socialism, and facism abroad, the passing of both the New and Fair
Deals, and the advent of a Republican government, elected by a
weary and disillusioned electorate, at home. Richard Weaver was
affected, and James Burnham slightly touched, by it. So even was the
dour Russell Kirk; who, in a kind of postscript to *The Conservative
Mind* (revised in 1967 for a new edition), outlines what he terms
"Conservatives' Promise." Here, Kirk considers the sickness of
radicalism in the 1950s, the rise of the mangerial elite, and the
conservative as poet (T. S. Eliot, John Betjeman, and Robert
Frost). His conclusion will cause the sympathetic reader today—
fifty years later when, at the onset of the twenty-first century, virtually every conservative idea, tendency, and instinct has been
overridden by the Gadarene rush into postmodernity—to feel the
pang that accompanies the backward look toward a time, not so
very long ago, when conservatives *had* hope, and the recognition
of how much ground they have lost since then, and how fast.

Writing in 1967, Kirk identifies 1950 as the year in which "the
intellectual recovery of conservative ideas commenced." Figuring
a generation to be necessary for infused ideas to reach fruition in

action, he calculates Americans to be at the midway point in their journey toward conservatism. They had, as he perceives the situation, a strong foundation on which to build. "How much conservatives have lost since July 14, 1789, has been suggested in the preceding chapters of this essay. What they have retained, in Britain and America, remains far greater than what they have forfeited. . . . [T]he indispensable basis of any conservative order, religious sanction, remains tolerably secure."

So, Kirk believes, with respect for property rights in America and Britain; and so also with "established usage and longing for continuity." Of the six premises for conservative belief set forth in his introductory chapter, four continue to "animate the social impulses" of a great many Britons and Americans. In Great Britain, the institutions of Parliament and the monarchy are still mainly unchallenged, while "[i]n America, the Federal Constitution has endured as the most sagacious conservative document in political history; the balance of interests and powers still operates, however threatened by recent centralization; and almost no one advocates a radical revision of political establishments in America." Kirk does, however, feel compelled to add a caveat: "A task for conservative leaders is to reconcile individualism (which sustained nineteenth-century life even while it starved the soul of the nineteenth century) with the sense of community that ran strong in Burke and Adams. If conservatives cannot redeem the modern masses from the sterile modern mass-mind, then a miserable collectivism impoverishing both soul and body impends over Britain and America."

In the nearly four decades that have passed since Russell Kirk wrote these lines, consumer socialism united with the "colossal state created chiefly for its own sake" has allowed the mass-mindedness he warned against to transform America (and the British Isles) to a degree Kirk could not have imagined in the late 1960s. In 2004, no true conservative can argue that religious sanction is secure in a post-Christian age, that the balance of powers still operates in a government in which the judiciary has usurped the powers of the legislative branch, and that "respect for established usage and longing for continuity" exists in a nation

submerged in suburbia, informality, and a culture that is atom-
ized by the collapse of the family structure and inundated by
mass immigration representing scores of foreign cultures. The discrepancy between Kirk's vision of the 1950s and 1960s and today's
reality is staggeringly apparent—as indeed it had become to Kirk
himself at the time of his death in 1994.

"If conservatively inclined men of affairs can rise to the summons of the poets, the norms of culture and politics may endure
despite the crimes and follies of the age." Half a century later,
nothing of the sort has happened: "Conservatively" inclined men
of affairs have risen rather to the summons of corrupt corporate
executives, scheming global democratic capitalists, demagogic
"civil rights" leaders, and clever, vindictive journalists advocating
the deconstruction and transformation of Western civilization.
And yet, the providentiality of history, though it appears at times
to be a pipe dream, remains a dream that conservatives must continue to believe in, and even to affirm.

11

THE LIBERAL MIND

by Kenneth R. Minogue

1963

The Liberal Mind, written by a professor at the London School of Economics and Political Science, has achieved the status of a classic since its publication in 1963, sufficiently ahead of the solidification of political correctness to establish itself securely in reading lists for political philosophy and political science courses. Kenneth R. Minogue (1930–) is an accomplished stylist, an elegant writer possessing the ability to explicate complex and sophisticated ideas clearly. Even so, his book requires close attention, better yet study. Philosophers have a trick of using ordinary words in ways that depart by a few degrees from the ordinary, causing the nonprofessional reader a certain perplexity produced by misled expectations. And Minogue does appear somewhat eliptical in his approach to his subject—before we remember that the author's specified concern is not liberal doctrine, or liberal politics, or even liberalism itself, but instead the *mind* capable of producing these phenomena. After that, it is easier to discern the glimmering hints at Minogue's intent and direction; until near the end of chapter 2 ("The Anatomy of Liberalism") the trap is sprung and the galvanized corpse of liberalism, tongue protruding and eyes bulging, dangles at the end of the hangman's rope. Finally, there is left only the brain autopsy for Professor Minogue to perform with skill, humor, and a certain sympathy for the victim that (as he is only too well aware) will be up and about again in no time: an earnest zombie brimming with false optimism and a shallow metaphysics, stalking the world in search of "suffering situations" to alleviate and transform.

"The aim of this book," Minogue writes in his preface, "is to analyze the long tradition of liberalism. It regards the current fluidity of political boundaries as due to the fact that an enlarged and somewhat refurbished liberalism has now succeeded the ideologies of the past. It maintains that this liberalism provides a moral and political consensus which unites virtually all of us, excepting only a few palpable eccentrics on the right and communists on the left." Contemporary liberalism combines classical liberalism's emphasis on individual liberty with modern liberalism's commitment to state paternalism.

Additionally, Minogue identifies two elements of liberalism as a whole: "libertarianism," which is disposed to subject all of life to critical inquiry and hence is dangerous to all authorities, traditional or modern, and "salvationist liberalism," which works from the assumption that, while the present is revolutionary and the near future likely at least to remain so, history must arrive nevertheless at a definite end in the perfection of human society. Liberalism at its core is a balanced and prudent doctrine. Libertarianism, however, when elevated to a doctrine in its own right, succumbs to irrationalism and romantic fantasy, under the influence of which it tends toward violence and destruction. Both elements, Minogue argues, are integral to liberalism as it has existed over the past several centuries, resulting in the ideological incoherence that is a feature of every ideology. "For liberals are simultaneously to be found praising variety and indeed eccentricity of opinion and behavior; and gnawing industriously away at the many sources of variety in an attempt to provide every man, woman, child and dog with the conditions of the good life. They are to be found deploring the tyrannical excesses of totalitarian government, and yet also watching with birdlike fascination the pattern of order and harmony which those excesses are explicitly designed to promote." Instinctually recognizing the incoherence of liberal movements, traditional societies have rightly done all they could to ward off the liberal infection. "For once liberalism gains a hold, a sort of traditional innocence is lost." What is more, liberalism is a culturally specific ideology. "The political consequences of liberal ideas may be the establishment of a liberal democratic society of the western European kind. But this outcome requires the cooperation of social and economic circumstances, or perhaps simply elements of good fortune, which are far from being universally distributed."

Liberalism since the seventeenth century, Minogue argues, has been disposed by its commitment to the concept of natural rights and of a social contract predating the formation of government to regard the individual as an autonomous political institution. "It created a policy of the individual and called it ethics." "The liberal view of man must be regarded not as inadequate or as unfruitful but simply false, because of the superior logical status it accords to a grouping of interests or desires called the individual self." In identifying these interests and desires, liberal theory has created a hypothetical entity, or model, Minogue calls "generic man," who exhibits, always and everywhere, such desires and interests, while depending on the fulfillment of "needs." The problem here is the assumption that every individual may be explained psychologically and that all social institutions are comprehensible in terms of the individuals who comprise them; while, in reality, "the starting point for [social and institutional] explanation must not be the rationalist essence of the individual, but the complex situation we are trying to explain."

"Generic man," the conceptual basis of liberal thought, of course is an abstraction. He is, however, an abstraction highly useful to liberalism and to liberals. The notion of "generic man" gives the liberal concept of "progress" plausibility, while answering liberalism's need to identify a single point of view that will serve to harmonize all human relations and provide liberal doctrine with a system. (" 'Sophistry,' " Hilaire Belloc writes in *The Free Press*, "consists in making up 'systems' to explain the world.") Also, it reflects the fact that liberalism does not take reality for its starting point, for the very good reason that it has, finally, no interest in or concern for present reality, but only the realization of a new reality and the transformation of human existence. Liberals do not devise their melioristic and reformist policies in accordance with their concept of society; instead, they form those concepts in accordance with the policies they wish to devise and apply. For liberals and liberalism, solutions typically precede problems, because solving the "problem" is not in any particular instance an end in itself but a means to realizing a replacement society to which the immediate "problem" necessarily bears no relation.

"[T]he idea of a social problem," Minogue goes on to say,

> appears to come from no particular location in society. It is a social incoherence arising out of an ideal; and this ideal can be most persuasively put in moral terms. . . . The "real question," in liberal terms, is "whether the social order actually serves our needs." . . . Here we have illustrated the use of "needs" as something mysteriously outside the social order and acting as a moral criterion of the "social order." But what is the "social order"? If "society" is simply the "complex of social relationships" then it is not a single manipulative order. In so far as there is a single order, then it is that imposed by the State and expressed in laws. Similarly, when we read that "the true nature of society" is that it is a "human organization for common needs," we can only observe that a complex of relationships is not an "organization" at all—only the State and the institutions it sanctions are "organizations" in that sense. But it is precisely the aim of liberalism to *make* society into a single complex *organization*.

"Where there's no solution," James Burnham used to say, "there's no problem." In a similar vein, Minogue notes that any particular situation presents a problem only to someone of a certain character—in the liberal instance, one who believes that a "solution" is not only possible but desirable, on a scale vastly exceeding the level at which the problem exists. Apathetic persons, he quips, are simply people who aren't concerned with the things that concern liberals; totalitarianism, by his definition, is "the attempt to find an absolute solution to a bogus problem." Once again, we find ourselves confronted by the question of incoherency in an ideology that has, however indirectly, been the cause of brutal inhumanity and degrading misery (surpassing anything previously known to history) in its quest for a utopia of freedom, tolerance, and love—in brief, for universal happiness.

At this point, rather than pursue the incoherence of liberalism, we should examine the contradiction that is both related to the incoherence and integral to the ideology itself: a contradiction that can be simply stated by saying that freedom, which is both part of the liberal's conception of universal happiness and a synonym for it, lies beyond the end-means context by which liberals expect to achieve it.

Liberals are preoccupied with the conditions of freedom and the means to create or enhance these. But their preoccupation betrays a naïveté amounting, really, to ignorance. "For if we are seeking the conditions of freedom," Minogue explains,

we must look not to those circumstances which happen to accompany it, but to the manner it which it has been attained. And we will find that it has always been attained because of a spontaneous growth of interest in truth, science, or inventiveness; a spontaneous growth of moral principles appropriate to freedom; a spontaneous construction of the political arrangements which permit of free constitutional government. Spontaneity indicates that free behavior has arisen directly out of the character of the people concerned, and that it is neither a mechanical process, nor a "natural reaction" to an environment, nor a means to the attainment of some end. Free behavior, in other words, is its own end.

As its own end, freedom provides or creates the materials necessary to its continuance into the future. From this reasoning, we can devise four theorems: 1. "[A] political policy which aims at attaining any of the supposed conditions of freedom is likely to destroy free behaviour." 2. "[T]he political pursuit of freedom is

always the pursuit of something else." 3. "[Freedom] is a question, not of what is done, but of how it is done and who does it."
4. "A populace which hands its moral intiative over to a government, no matter how impeccable its reasons, becomes dependent
and slavish."

Liberalism, as James Burnham concedes in *Suicide of the West,*
has made definite contributions to Western institutions, chiefly by
attacking and removing certain of their less attractive and re-
formable features. Minogue, for his part, allows that policy based
on faulty or false assumptions and principles need not *necessarily*
produce bad effects. The presumption, however, must be that
they will—if not in this instance, then in the next, or the next after
that, since no human society grounded on a philosophy of unreality—in particular, one that is by its nature essentially destructive—
can survive indefinitely. Conservatism, from its acute awareness of
the perverse frailty of man and the fragility of human institutions,
is always disposed to the tragic sense. What was built up over two
thousand years can be destroyed in two hundred (or less), without hope of resurrection or re-creation. How, after all, does one
create spontaneity? It is as easy, Kenneth Minogue suggests, to
create a nation of mystics. Or of "happiness." On the other hand,
we all have a fair idea how to go about building a people's republic of gulags, gas ovens, and terror.

12

IDEAS HAVE CONSEQUENCES

by Richard M. Weaver

1948

A bookish and reclusive Southerner who spent most of his working life at the University of Chicago and died in 1963 of a heart
attack, aged fifty-three, Richard M. Weaver would have been astonished had he lived to know the celebrity that his quotable phrase
won him during the Reagan administrations. Then the words
"Ideas have consequences, you know!" tripped blithely from the
lips of everyone in the triumphant neoconservative establishment
in Washington, D.C., and New York City who considered himself
an intellectual. (And that *was* everyone.)

Rereading the book today, one wonders whether these enthusiasts for Weaver ever read his book to begin with; so unlikely it
seems that they could have failed to recognize themselves among
the "hysterical optimists" the author finds emblematic of the
modern West. Richard Weaver himself was no *historical* optimist.
That is to say, he would have deplored the "national greatness
conservatism" currently being pushed by neoconservatism and its
madeover vehicle, the Republican Party. Weaver was never a Cold
Warrior in his day (he argued against registering communists in

the McCarthy era), and he would not have favored exploitation by the United States of its position as Sole Superpower in our own. As a Southerner, Weaver was all too familiar with the aggressive tendency and destructive nature of mass industrial democracy, which had largely succeeded in deconstructing his native region and melding it with the Northern behemoth. (*The Southern Tradition at Bay*, published posthumously, is one of the best defenses of the South and its civilization ever written.) For Weaver, a national political program dedicated to mass, size, power, and influence was a grandiose example of the materialist heresy that had wrecked human community and destroyed civilization in the West, while reducing man himself to the stature of a "moral idiot."

The neoconservatives' optimism is grounded in a misapprehension of America's—and the West's—relationship to the rest of the world, which they regard as unassailable and, therefore, permanent. To them, the collapse of the Soviet Union and the spread (such as it is) of democratic capitalism signify "the end of history" (Francis Fukuyama's famous phrase), with the international status quo frozen in place. This vision of reality is as blinkered and shallow as it is self-induced, but that is hardly the issue here. The point, rather, is that the "triumph" of democratic capitalism over communism amounts to the defeat of idealistic materialism by materialistic idealism—of dialectical thinking over the pragmatic, positivistic variety representing the *true* materialism that, over a period of centuries, has undone and (quite literally) unmanned Western civilization.

And so, writing only three years after the unconditional Allied victory over the Axis powers, Weaver concedes in his introduction that "[t]his is another book about the dissolution of the West. . . . I present an account of that decline based not on analogy but deduction. It is here the assumption that the world is intelligible and that man is free and that those consequences we are now expiating are the product not of biological or other necessity but of intelligent choice." His book, he tells us, is "not primarily a work of philosophy"; rather, it is "an intuition of a situation," of "a world which has lost its center, which desires to believe again in value and obligation. But this world is not willing to realize how it has lost its belief or face what it must accept in order to regain faith in an order of goods."

For Weaver, the crucial event in the history of Western culture occurred when a protracted medieval debate concluded with the defeat of logical realism by the doctrine of nominalism, first set forward by William of Occam in the late fourteenth century. Nominalism, by denying the real existence of universals, posed the question of whether man is both the source and the measure of truth. Formally resolved or not, that debate had the effect of leading men to deny the reality apprehended by the intellect in favor of reality as it presents itself to the senses. "With this change in the affirmation of what is real, the whole orientation of culture takes a turn, and we are on the road to modern empiricism."

Nominalism amounted to the denial of transcendentals, which leads to the denial of truth, which leaves man the measure of all things.

> Thus began the "abomination of desolation" appearing today as a feeling of alienation from all fixed truth. Now, nature no longer was recognized as an imperfect imitation of a transcendent model: a development which vitiated the doctrine of forms, and that of forms imperfectly realized. In man's eyes, the universe lost the dimension of mystery that supported and gave meaning to the teaching of original sin. With nature reduced to mere intelligibility and man forced uncompromisingly into the narrow setting of intelligible nature, the natural goodness of man followed as an obvious conclusion. There being now no need for man to look beyond the world, rationalism was elevated to philosophy, whose basis was the systematization of phenomena. In these circumstances, Christianity withered into deism. But this religion, like all those which deny antedecent truth, was powerless to bind: it merely left each man to make what he could of the world open to the senses.

There followed materialism, and from materialism the necessity to explain man in terms if his environment (Darwinism and Marxism). "With the human being thus firmly ensconced in nature, it at once became necessary to question the fundamental character of his motivation," and so the survival of the fittest was proposed as the *causa causans.* "Finally came psychological behaviorism, which denied not only freedom of the will but even such elementary means of direction as instinct." And so man finds himself at last degraded to the condition of "abysmality" in result of one abdication succeeding another, in course of which "[h]e has found less and less ground for authority at the same time he thought he was setting himself up as the center of authority in the universe; indeed, there seems to exist here a dialectic process which takes away his power in proportion as he demonstrates that his independence entitles him to power."

If philosophy begins in wonder, then sentiment, Weaver reasons, must antecede reason. And it is through sentiment that men intuit what he calls "the metaphysical dream," or apprehension of immanent reality, lacking which men cannot for long coexist harmoniously. Man does not live, of course, by sentiment alone; he requires the use of his reason to deal with the material given of this world. Yet, reason in directive support of sentiment allows man to avoid sentimentality by means of "the unsentimental sentiment." Reason acting on sentiment allows us to comprehend measure, in the absence of which forms, made possible by ultimate conceptions, are impossible and give way to confusion and chaos induced by the lack of control characteristic of the civilized man, who is capable of the necessary feat of abstraction allowing him to see that form is the enduring part of reality. By contrast, the barbarian or Philistine ("the barbarian living amid culture") demands immediacy of apprehension and experience: the thing direct, divested of the veil that reveals even as it conceals. And so we are everywhere aware today of the "desire to get ever closer to the source of physical sensation," "the substitution of sensation for reflection," as accompanying signs that "culture, as such, is marked for attack because its formal requirements stand in the way of expression of the natural man." And not just "culture," but all human relationships as well suffer from the deteriorative force created by the decay of sentiment and the "passion for immediacy" produced, like swamp gas, by the process of decay.

Modern man's incomprehension of, and disrespect toward,

forms is responsible for what Weaver calls "[t]he most portentous general event of our time," the breaking down of all those distinctions that create a society. "Rational society is a mirror of the logos, and this means that it has a formal structure which enables apprehension. The preservation of society is therefore directly linked with the recovery of true knowledge." Those people who charge (to the outrage of liberal opinion) that there are "subversives" among us, tunneling beneath and undermining society, have it exactly right, Weaver affirms. "Since subversive activity is the taking away of degree, it is logical that conservatives should treat as enemies all those who wish to abolish the sacred and secular grounds for distinctions among men." Fraternity, not equality, he insists, has always been what unites men by creating and sustaining affection among them, while equality is ever at war with fraternity. Social hierarchy corresponds with a hierarchy of values. There is no way save education to open men's eyes to that hierarchy; yet, "it is precisely because we have lost our grasp of the nature of knowledge that we have nothing to educate with for the salvation of our order."

And we can renew our grasp on knowledge only by a return to the metaphysical or theological center, however we conceive it. This is because the West, for centuries now, has been in flight toward the periphery, prompted by what Weaver terms "the centrifugal impulse of our culture." From the Middle Ages to the present day, the paradigm of learning and enlightenment—the keeper of the culture, so to speak—has degenerated from the philosophic doctor to the gentleman to the specialist, an arc that traces the downward course from a concern with ultimate matters to the knowledge, however circumscribed, that is power, dedicated to ad hoc ends. "It should be plain," Weaver suggests, "that modern man is suffering from a severe fragmentation of his world picture. This fragmentation leads directly to an obsession with isolated parts," in which the modern discovers a certain security within his insecurity. It is all a matter of substituting means for ends, and yet, "[s]anity is a proportion with reference to purpose; there is no standard of sanity when the whole question of ends is omitted." And the specialist has nothing to say on the subject of ends, of which only the philosophic doctor is qualified—and, indeed, inclined—to speak.

The ignorance of ends has been accompanied by ignorance in another form, "that form of ignorance which is egotism." Knowledge, for the medieval idealists, was humility. Francis Bacon destroyed that equivalence in three words when he declared that "knowledge is power," thus making the aim of knowledge domination instead of understanding. Now, domination relies on what is utile, not what is necessarily true, which means that the commitment to domination implies a turning away from knowledge and therefore from work, defined as "a bringing of the ideal from potentiality into actuality." And since there is no necessity without truth, the modern worker's egotism prevents him from understanding that he is a creature under obligation to rational and responsible employment. The injunction *"Labore est orare"* ("To labor is to pray") is meaningless for the egotistical worker of modern times, whether he be a poet, a politician, or a union member. Yet, "[e]gotism in work and art," as Weaver reminds us, "is the flowering, after long growth, of a heresy about human destiny."

Employing a celebrated metaphor, Weaver describes in his chapter "The Great Stereopticon" how "[t]he vested interests of our age, which, from all kinds of motives, desire to maintain traditional values or to get new values set up in their place, have constructed a wonderful machine, which we shall call the Great Stereopticon," whose function is "to project selected pictures of life in the hope that what is seen will be imitated" by the masses. The Great Stereopticon amounts, of course, to what are called The Media today. It represents an understandable response to the problem the elite class faces in persuading the members of a disintegrated culture to engage themselves communally in the absence of a unifying belief binding them together as one people. However, the Stereopticon is also the chief purveyor of the sickly metaphysical dream: "the great projection machine of the bourgeois mentality," itself "psychopathic in its alienation from reality." In its campaign to promote the popular dream of materialism and success, moreover, it makes war against memory and the past, just as the World State in Aldous Huxley's *Brave New World* does. "The successive perception of successive events is empiricism; the simultaneous perception is idealism. Need we go further to account for the current dislike of long memories and for the hatred of the past?" The Great Stereopticon is one of the principal creators, molders, and sustainers of "The Spoiled Child Psychology" characteristic of the mass man, who has been taught for centuries by scientists that there is nothing he cannot know and by demagogues that there is nothing he cannot have, and of whom Richard Weaver writes, in one of the more famous passages in his book, "No one can be excused for moral degradation, but we are tempted to say of the urban dweller, as of the heathen, that he never had an opportunity for salvation. He has been exposed so unremittingly to this false interpretation of life that, though we may deplore, we can hardly wonder at the unreasonableness of his demands."

In the conviction that "man should not follow a scientific analysis with a plea of moral impotence," Weaver closes with the suggestion that the right to private property—"The Last Metaphysical Right," in the sense that it is the one right remaining to us that needs no justification beyond itself—be made the support on which the ladder of ascent back to our former, higher condition is set up. He advocates the teaching of poetry and rhetoric as a means to developing sentiment and apprehending reality and to respecting words as things, and the cultivation of piety, defined as "a discipline of the will through respect" for the substance of the world, of other beings, and of the past. Still, Weaver sees an uphill road. "With ignorance virtually institutionalized, how can we get man to see?" The salvation of the modern world lies in its willingness to survive—which, he admits, is not something to be taken for granted, since modernity shows signs, rather, of pushing the periphery ever outward in its continued flight from reality.

Ideas Have Consequences, a mere 189 pages long in the University of Chicago paperback edition, is among the most thoroughgoing philosophical treatises on the modern predicament ever written. It can be read, also, as a devastating attack on the middle class (the villain of Weaver's story, though it is ordinarily regarded by antiliberals as the avatar and mainstay of the modern West), which he accuses of rebellion against metaphysical reality. "That series of subversive events which raised the middle class to a position of dominance allowed it not only to prescribe the conditions of labor but also to frame the world of discourse in terms of economics."

13

I'll Take My Stand: The South and the Agrarian Tradition

by Twelve Southerners

1930

Edward Abbey called growth for growth's sake "the ideology of the cancer cell." Though Abbey was an outdoorsman and an environmentalist rather than a farmer, his lifelong loathing for industrial capitalism was congruent with the disposition of the Southern Agrarians: a dozen men "well acquainted with each other" (as they describe themselves in their introduction) "and of similar tastes, though not necessarily living in the same physical community and perhaps only at this moment aware of themselves as a single group," who collaborated to produce a famous volume of essays, originally published in 1930. A few of the twelve in later years achieved national and international literary reputations; others, lesser known, earned distinguished ones; a few have scarcely been heard from since. They are John Crowe Ransom (1888–1974), Donald Davidson (1893–1968), Frank Lawrence Owsley (1890–1956), John Gould Fletcher (1886–1950), Lyle H. Lanier (1903–1988), Allen Tate (1899–1979), Herman Clarence Nixon (1886–1967), Andrew Nelson Lytle (1902–1995), Robert Penn

Warren (1905–1989), John Donald Wade (1892–1963), Henry Blue Kline (1905–1951), and Stark Young (1881–1963). Of these twelve, only one ever disavowed the ideas set forth here: Robert Penn Warren, who changed his tune after moving north of the Mason-Dixon Line to become a literary lion—and a Yankee.

It is important to state at the outset that *I'll Take My Stand: The South and the Agrarian Tradition* is not a call to a second War Between the States. The book does not argue for secession, nor even contemplate such a thing. Its authors are not concerned with the prospect of Dixie creating an existence separate from that of the North, but instead with the extent to which the South ought to transform itself in the Northern image. Or, as the authors express it, "how far shall the South surrender its moral, social, and economic autonomy to the victorious principle of Union?" Hitherto, they note, the South has been jealous of its minority right to live its own distinctive life. "Of late, however, there is the melancholy fact that the South has wavered a little and shown signs of wanting to join up behind the common or American industrial ideal. It is against this tendency that this book is written. The younger Southerners, who are being converted frequently to the industrial gospel, must come back to the support of the Southern tradition. They must be persuaded to look very critically at the advantages of becoming a 'new South' which will only be an undistinguished replica of the usual industrial community."

As the Agrarians understood America in 1930, the communist menace was real—only the real communists were America's industrialists, intending to set up "an economic super-organization" that would itself become the government. "[I]t is simply according to the blind drift of our industrial development to expect in America at last much the same economic system as that imposed by violence in Russia in 1917."

As with the Red version, American communism was the enemy of civilization in its totality. Endlessly accelerated consumption—the endless end of industrialism—cannot lead to human satisfaction but instead to satiety, aimlessness, and loss of vocation. Industrialism wars against religion, by its assault on nature and on man's sense of the inscrutability of nature, from which religion arises and on which it depends. Since art, too, is reliant on a right attitude toward nature, industrialism is inimical as well to the arts, which cannot, under industrialism, have "a proper life." And, since relations between men are inextricably bound to the relationship between man and nature, "The amenities of life also suffer under the curse of a strictly-business or industrial civilization." Humanism, industrial civilization's equivalent of traditional learning and cultivation, the Agrarians regard as an abstraction: "We cannot recover our native humanism by adopting some standard of taste that is critical enough to question the contemporary arts but not critical enough to question the social and economic life which is their ground." Industrialism's most significant developments—advertising and personal salesmanship—represent for them "the great effort of a false economy to approve of itself," operating in total disregard of the welfare of laborer and consumer alike. Indeed, the Agrarians argued, the industrial system always exhibits complete unconcern for individuals and their wants. In an agrarian society, agriculture would be the primary vocation, though urban vocations, the cities in which they thrive, and the industry that gives rise to both would have their use as well. For the Agrarians, agriculture was the form of labor most compatible with intelligence and leisure: a model for all other forms. "But an agrarian regime will be secured readily enough where the superfluous industries are not allowed to rise against it. The theory of agrarianism is that the culture of the soil is the best and most sensitive of vocations, and that therefore it should have the economic preference and enlist the maximum number of workers."

The classic essays in *I'll Take My Stand* are Ransom's "Reconstructed but Unregenerate," Davidson's "A Mirror for Artists," Tate's "Remarks on the Southern Religion," and Lytle's "The Hind Tit," of which Tate's is the greatest and Lytle's the most charming.

Ransom argues that "[t]he South is unique on this continent for having founded and defended a culture which was according to the European principles of culture; and the European principles had better look to the South if they are to be perpetuated in this country." European cultures, he argues, contended against nature only to the point at which nature afforded them a comfortable living; thereafter, they declared a truce and devoted their energies to the cultivation of religion, the arts, and philosophy. By contrast, modern societies in general, but America especially, have engaged in a perpetual struggle with nature that is irrational in terms of the human advantage to be gained and the dislocation sustained by it. "This is simply to say," Ransom concludes, "that Progress never defines its ultimate objective, but thrusts its victims at once into an infinite series. . . . [O]ur progressives are the latest version of those pioneers who conquered the wilderness, except that they are pioneering on principle, or from force of habit, and without any recollection of what pioneering was for."

Davidson, in his chapter, attacks what he calls "the industrial theory of the arts," which holds that the wealth and leisure created by industrialism will produce a renaissance in which not only the wealthy but also the plain people will share. This theory, Davidson—himself a distinguished poet and friend of Robert Frost—argues, is completely untenable. "Industrialism cannot play the rôle of Maecenas, because its complete ascendancy will mean that there will be no arts left to foster; or, if they exist at all, they will flourish only in a diseased and disordered condition." Indeed, industrial society must extinguish the meaning of the arts as they have traditionally been understood, by altering the conditions of life in which art has meaning at all. "For they have been produced in societies which were for the most part stable, religious, and agrarian; where the goodness of life was measured by a scale of values having little to do with the material values of industrialism; where men were never too far removed from nature to forget that the chief subject of art, in the final sense, is nature."

In "The Hind Tit," Andrew Lytle (the novelist and long-time editor of *The Sewanee Review* whose novels include *The Velvet Horn* and the wonderful *At the Moon's Inn*) restates Ransom's thesis when he writes that "[t]he South long since finished its pioneering. It can only do violence to its provincial life when it allows itself to be forced into the aggressive state of mind of an earlier period." Moreover, in the divided world of the New South—divided, that is, between the agrarian way of life and the industrial one—the Southern farmer has become the runt pig in the sow's litter, compelled to make do with the hind tit when he is lucky enough to avail himself even of that. Politically speaking, there is a single means of recourse: To join with the populist agrarian West and conservative communities scattered around the country in united resistance to "industrial imperialism."

The boldest chapter, however, is also the most original and brilliant. In the view of Allen Tate—among the greatest American poets and critics of the twentieth century, and the author of one of its greatest novels (*The Fathers*)—the War Between the States was of itself a trivial setback to Southern civilization. "The South," he insists, "would not have been defeated had it possessed a sufficient faith in its own kind of God. It would not have been defeated, in other words, had it been able to bring out a body of doctrine setting forth its true conviction that the ends of man require more for their realization than politics." Here, Tate directly counters Ransom's claim that the South represented the European principle. The South, he argues instead, epitomized the split-mindedness that has always bedeviled the Western mind, precariously balanced between reason and intuition, practicality and tradition. The two were in balance only once in Western history, during the Middle Ages; as for the Old South, it was a feudal society without a feudal religion. The South, Tate believes, failed to create an "appropriate religion" for the reason that its religious impulse was inarticulate, owing to its commitment to the traditions of Protestantism: the religion of a trading and commercial, rather than of an agrarian, society. And since religion determines a society's economic structure, and the economic structure determines the social one, the southern religious system was necessarily out of alignment with its secular system. The result was the development of dangerous social strains to which the South, two generations after the War, showed signs of succumbing.

"How may the Southerner take hold of his Tradition?" Tate asks in conclusion, and provides an answer that seems shocking in context: "[B]y violence."

The reader might suppose Tate to have in mind here violence in its metaphorical or spiritual form, as represented in the biblical text that Flannery O'Connor—herself a close friend of Tate's wife, the novelist Caroline Gordon, and a Southerner—chose as the epigraph for her eponymous novel. ("From the days of John the Baptist until now, the kingdom of Heaven suffereth violence, and the violent bear it away."—Matthew 11:12) As Tate proceeds to show, however, the solution he intends is "political, active, and, in the nature of the case, violent and revolutionary." Because he cannot fall back on an articulated religious belief, the Southerner, Tate explains, "is faced with the paradox: He must use an instrument, which is political, and so unrealistic and pretentious that he cannot believe in it, to reestablish a private, self-contained, and essentially spiritual life."

What precisely this instrument might be, Tate leaves to our imagination. Presumably, he envisioned political action of the sort advocated today by Clyde N. Wilson (the Calhoun scholar from South Carolina), who argues that only a recommitment to the doctrine of states' rights can save the South, and with it the United States of America. Unlikely as the prospect for a return to true federalist principle might appear, it still seems more imaginable than the instauration of the agrarian society advocated by the Twelve in their manifesto.

If *I'll Take My Stand* had a somewhat unreal quality in 1930 (as indeed some readers noted at the time), that aspect has only been enhanced by the passage of nearly three-quarters of a century, after the industrial system has been succeeded by postindustrialism and the farm population has declined to 1 or 2 percent of the American population. Yet, the Agrarian critique of industrialism was perfectly sound; it is the industrial system itself, whether we are stuck with it or not, that is fundamentally unsound. ("Our only hope," Abbey once remarked, "is catastrophe.") Social or political criticism is not wrongheaded or worthless simply because it offers no immediate practical application. If, as Alexander Pope thought, the proper study of man is man, then knowing where it has taken the wrong road is critical to a civilization's understanding of itself, regardless of whether the possibility exists for it to retrace its steps back to the critical junction and choose the other one. Perhaps, even, that knowing amounts to conservatism's central and essential function.

14

BURDEN OF EMPIRE: THE LEGACY OF THE ROOSEVELT-TRUMAN ERA

by Garet Garrett

1953

" 'Whose hand shall control the instrument of war?' It is late to ask. It may be too late, for when the hand of the Republic begins to relax another hand is already putting itself forth." The voice is as fresh as Patrick Buchanan's, as relevant to the American situation today as that of Paul Craig Roberts or Charley Reese. Yet, those words were written in 1952, a dozen years before the Tonkin Gulf Resolution and nearly two decades before even neoconservatives knew what a neoconservative was. (Which only goes to show how far we've progressed as a country over the last half-century.)

Garet Garrett (1878–1954), from good Middle American stock, was raised in the very middle of the middle of the country. Born in rural Illinois, he grew up in Burlington, Iowa, and learned to handle a team by the age of ten, having quit school after the third grade. He apprenticed himself to a Burlington printer and worked for a time at that trade before, having grown restless, he hitched a boxcar over to Cleveland, where he was hired on by the *Cleveland Plain Dealer*. Later, he went to Washington to work for the *Washington Times* and ended up in New York City, writing for the financial pages of all the big papers there and hobnobbing with the likes of Bernard Baruch. After reporting on World War I from Germany, Garrett returned to New York, where he assumed the position of executive editor at the *Herald-Tribune*. Though his eight books include a history of the United States and two novels (about the business world), Garet Garrett was mainly a financial writer—which explains why, despite the enormous political sagacity displayed in *Burden of Empire: The Legacy of the Roosevelt-Truman Era*, his work gives the impression that an economist, rather than an historian or a political journalist, is doing most of the talking. (To the extent that Garrett is known today, he owes his readership largely to the efforts of libertarian conservatives like Justin Raimondo and the late Murray Rothbard—an economist—who have helped to keep his reputation, and his name, alive.)

An enthusiastic supporter of President Wilson's decision to commit the United States to the Great War, Garrett was subsequently among the earliest observers to perceive the deeper meaning of the New Deal, the darkest intentions of President Franklin D. Roosevelt, and (later) the degree to which America's part in World War II and the Cold War represented the extension of a "revolution within the form" handily accomplished by Roosevelt and his Brains Trust ("a bund of intellectual revolutionaries," to Garet Garrett). Like John T. Flynn, Garrett was targeted (along with the *Saturday Evening Post*, to which he contributed anti–New Deal copy) for destruction by a vengeful Roosevelt; after Pearl Harbor, when the *Post* announced its unconditional support of the president in wartime, he resigned from the magazine's staff and later accepted the editorship of *American Affairs*, a publication of the National Industrial Conference Board. *The Revolution Was*, though written in 1938, did not see print until six years later. This pamphlet, together with its sequels *Ex America* and *The Rise of Empire*, was released in 1953 by the Caxton Printers as a trilogy entitled *The People's Pottage*.

Garrett wrote what he saw, with the prophet's brutal clarity

and forcefulness, facilitated by a quirky, colloquial style that
seems wholly American. Written three years before the publication of *The Managerial Revolution:What Is Happening in the World*,
The Revolution Was offers a startling counterthesis to that of James
Burnham's far better known classic: The managerial revolution
was effected, not in an evolutionary way but directly, by a revolutionary presidential administration in Washington, D.C.

To those who in the 1930s warned of political revolution in
progress and called for holding the pass against it, Garrett's message was blunt: They were staring in the wrong direction. "The
revolution is behind them. It went by in the Night of Depression,
singing songs to freedom." To fault the New Deal (Garrett insisted) on grounds of ignorance, contradiction, incompetence,
and senselessness was irrelevant, since it never intended to make
the kind of sense that an American basis would have presupposed
for it. "It took off from a revolutionary base. The design was European. Regarded from the point of view of revolutionary technique
it made perfect sense. Its meaning was revolutionary and it had
no other. For what it meant to do was from the beginning consistent with principle, resourceful, intelligent, masterly in work-
manship, and it *made not one mistake.*"

The fact of the revolution's overwhelming success proved, for
Garet Garrett, the American people's political immaturity. "To
the revolutionary mind the American vista must have been almost
as incredible as Genghis Khan's first view of China—so rich, so
soft, so unaware." Not only had America no revolutionary tradition, but the American government belonged to its people. "Why
should anyone fear government?"

Yet, since the turn of the twentieth century, American society
had been evolving a class of European-style intellectuals infected
with a resentful and bitter radicalism: "a prepared revolutionary
intelligence in spectacles. There was no plan to begin with. But
there was a shibboleth that united them all: 'Capitalism is finished.' There was one idea in which all differences could be resolved, namely, the idea of a transfer of power. For that a united
front; after that, anything. And the wine of communion was a pas-

sion to play upon history with a scientific revolutionary technic."
Unlike the Communist Party, the native radical elite could produce a Gracchus almost on demand, when the times were most
favorable for his success. And in 1932, at last they were. Economic distress was rife, but it amounted more to a national psy-
chosis than it did to actual misery, at least by comparison with the
rest of the world. The national wealth was fabulous, and it was
conveniently embodied in the modern, abstracted form. The political unsophistication of the American citizenry was demonstrated by the voters' having passed a law against the violent
overthrow of its government; and the elite was dedicated to Aristotle's "revolution within the form"—meaning, a change of power
within the framework of existing law. Given the conditions, the
revolutionaries confronted a set of problems, in a given sequence:
These were: 1) the capture of the seat of government; 2) the seizure
of economic power; 3) the mobilization of political and social hatred by modern propaganda; 4) the reconciliation and attachment
of the two great classes (farmers and industrial workers) whose
support was as indispensable as their interests were mutually antagonistic; 5) a solution to the "problem" of business; 6) "the do-
mestication of individuality" (Burckhardt's phrase); and, finally, 7)
the reduction, if not the elimination, of other rival authorities.

Now, Garrett observes, each of these problems was like a coin
with two sides. One side was engraved with the slogan of Recovery, the other with the policy of Revolution. The Roosevelt administration had an alternative to every decision it made, whether
to go with one side or the other. Guess which side it chose?

"[T]he choice," Garrett argues, "was one that could not fail:

(a) To ramify the authority and power of executive government—its power, that is, to rule by decrees and rules and regu-
lations of its own making;
(b) To strengthen its hold upon the economic life of the nation;
(c) To extend its power over the individual;
(d) To degrade the parliamentary principle;
(e) To impair the great American tradition of an independent,
Constitutional judicial power;

(f) To weaken all other powers—the power of private enterprise, the power of private finance, the power of state and local government;

(g) To exalt the leader principle.

The result was revolution in the form effected over a period of two decades, in part by the creation and manipulation of a series of countersymbols that recall George Orwell's warning that when words lose their meaning, people lose their freedoms. The object was power, of which the revolutionists never lost sight. Hating free enterprise, they did their best to destroy the capitalist system; failing that, to shackle it by federal control of finance and the money supply. In all of this, the New Deal—expression and embodiment of the revolutionary technic applied to America—operated beyond morality and legality, for neither of which it had the least concern. "Its cruel and cynical suspicion of any motive but its own," Garrett says in a fine phrase, "was a reflection of something it knew about itself." Anyhow, "the revolutionaries were inside; the defenders were outside. A government that had been supported by the people and so controlled by the people became one that supported the people and so controlled them. Much of it is irreversible."

The replacement of the old American Republic by the new centralized social-democratic state led directly, and in almost no time, to the creation of the American Empire. Both of these things were made possible by the government's taking control of the money supply and by its discovery of money as a means to abuse and expand its powers. "That is why," Garrett explains in *Ex America*, "every government in the secret recesses of its nature favors inflation. Inflation provides the means. Under pretense of making money cheap for the people, the government creates money for itself. When it goes into debt for what it calls public welfare it fills its own purse first and then, as it spends the money, it extends its authority over the liberties of its people. It suborns them." And not just its own people, either.

America's unprecedented wealth, in its real assets and its inflated currency, meant that her newly minted government was now free. "Free from what? Free from the ancient limitations of money." Without the government's magic wand to command billions whenever it wished, World War II might not have been possible; the Marshall Plan would have been unthinkable. Even so, there was left one thing wanting to "the government"—meaning, now, the executive—and that was the power to declare war: a power Roosevelt himself dared not grab, but left to his much weaker successor to claim (successfully) in the Korean "crisis." "'Whose hand shall control the instrument of war?' . . . [W]hen the hand of the Republic begins to relax another hand is already putting itself forth." That hand, of course, is the hand of empire.

The historian Clyde Wilson argues, in *From Union to Empire,* that a republic may be said to have passed over into empire "when political activity is no longer directed toward enhancement of the well-being of a particular people, but has become a mechanism for managing them for the benefit of their rulers." Garet Garrett is more specific. In his mind, empire is characterized by: the dominance of the executive power of government; the subordination of domestic policy to foreign policy; the ascendancy of the military mind, and its intimidation of the civilian one; the acquisition of satellite nations to serve as the empire's "hired guard;" a complex of "vaunting and fear" in the mind of both the government and its people; and the imperial nation's becoming, at last, "a prisoner of history."

The way of empire is fraught with burden, contradiction, and distraction, benefitting none but a restricted imperial elite. Every republic belongs to itself; empire, owing to its global extent and stature, belongs to history. A republic has no responsibilities beyond itself; empire has a mission to instruct and reconstruct the world. Empire vaunts itself: It takes untold satisfaction from the thought, "It is our turn." Our turn to assume international moral leadership. Our turn to save civilization and serve mankind, in the name of peace—"Peace by grace of force," naturally. Of course, that force requires to be perpetually exerted. For empire, there is no getting off the track, no going back. The empire must always go on. "What does going on mean? You never know."

Yes, the Roman Empire and the British Empire were Bad

Things. (Roosevelt disliked and mistrusted Winston Churchill as a Tory imperialist, while entertaining a fondness for Uncle Joe Stalin and admiring the "progressive" spirit of the Soviet Union.) But the American Empire would be "Empire in a new sign. For the first time in the history of mankind it happens that the paramount power of the world is in the keeping of a nation that has neither the will to exploit others nor any motive to increase its wealth at their expense. It wants only to chain the aggressor down, and then a world in which all people shall be politically free to govern themselves and economically free to produce and exchange wealth with one another on equal terms." That passage was written more than a half-century ago. Five decades later, it is not only the political heirs of the New Dealers and the Fair Dealers who think this way: Instead, they have been joined by the Republican Party in a bipartisan push (or should it be putsch?) for empire that is challenged only by the wilderness party, when the imperialist plans of the party in power go awry (as occurs today in the Iraq War). Unfortunately, the empire, as Garet Garrett recognizes, is indeed under a new sign, and that sign is eventual bankruptcy. "This is the Imperialism of the Good Intent. . . . Empire of the Bottomless Purse."

So much for empire, then. How might it be dissolved, and the republic restored? "Do not ask," Garrett exhorts, "whether or not it is possible. Ask yourself this: If it were possible, what would it take?" His answers are: the necessity for the American people to relearn the habit of thinking for themselves; for foreign policy issues to be submitted once again for public debate; for the control of the public purse to be taken from the executive branch and restored to the legislative one; for the "Fallacious Serpent" (planned inflation) to be reduced to an impotent shadow; and for the fortitude required to take the momentous step to decelerate an economy fueled by perpetual war and inflation and to suffer the relatively short-term but unpleasant consequences resulting from that crucial commonsense policy.

Realists will object that democracy is inherently inflationary, and that, just as Garrett concedes that the American people ac-

quiesced in political revolution after the fact, so in the fifty years
since he wrote have they acquiesced in empire; therefore, to alter
or reverse course at the beginning of the twenty-first century is
impossible. For such people, Garet Garrett has an answer as good
for 2004 as it was for 1953: "If that were true, then a piece of
writing like this would be an exercise in pessimistic vanity."

15

SUICIDE OF THE WEST: AN ESSAY ON THE MEANING AND DESTINY OF LIBERALISM

by James Burnham

1964

James Burnham (1909–1987) ranks unquestionably as one of the most original and penetrating thinkers of the twentieth century, not alone in the context of modern conservative literature but in the history of Western thought in the twentieth century. Indeed, it was probably not until late in his career that Burnham regarded himself as a "conservative" at all (if indeed he ever did) for the reason that the term seems too warmly emotional to describe his dispassionate, nearly scientific attitude toward human affairs.

The son of a wealthy New York City railroad executive, Burnham became a Trotskyite and a member of the inner circle of *Partisan Review* before breaking with the Left and devoting the remainder of his life to resisting the communist assault on the West. A man of vast erudition, Burnham was for many years a professor of philosophy at New York University, and in 1955 became a founding editor of the young William F. Buckley Jr.'s *National Review*, to which he contributed a regular column, "The Protracted Conflict," until 1977, almost the end of the Cold War. Had his career extended through another decade, Burnham might well have prevented *NR*'s slide leftward into neoconservatism, where the magazine is presently moored.

As the dominant intellectual presence at *National Review,* Burnham was admired by staff and readership alike for his lucidity of mind and prose; though one could argue that, in abandoning the Marxist dialectic for conservative anticommunism, he threw out the previous content of his mind without changing its mold. In fact, the intellectual rigidity so characteristic of the man ("Who says A must say B . . .") may well have intensified in later life. In 1977, James Burnham suffered a crippling stroke that made reading and writing impossible for him thereafter. He died just two years before the collapse of his archenemy, the Soviet Union; yet, it seems probable that, had he lived, the sudden demise of the system he had argued for thirty years was destined to rule the world would have caught him entirely by surprise.

Suicide of the West: An Essay on the Meaning and Destiny of Liberalism, first published in 1964, has affinities with Kenneth R. Minogue's *The Liberal Mind,* released a year earlier in England. While the two books make overlapping statements regarding the nature of liberalism as an ideology, as between the two, Burnham's is the more accessible to the general public, though written by a man with academic philosophical credentials to match Minogue's own. More important, Burnham, after delineating the logic of liberalism and analyzing the liberal mentality, goes on to suggest the implications pervasive liberalism has for the future of the United States and for geopolitical arrangements in the coming decades.

Burnham tells us in his preface that this is a "third-generation" book, revised and expanded over a period of four years from two sets of university lectures. Following his classic *The Managerial Revolution* by nearly a quarter-century, *Suicide of the West* reveals a more relaxed and humorous writer than the man who put his name to the earlier work. By 1964, James Burnham had worked as a journalist for nine years in the offices of *National Review.* Time and journalistic practice honed his polemical skills, while modifying somewhat the professorial pretense to scientific dispassion and disengagement. *Suicide of the West* is an eminently readable, mordantly witty, and genuinely unpleasant book, though it closes on a slightly more optimistic note than *The Managerial Revolution* does. "There are a few small signs, here and there," Burnham writes in his concluding lines, "that liberalism may already have started fading. Perhaps this book is one of them." It wasn't.

Burnham's thesis is straightforward. "Liberalism," he writes, "is the ideology of western suicide. When once this initial and final sentence is understood, everything about liberalism—the beliefs, emotions and values associated with it, the nature of its enchantment, its practical record, its future—falls into place. Implicitly, all of this book is merely an amplification of this sentence." That is not to say, Burnham adds, that liberalism is "'the cause'" of the contraction and probable death of Western civilization. ("The cause or causes have something to do, I think, with the decay of religion and with an excess of material luxury; and, I suppose, with getting tired, and worn out, as all things temporal do.") Rather, "liberalism has come to be the typical verbal systematization of the process of Western contraction and withdrawal; . . . liberalism motivates and justifies the contraction, and reconciles us to it." Furthermore, liberalism's hold on public opinion and policy makes it extremely difficult for the Western nations to invent—and even to imagine—a strategy equal to the challenge to its existence by which the West is presently confronted.

Burnham categorizes liberalism, though a looser concept than Marxism and socialism, as ideological in nature—unlike its still more loosely conceived opponent, conservatism. Ideology, by his definition, is "a more or less systematic and self-contained set of ideas supposedly dealing with the nature of reality (usually social reality), or some segment of reality, and of man's relation (attitude, conduct) toward it; and calling for a commitment [i.e., agendum] independent of specific experience or events." Liberalism, heir to the "main line . . . of post-Reaniassance thought" and dominated in its formative phase by Francis Bacon and René Descartes, is *rationalistic* by nature. Considering human nature to be plastic, rather than pure or corrupt, it finds no reason to believe humanity incapable of achieving the peace, freedom, justice, and well-being embodied in the liberal dream of the "good society," and rejects therefore the tragic view of man held by non-Christian, as well as Christian, thinkers before the Renaissance. It is also *antitraditional*, believing that ideas, customs, and institutions held over from the past are suspect, rather than worthy of respect. Suspicion of hoary error and injustice makes liberalism *progressive*, a characteristic that, as John Stuart Mill observes, "is antagonistic to the law of Custom, involving at least emancipation from that yoke."

"Professor Sidney Hook," Burnham remarks with good-humored malice, "has squeezed the entire definition of liberalism into a single unintentionally ironic phrase: 'Faith in intelligence.'" The dig, despite its humorous intent, explains why liberalism's commitment to rationality has never precluded an exuberant irrationalism of its own: To the extent that modern liberalism has replaced reason with religious faith as its foundation, its faith in reason is unreasonable. Assured that all human wrongheadedness and intransigence can be cured by education and that the social expressions of these undesirable qualities signify "problems" to be solved by political action, liberals envision politics as "simply education generalized" and the end of politics as social perfection (entailing, as Michael Oakeshott notes, social uniformity). Yet, the human record demonstrates that human beings, individually and collectively, are *not* perfectible and that every attempt to prove experience wrong has had highly unpleasant effects. For liberals, the fact of human imperfectibility would be tragic—if liberal ideology were inclined to understand history as tragedy, which it isn't.

Moreover, the excessive rationalism of liberalism commits it paradoxically to a relativistic theory of truth, which holds that no objective truth exists and that, if it does, we could never prove that objective truth was, in fact, what we had hold of. This reasoning amounts to a form of anti-intellectualism that is wholly unexpected from the premier intellectual tradition of modern intellectualism. It amounts also to what Burnham perceives as "an inescapable practical dilemma" for liberalism. "Either [it] must extend the [liberal] freedoms [of speech, conscience, association, etc.] to those who are not themselves liberals and even to those whose deliberate purpose is to destroy the liberal society . . . or liberalism must deny its own principles, restrict the freedoms, and practice discrimination." This dilemma, Burnham notes, is particularly sharp in our own day, when liberal societies have been infiltrated by agents of aggressive totalitarianism. "Surely there would seem to be something fundamentally wrong with a doctrine that can survive in application only by violating its own principles." It is why, he suggests, so many liberals tend to shrink from any explicit statement of the fundamental principles of liberalism.

Liberalism, though surely a *rational* system, is not by virtue of its rationality a *reasonable* one. Liberalism amounts to a fasces of propositions (Burnham lists nineteen), not all of which all liberals accept. So logical is the structure of liberal ideology, however, that if certain of these liberal beliefs can be shown to be false or problematical, logical argument based on the chain of logical propositions simply dissolves. And so, "[t]he liberals, whether they like it or not, are stuck with liberalism." As with Frank Sinatra, for them it's "All, or nothing at all"—a desperate situation in politics, as well as love.

The ideology of reason, Burnham shows, in reality lives by faith; the ideology of rationality harbors deeply irrational tendencies. Guilt, Burnham argues, is integral to liberalism, in which it is a motivating force. But while the liberal's conviction of his own guilt in the face of oppression and misery may or may not bespeak some moral obligation on his part, neither the guilt nor the obligation can be derived from liberalism's own principles, since liberal theory is atomistic and rejects the organic view of society on which the notion of collective guilt depends. Therefore, liberal guilt is not only irrational, it is irrational "precisely from the point of view of the liberal ideology itself." The genius of liberalism in relieving the burden of personal guilt—though without ever absolving anyone from it, and forbearing to exact penance—is, Burnham concedes, a "significant achievement, by which [liberalism] confirms its claim to being a major ideology." Nevertheless, in the context of his argument and of the condition of the Western world today, the problem of liberal guilt comes down to this: "that the liberal, and the group, nation, or civilization infected by liberal doctrine and values, are morally disarmed before those whom the liberal regards as less well off than himself."

The element of guilt, added to liberalism's egalitarianism, universalism, and internationalism, is the activating ingredient that makes the liberal compound such a deadly one for the Western world. Guilt, when it becomes obsessive for the liberal, flowers as a generalized hatred for his own country and the wider civilization of which it is a part; it is hatred that causes him to sympathize with their (and his) enemies, toward whom he is already inclined by the fact of liberalism's intellectual kinship with socialism and communism. The relationship (which is instinctively felt by liberals, though never acknowleged by them) explains why, for the liberal, the implicit rule of thumb is *"Pas d'ennemi à gauche"*— which translates as "No enemy to the left" and means "The preferred enemy is always to the right."

This inclination, Burnham insists, "is in a pragmatic sense a legitimate and inevitable expression of liberalism as a social tendency. It is not merely arbitrary prejudice or quirk of temperament." A partial explanation has to do with liberalism's anti-statism in the nineteenth century, before it *was* the state; and the discomfort—even disbelief—experienced by an historically anti-establishment movement in having *become* the establishment, after seizing the apparatus of government and accepting the role of despised authoritarian from the Right. (Something else to feel guilty about, perhaps.) Be that as it may, it remains a fact of history that liberalism, both as an active movement and an ideological doctrine, has nearly always opposed the existing order. In result, Burnham says, "[l]iberalism has always stressed change, reform, the break with encrusted habit whether in the form of old ideas, old customs or old institutions. Thus liberalism has been and continues to be primarily negative in its impact on society: and in point of fact it is through its negative and destructive achievements that liberalism makes its best claim to historical justification."

Universalism, relativism, materialism, moral perfectionism, guilt, self-criticism amounting to self-hatred, ideological reflex self-disguised as scientific thinking, antiestablishmentarianism, perpetual social and spiritual restlessness, endless reform, and the ceaseless sturm und drang accompanying it—plainly, liberalism is not the governing philosophy appropriate to a beleaguered civilization engaged in the greatest struggle for existence in its history. What is wanted, rather, is confidence arising from a proud sense of self-appreciation and self-worth, and a value system transcending affluence and comfort, such as men are willing to die for. "Quite specifically, [what the West needs is] the pre-liberal conviction that Western civilization, thus Western man, is both different from and superior in quality to other civilizations and noncivilizations. . . . [Also, it requires] a renewed willingness, legitimized by that conviction, to use superior power and the threat of power to defend the West against all challenges and challengers."

Such conviction and willingness are things liberalism by its nature is incapable of providing, even in the face of what Burnham identifies as the three crucial challenges to civilization: the "jungle" overtaking society, explosive world population growth and political activization in the Third World, and the communist drive toward world domination. Against these dangers, Burnham sees, liberalism in its Gaderene stampede from reality is worse than ineffectual: It is, quite literally, suicidal. For him, the mixture of utopian social policies at home and a foreign policy whose survivalist instincts are often confused and sometimes negated by moralistic and ideological tendencies amply demonstrates that fact.

Suicide of the West bears directly on a contemporary internecine debate sparked by the left wing of the antiliberal alliance, members of which have recently claimed this distinguished social critic, political commentator, and geopolitical strategist as "the first neoconservative." The case for Burnham as a "neocon" appears limited to his frequent advocacy of global interventionism—armed, if necessary—by the United States to protect and forward American and Western security. This tendency (so the argument goes) places him squarely in the camp of the global democrats, multinational capitalists, and "American greatness conservatives" of the present day, all of whom are eager for Washington to impose American values and institutions on a reluctant world. A closer look from a less parti pris standpoint suggests otherwise.

To begin with, Burnham was concerned with the survival of the United States and the West, and not with the welfare of the world. He wished Third World and other backward countries to be controlled by the West in the West's best interests, not reformed by it, and doubted that most—if any—of these so-called developing nations were capable of being trained up to civilization at the Western level. While Burnham called for the preservation—not the exportation—of Western civilization, there is no evidence that he considered consumer capitalism and mass culture, American style, to be among its glories. Unlike the neoconservatives, Burnham did not see the founding fathers as sharers in the European Enlightenment's optimistic (i.e., liberal) view of human nature. Rather, he seems to have taken them at their word on the subject, as when John Adams wrote that "human passions are insatiable," that "self-interest, private avidity, ambition and avarice will exist in every state of society and under every form of government," and that "reason, justice and equity never had weight enough on the face of the earth to govern the councils of men." For himself, James Burnham, espousing the tragic view of history, had no use whatsoever for neoconservative triumphalism. So far from believing the United States would prevail over all, he appears to have expected it, and with it the West, to become in time something other than the West—that is, to perish. Burnham in maturity was a realist rather than an optimist, a thinker rather than a careerist. He never told you what he thought you wanted to hear or what would make him rich and powerful to say. He gave you the truth as he saw it, and went on to write another book.

16

WITNESS

by Whittaker Chambers

1952

All great books are in some sense a part of history. *Witness,* however, is directly a part of the political history of its time, which it summarizes, explains, and exemplifies. Whether it is as well a work of great literature is debatable, for reasons largely irrespective of the character of its author who for the past half-century has been alternately praised as a hero, prophet, genius, and saint; damned for a compulsive liar, reckless slanderer, grand provocateur, and political psychopath; or, somewhere in between, deprecated as a sentimental megalomaniac and self-dramatizing poseur, whose fondest image of himself was that of a solitary and heroic figure caught between combatants in the War of the Titans that dominated and defined world history from 1917 to 1989.

Whittaker Chambers (1901–1961) himself appears to have been sensitive to an unprepossessing aspect of his nature as reflected in the confessional self-indulgence that detracts from the felt sincerity of *Witness.* In his copy of Chambers's book, the late Neil McCaffrey (a conservative publisher who did promotional work for *National Review* in the magazine's early days) noted beside the passage where Chambers justifies his untruthful denial—under oath—that he had direct knowledge of espionage, by invoking a God of Mercy over a God of Justice: "Here, too, is the good man adrift without a set of principles: justifying perjury." (On the page immediately previous, Chambers has just concluded a fairly casual and self-exculpating account of his failed suicide attempt.) Similarly, in the book's opening pages, he offers a self-referential explanation of the communist temptation, which he attributes (rather in the spirit of misplaced Christian charity, or indeed Divine Mercy) to communism's "profound appeal to the human mind"—not just *certain* human minds, but the human intellect itself! Again, Chambers describes the communist faith as the "great alternative faith of mankind," based on the vision of Man without God; strikingly, he refuses to call this "faith" by its real name, which is heresy of the most radical sort. Given the author's apocalyptic vision of a War of the Worlds between communism and "freedom" and his insistence on the radical evil communism represents, Chambers's insistence on the intellectual honesty of many individual communists, however misguided, seems worse than self-serving; it is almost unclean. Yet, this tawdriness displays a reverse side: the self-made greatness of a deeply flawed man who achieved, finally, the heroic stature for which he was in many ways unsuited. It is possible to conclude from reading *Witness* that its author is a slightly hysterical monomaniac under the spell of the noisiest Romantic composers and of Quaker piety. It is nearly impossible for a fair reader to doubt, in the end, that Whittaker Chambers did what he said he did, knew whom he said he knew, and saw what he said he saw. In this respect, *Witness* is absolutely compelling—in some of the most expressive prose written in the last century.

Witness is the story of the mythic Alger Hiss-Chambers case, written by the man to whom it owed its making. The basic facts of the case are well known. In August 1948, a senior editor at *Time* testified at a hearing held by the House Un-American Activities Committee that Alger Hiss (socialite; president of the Carnegie Foundation for World Peace and darling of the Washington establishment; former assistant to Assistant Secretary of State Francis Sayre; a participant at the Dumbarton Oaks Conference at Yalta and at the San Francisco conference that came up with the charter for the United Nations) had belonged to the communist apparatus functioning in Washington before World War II. Chambers himself had joined the Communist Party in 1925 and, in spite of recurring misgivings, remained a member until the spring of 1938, when he "broke" and went into hiding with his family for a year. His closest friends within the party (so Chambers stated, and later wrote) had been Alger Hiss and Hiss's second wife, Priscilla; neither of whom he had seen (he claimed) since 1938, when he visited the Hisses at their home in Washington, informed them of his break, and pleaded with Hiss also to desert the Communist Party. Hiss sued Chambers, claiming slander. Chambers countered by producing classified State Department documents, or copies of such, allegedly given him by Hiss that Chambers had afterward deposited for safekeeping in a hollowed-out pumpkin on his farm in Maryland. The hearings (which established the career of Representative Richard M. Nixon from California, then a member of HUAC) led eventually to Hiss's indictment on two counts of perjury by a federal grand jury in New York on December 15, 1948.

His first trial produced a hung jury in July 1949; at the conclusion of the second trial, the jury found the defendant guilty as charged and the judge sentenced Alger Hiss to five years in prison. Hiss served his time, while refusing to admit guilt in the case. Indeed, he continued to profess innocence straight through to the end of a very long life, during which he remained a cause célèbre on the American Left. Similarly, Whittaker Chambers, though he died a broken man at the age of sixty in 1961, lived the remainder of his life as an icon of the postwar conservative movement, enjoying an intimate friendship with William F. Buckley, Jr. and with Buckley's *National Review,* founded in 1955. Senator Joseph McCarthy's charge that the State Department was infiltrated by communists after "twenty years of treason" in Washington, coming as it did a year after Hiss's conviction to ignite a violently divisive political controversy that is not completely ended after half a century, is partly responsible for the case's longevity—but only partly.

"[A] man," Chambers writes in his foreword, "A Letter to My Children," "may . . . be an involuntary witness. I do not know any way to explain why God's grace touches a man who seems unworthy of it. But neither do I know any other way to explain how a man like myself—tarnished by life, unprepossessing, not brave— could prevail so far against the powers of the world arrayed almost solidly against him, to destroy him and defeat his truth. In this sense, I am an involuntary witness to God's grace and to the fortifying power of faith." The daughter of a German diplomat in Moscow, attempting to explain to Chambers why her father had renounced communism to become a fervent anticommunist, told how "one night—in Moscow—he heard screams. That's all. Simply one night he heard screams." In Chambers's case, his conversion was accomplished by the sight of his young daughter's perfectly formed ear: for him, an irresistible witness to the force of Design in the universe and to the eternal existence of a Great Designer.

In breaking with the communist world revolution and allying himself with "freedom," or the West, Chambers believed that he was abandoning the winning side of history for the losing one. His subsequent treatment by the "progressive" American establishment only confirmed him in that belief. "Every public failure to understand my purpose, every official effort to shut off my testimony or to penalize me for testifying, pled that the Communists were right and that I was wrong, pled that I was a fool not to know that it is a law of history that no one can save those who will not save themselves, whose plight is the proof that they have lost the instinct of self-preservation." The working class—an acquaintance remarked to Chambers—are Democrats, the middle class are Republicans, and the upper class are communists. Chambers thought he had correctly divined the course of history; he never imagined, however, that victory would be achieved, by one side or the other, this side of a titanic struggle. Thus, not he alone but his children and indeed all people alive were called to be involuntary witnesses to the clash of the "two great faiths of our time." "In nothing," Chambers promised his children, shall I be so much a witness, in no way am I so much called upon to fulfill my task, as in trying to make clear to you (and the world) the true nature of Communism and the source of its power, which was the cause of my ordeal as a man, and remains the historic ordeal of the world in the 20th century. For in this century, within the next decades, will be decided for generations whether all mankind is to become Communist, whether the whole world is to become free, or whether, in the struggle, civilization as we know it is to be completely destroyed or completely changed. It is our fate to live upon that turning point in history.

It might seem reasonable, at the beginning of the third millennium and more than a decade after the collapse of the Soviet Union, to throw Whittaker Chambers's pessimism up to his shade. In fact, his prophetic vision can be stretched to include even that epochal event, as a further passage in *Witness* suggests. "The crisis," he writes,

> of Communism exists to the degree in which it has failed to free the peoples that it rules from God. Nobody knows this better than the Communist Party of the Soviet Union. The crisis of the Western world exists to the degree in which it is indifferent to God. It exists to the degree in which the Western world actually shares Communism's materialist vision, is so dazzled by the logic of the materialist interpretation of history, politics and economics, that it fails to grasp that, for it, the only possible answer to the Communist challenge: Faith in God or Faith in Man? is the challenge: Faith in God.

Had Chambers lived into the 1970s, he would have been unsurprised by emerging signs of "convergence," suggesting that the Soviet Union and the United States were on approach to one another—politically, economically, and socially—as the Soviets attempted to re-create for themselves the economic miracle the Americans had achieved, and the Americans sought to extend the concept of "socialism in one country" to their own. Since the Union of Soviet Socialist Republics conveniently removed itself from the

international stage in 1989, the United States of America has succeeded it as the paradise, beacon, and hope of the Left; which, by
co-opting capitalism instead of destroying it, is moving rapidly to
accomplish its agenda, both international and domestic. No nation today is more ideologically driven than "the indispensable
nation," no nation today acts more aggressively in seeking to impose its secular-capitalist-democratical beliefs on foreign nations
and un-American societies. The spirit of the old Soviet Union abhorred by Whittaker Chambers lives on, in substantial degree, in
the semipossessed body of its "victorious" rival, the United States.

Chambers concedes (perhaps he concedes too much) that
communists are "sincere" in their faith, by which he appears to
have understood "well-meaning." Beyond doubt, however, the
members of the crowd that opposed him with ridicule, contempt,
and slander were at the very least dishonest, in the sense that they
were much less than candid about who they actually were, where
their sympathies lay in the world struggle, and how they planned
to realize those sympathies. Chambers knew exactly why: To him,
the explanation was obvious enough:

> It was the forces of this [communist] revolution that had smoth-
> ered the Hiss Case (and much else) for a decade, and fought to
> smother it in 1948. These were the forces that made the phene-
> menon of Alger Hiss possible; had made it possible for him to
> rise steadily in Government and to reach the highest post *after*
> he was already under suspicion as a Communist in many quar-
> ters, including Congress, and under the scrutiny of the F.B.I.
> Alger Hiss is only one name that stands for the whole Com-
> munist penetration of Government. He could not be exposed
> without raising the question of the real political temper and
> purposes of those who had protected and advanced him, and
> with whom he was so closely identified that they could not tell
> his breed from their own.

Half a century later, Chambers's insight was corroborated in
more explicit terms by Samuel Francis (the contemporary author
and columnist) in respect of the McCarthy phenomenon that followed on the heels of the Hiss-Chambers case. By way of explain-

ing the despisement and hatred of the senator from Wisconsin expressed by American liberals, Francis suggests that McCarthy put them in the position of having to explain how—precisely—liberalism differs from communism in its essential nature. Granted that liberalism pursues an obviously milder agendum than communism, in what other respects do the two differ? Are the differences between them generic or are they a matter of degree only? Liberals in McCarthy's time, and since, have been unable to answer that question without embarassing themselves and compromising their program—which is why the man who put them in the hot seat has always been anathema to them and always will be, so long as they succeed in keeping his memory alive.

17

THE HARVEST OF SORROW: SOVIET COLLECTIVIZATION AND THE TERROR-FAMINE

by Robert Conquest

1986

Robert Conquest (1917–) is a published poet, novelist, and translator (of Aleksandr Solzhenitsyn's *Prussian Nights)*, as well as a prolific historian of Russia. As a work of historical research, his account of the Soviet program of rural collectivization and dekulakization in the 1920s and early 1930s is a monument to genius, while the richness of grotesque, horrific, and ironic detail gives this book the specificity and particularity on which literature depends. Compounding these qualities, Conquest's narrative skills—his sense of economy and pacing, especially—ensure a gripping narrative that succeeds in overwhelming the reader with a diabolical reality covered over, disguised, denied, rationalized, and explained away for decades by the international Left.

The Harvest of Sorrows: Soviet Collectivization and the Terror-Famine is a book of horrors recounting the arrest, imprisonment, deportation, and execution of the kulaks, or well-off peasants of the Ukraine; the campaign to "settle" and collectivize the nomadic Kazakhs for the purpose of eradicating "the economic and cultural anachronisms of the nationalities," which, between 1929 and 1936, reduced the number of Kazakh households from 1,233,000 to 565,000; the death of millions of families by slow starvation; the liquidation of the Ukraine's blind bards, invited to a congress where they were arrested and subsequently shot; and the destruction or maiming of a generation of children in the Ukraine (indeed, in the Soviet Union), by means including the solution of the "problem" of homeless juveniles by their "liquidation"—all combining to produce a death toll of as many as fifteen million human beings.

The profound importance of *The Harvest of Sorrow* lies in its implicit thesis that communism is as evil in theory as it is in practice: a mental act of intellectual rebellion, mayhem, and destruction as wicked, deranged, and inhuman as the physical violence and brutality it encourages. Nothing so enrages liberals as the observation that, after all, liberalism is on the same continuum as communism, with all its overt terrors. Yet, Conquest implies as much in his chapter "The Record of the West," where he concludes that "[t]he scandal is not just that [a large body of influential Western liberals and socialists] justified the Soviet actions [which many did], but that they refused to hear about them, that they were not prepared to face the evidence." If liberalism were not in fact akin to communism, then liberals would not have invested so much emotional capital as in fact they did in the success of Soviet Russia; they would not, and could not, have allowed themselves to be taken in by Soviet propaganda and their own wishful thinking, which amounted to a program of self-propagandization. "This lobby of the blind and the blindfold"—which included Sidney Webb and Beatrice Webb, George Bernard Shaw, Anna Louise Strong, and, most notoriously, the *New York Times*'s Soviet correspondent, Walter Duranty, who was not blind at all but a conscious liar—"could not actually prevent true accounts by those who were neither dupes nor liars from reaching the West. But they could, and did, succeed in giving the impression that there was at least a genuine doubt about what was happening and insinuating that reports of starvation came only from those hostile to the Soviet government and hence of dubious reality." Their falsifcations, moreover, were lasting in their effect, persisting at least into the 1940s and winking out, finally, only in the post-Soviet period. Three years before *The Harvest of Sorrow* was first published in 1986, the *New York Times*'s Company Annual Report of 1983 printed a list of Pulitzer Prizes received by its writers to date, including the one awarded to Duranty for "dispassionate, interpretive reporting of the news from Russia." By 1983, Duranty was well known—even by the *Times*—to have been the Prince of Journalistic Liars in his, or anyone else's, century. Even so, as late as 2003, the Pulitzer Prize Board refused to revoke Duranty's award on the grounds that there exists "no clear and convincing evidence of deliberate deception" by the reporter in those articles cited by the board in 1932.

"Fifty years ago as I write these words," Conquest begins his story,

> the Ukraine and the Ukrainian, Cossack and other areas to its east—a great stretch of territory with some forty million inhabitants—was like one vast Belsen. A quarter of the rural population, men, women, and children, lay dead or dying, the rest in various stages of debilitation with no strength to bury their families or neighbors. At the same time (as at Belsen), well-fed squads of police or party officials supervised the victims.
>
> This was the climax of the "revolution from above," as Stalin put it, in which he and his associates crushed two elements seen as irremediably hostile to the regime: the peasantry of the USSR as a whole, and the Ukrainian nation.

The narrative covers the events related to that revolution, which occurred during the four years from 1929 to 1933. The first three witnessed the Soviet Communist Party's "double blow" at the Soviet peasantry in total: dekulakization—the killing or deportation of millions of peasants with their families to the Arctic—and collectivization, meaning the abolition, effectively, of private property in land. Between them, these two programs produced millions of deaths. The fourth year, 1932–1933, saw a "terror-famine" delivered to the collectivized peasantry of the Ukraine and of the Kuban, whose population was also chiefly Ukrainian. The catastrophe, deliberately and coldbloodedly engineered by the party, was effected by means of setting impossibly high grain quotas for the peasants to meet, withdrawing from them all food supplies, and blocking all outside aid from reaching the starving population. Concurrently, Joseph Stalin launched an all-out attack on Ukrainian cultural and intellectual centers and institutions, including the churches. He justified these actions by claiming that the peasants were guilty of deliberately withholding their grain from the requisition from nationalistic motives: "All of which," Conquest notes, "was in accord with Stalin's dictum that the national problem was in essence a peasant problem. The Ukrainian peasant thus suffered in double guise—as a peasant and as a Ukrainian." Before the war against the peasantry ended, the loss of life was greater than that suffered by all the belligerents in World War I taken together.

This "Second Revolution" was the result of intentions long held by the Communist Party and the frustrations it met with in trying to realize them. From the beginning, the party was determined to end individual farming and the rural market economy in the Soviet Union. In 1921, V.N. Lenin, realizing that his regime faced economic ruin, proclaimed the New Economic Policy, postponing the socialization of the countryside while the party consolidated its political power. Seven years later, Stalin, faced by a disequilibrium in the grain market amounting (he insisted) to a crisis, made the decision to requisition grain supplies that had been produced for profit under what the producers had understood to be guaranteed market conditions. Stalin, placing full blame for the crisis on the kulak, declared that "the solution lies in the transition from individual peasant farming to collective, socially conducted agriculture," and in "a struggle against the capitalist elements of the peasantry, against the kulaks." Refusing to recognize that the peasantry, in producing less grain for the market, was responding normally to artificially low prices set by Moscow, the party discovered by the end of the year that both grain and livestock production were in decline. In the conviction (as one Soviet economist put it) that its task was "not to study economics but to change it," the government followed its demoralizing policy of temporary compulsion with further force, and, when force failed, resorted to collectivization to ensure that the party controlled crop production from the start—a far sounder plan, from an ideological point of view, than NEP had offered.

"In effecting these ends," Robert Conquest explains, "the Party had relied continually on a spurious doctrinal analysis to show it a supposed class enemy of a minority in the countryside, whereas in fact almost the entire peasantry was opposed to it and its policies. This doctrinal fantasy had, however, practical advantages, in that it could be used against the natural leaders of the peasantry [i.e., the kulaks: best defined as the most "prosperous" peasants, amounting to 3 to 5 percent of the peasant class, of whom a minority owned three or four cows and two or three horses] to cripple the villages' resistance." The results—an end to the partial independence of the peasantry, to market economics, and to the petit bourgeoisie, together with the extension of state power throughout the countryside—wholly satisfied the Communist Party, despite the substantial reduction in grain production; more, the revival of class warfare proved a stimulant to its self-identity and sense of purpose. On December 29, 1929, *Pravda* quoted Stalin's boast: "We have gone over from a policy of limiting the exploiting tendencies of the kulak to a policy of liquidating the kulak as a class."

A century of publicized atrocities and mass atrocities, many of them (not including the more politically embarassing ones) accorded excruciating coverage by the mass media, has dulled the reaction of the public by impressing it with a sense, less of the banality of evil, than of its unreality. No one who has read Solzhenitsyn will be *surprised* by what he reads in *The Harvest of Sorrow*, though Conquest's book in instances surpasses even Solzhenitsyn's material in its graphic hideousness. But the twentieth century was, more still than the century of mass physical brutality, the century of mass metaphysical violence, the violent metaphysical lie. Physical violence on a large scale, so far from being new to history, is almost the stuff of it; mental or cognitive violence on a similar scale *is* something new, owing to its enablement by modern technology to dominate, pervert, and destroy societies and civilizations. From this perspective, the confiscation by a Soviet official of a starving peasant's cannister of flour mixed with ground bark seems less horrific than the deportation of kulaks who prospered felling timber in detention camps to the degree that they had to be dekulakized and deported for a second time; the party's invention of the socially meaningless term "subkulak" to identify people marked for liquidation; the declaration by the Bolshevik economist who declared, "We are bound by no [economic] laws. . . . The tempo is subject to decisions by human beings"; or the explanation for dekulakization given by a brave Russian novelist in 1934 ("Not one of [the kulaks] was guilty of anything; but they belonged to a class that was guilty of everything").

The root of every kind of sin is pride, and the greatest pride is the sin against metaphysical truth. In Christian terms, this amounts to blasphemy against the Holy Ghost; which, because it is the one sin for which there can be no divine forgiveness, inspires awe surpassing all understanding. Robert Conquest's stunning achievement in *The Harvest of Sorrow* is to have evoked a sense of that awe nearly beyond the bearing of it.

Part III
SOCIETY

18

HISTORICAL CONSCIOUSNESS:
OR, THE REMEMBERED PAST

by John Lukacs

1968

John Lukacs (1924–) is one the greatest historians of our time. Perhaps for that reason, he is additionally the bugbear of both his academic colleagues and of mainstream conservatives. The first group regards him as insufficiently "professional" (meaning, academic); the second as, at best, "not a team player," at worst a dangerous heretic. Nevertheless, Lukacs's stature is assured by his originality (always suspect by the "professionals") and independence of mind (much resented by movement conservatives); by his learning, which is vast in content as well as in scope; and finally by the grace, facility, and interest of his prose, which is unmatched by nearly all contemporary historians and most journalists.

A native of Budapest, Lukacs fled Hungary and emigrated to the United States in 1946 at the age of twenty-two. Since then, he has steadfastly avoided the lures, distractions, seductions, and weaknesses of establishment conservatism of the Anglo-American variety in the postwar era: its shameless careerism, its smug assurance that the world is its oyster, its boisterous nationalism and hysterical anticommunism, its philistine defense of consumer

capitalism and technocratic culture (viewed by Lukacs, with patrician disdain, as a particularly unpleasant modern heresy), and
its acceptance of free-market economics as its secular religion.
Despite his reputation in conservative circles as a naysayer and a
crank, John Lukacs is less an historical pessimist than an honest
Catholic philosopher who expects little or nothing from history
and is not afraid to say so. For more than half a century now, he
has documented "the passing of the modern age," the "devolu-
tions of its institutions and standards," and its succession by the
postmodern era, in which barbarism is renascent (though in a
form never before witnessed in history) and civilization (as distinguished from "culture") in free-fall.

While the end of the modern (or bourgeois) age is the central
theme of Lukacs's oeuvre taken as a whole, a glance at the listing
of his more than twenty books is enough to suggest the variety of
its breadth and development. Thus, among his works we find *The
Great Powers and Eastern Europe*; *Tocqueville: The European Revolution and Correspondence with Gobineau* (ed); *A History of the Cold
War*; *The Passing of the Modern Age*; *The Last European War: 1939–
1941*; *1945:Year Zero*; *Philadelphia: Patricians and Philistines 1900–
1950*; *Budapest 1900*; *Outgrowing Democracy: A History of the United
States in the Twentieth Century*; *The End of the Twentieth Century*;
Five Days in London: May 1940 (about Churchill's successful attempt to take Great Britain into World War II); and *Confessions of
an Original Sinner* (an autobiography). Published first in 1968
and since reprinted in two new editions (all three worth reading
nearly as separate books), *Historical Consciousness: or, The Remembered Past* remains—in its author's opinion, as well as that of most
of his critics and readers—John Lukacs's magnum opus.

Lukacs's thought is so complex, multifaceted, and divergent,
his sentences so full of fresh insights and mental grace notes, that
it is usually difficult to state in any kind of comprehensive or sat-
isfactory way what any particular one of his books is "about." In
Historical Consciousness—itself a richly complicated book—Lukacs
states his central thesis plainly enough at the outset, before proceeding to pull apart its many separate threads:

The principal theme of this book is that during the last three or four hundred years a movement—historical consciousness—has evolved, mostly in the West, which, though less recognized, may be at least as important as the other revolutionary movement—the so-called scientific revolution—for a number of reasons, one of them being that science is part of the history of man. Of this evolution the development of professional history has been but a portion, albeit an important one. Professional history followed in the wake of historical consciousness. In the eighteenth century people took history as a form of literature. In the nineteenth century history was regarded as a science, mostly by professional historians; it was then that the professionalization of history came about.

In the twentieth century, the majority of historians, uncomfortably aware that history is in fact *not* a science, tried to content themselves with the notion that it is, at least, a social scientific discipline. According to Lukacs, "A minority among historians, including this writer, believe that this is wrong, since not only the subject matter of history but the very condition of historical knowledge is different from the knowledge to which scientists, including social scientists, aspire."

The development of historical consciousness, Lukacs believes, is part of the development of personal consciousness in the modern individualized sense, as represented by psychoanalysis and the turn toward exploring interior consciousness in the arts; finally, toward self-knowledge. It is as well an aspect in the evolution of societies. History ("the remembered past") for Westerners has become a form of thought, a fact whose implications have yet to be recognized and understood: One of them is that "we may be outgrowing the scientific view of reality." Despite high intellectual talk about the present era in history being a posthistorical age, Lukacs believes, with the Dutch historian Johan Huizinga, that history is today "in our blood," and that the appetite for historical thinking will not disappear in the foreseeable future.

Furthermore, Lukacs argues, historical consciousness produces an ever-increasing intrusion of "mental element constructs in the formation of events"—analogously with Werner Heisenberg's principle that the act of observation alters the behavior of the object being observed. "What people think and what they believe is, more than ever, the main element of their histories." Contrary to Marxists and other economic materialists, "The main matter is what people think and believe, and the material organization and the material forms of their societies are but the superstructures of *that*." Lukacs's aperçu amounts, of course, to a devastating criticism of economic determinism. Ironically, it has got him into greater trouble on the Right than on the Left, for the reason that his profound historical and moral understanding has always prevented him from taking communism seriously, in spite of his youthful experience of it. For John Lukacs, the Union of Soviet Socialist Republics never was more than nationalist Russia swollen to historically greater proportions and motivated to a steroid aggressiveness. Communism (Lukacs has argued for nearly half a century now) has proved unconvincing and unappealing to nearly everyone: Historically, therefore, it is no more "subversive" than czarism was. Truly subversive of civilization are postbourgeois capitalism, scientism, consumerism, technicism, and a new form of nationalism—the democratic-capitalist variety—far more dangerous than the Russian variety ever was, by virtue of the vast economic and social power supporting it, the cultural prestige it enjoys, and the envy it has induced in Western and non-Western countries alike. For Lukacs, this is no more than historical truth, whose purpose is to achieve "understanding even more than accuracy, involving the reduction of untruth; . . . I can say that the *nature* of truth is inseparable from personal knowledge." For movement (or professional, or activist) conservatives concerned with concrete results ("defeating" communism, "defending" free enterprise and "freedom"), it was aid and comfort to the enemy. As so often happens, the Left perceived what John Lukacs was about more accurately than the Right did, and so this prophetic, provocative, and wholly original philosophical historian (as opposed, he would insist, to historical philosopher) has remained theoretically, politically, and professionally almost friendless throughout a long and hyperproductive career.

The historical form of thought, Lukacs insists, is an evolving product specific to our civilization, "involved as it has been with a specific kind of realism and with a particular tradition of rhetoric and with a certain conception of human nature." The reason is not difficult to find: It is the historicity of the West's two religions, Judaism and Christianity, culminating in God taking on Himself the form of a Man and becoming an historical character Himself. "Thinking about thinking is itself a form of thought, involving a certain kind of self-knowledge." Three to five centuries ago, following the end of the Middle Ages, an intellectual interregnum ensued. Now, we are experiencing another interregnum.

But,

History does not repeat itself. One distinct feature of our interregnum is that through excessive applications of scientific methods we may destroy ourselves. Another distinct feature of our interregnum is the condition that we may, historically thinking, recognize its existence. We know, *to some extent,* what is happening to our civilization—and this is something that our ancestors at the time of the Renaissance or at the end of the ancient world did not know. There are great potential dangers latent in this intellectual condition: for the notion of inevitability furthers the very progress of something that seems inevitable. Even more than the passing of the Middle Ages, the passing of the Modern Age has become inseparable from the idea of its passing. On the other hand we *may*—I am not saying that we *will*—confront our interregnum through our better understanding of ourselves: through the actual recognitions and the potential realism of our historical consciousness. The now present coexistence of widespread historical thinking with widespread intellectual confusion is unique: for, while intellectual confusion is characteristic of every great interregnum, historical thinking may be our principal heritage from the last three or four centuries, from "the Modern Age," "the bourgeois age," "the last age of reason," whatever we may wish to call it.

19

DEMOCRACY IN AMERICA

by Alexis de Tocqueville

1835, VOL. 1; 1840, VOL. 2

Russell Kirk, in *The Conservative Mind: From Burke to Eliot*, classifies Alexis de Tocqueville (1805–1859) as a "liberal conservative." Tocqueville, Kirk explains, "was not willing to let democracy become a cannibal; he would resist, so far as he could, the sacrifice of democracy's virtues upon the altar of democracy's lusts."

The great French aristocrat was guardedly optimistic about democracy, which he regarded as being, in its broad outlines at least, historically inevitable. "The gradual development of the equality of conditions," he wrote in the introduction to the first edition of *Democracy in America*,

is therefore a providential fact, and it possesses all the characteristics of a divine decree: it is universal, it is durable, it constantly eludes all human interference, and all events as well as all men contribute to its progress. Would it, then, be wise to imagine that a social impulse which dates from so far back can be checked by the efforts of a generation? Is it credible that the democracy which has annihilated the feudal system and vanquished kings will respect the citizen and the capitalist? Will it stop now that it has grown so strong and its adversaries so weak?

Several paragraphs on, Tocqueville reinforces his argument by suggesting that the democratization of societies is divinely willed:

It is not necessary that God Himself should speak in order to disclose to us the unquestionable signs of His will; we can discern them in the habitual course of nature, and in the invariable tendency of events. . . . If the men of our time were led by attentive observation and by sincere reflection to acknowledge that the gradual and progressive development of social equality is at once the past and future of their history, this solitary truth would confer the sacred character of a Divine decree upon the change.

To oppose the progress of democracy would therefore be to contend against God Himself.

Tocqueville was sent to the United States in 1831 by the French government to examine the American prison system. With his friend Gustave de Beaumont, he explored the regions between Boston, Green Bay, Sault St. Marie, Quebec, and New Orleans, before returning to France to write the magisterial work for which he is chiefly remembered. "Amongst the novel objects," he recalls, "that attracted my attention during my stay in the United States, nothing struck me more forcibly than the general equality of conditions." The more he studied American society, the more clearly he saw that this equality constituted the "creative element" from which all else American derived. Back in France, Tocqueville thought he perceived analogies between what he saw happening at home and what he had observed in the United States. Though the symptoms were less extremely developed in France, the trend to democracy, American style, was nevertheless making rapid advances toward power in Europe. "I hence conceived," he declares, "the idea of the book which is now before the reader"; written, Tocqueville adds, "under the impression of a kind of religious dread produced in the author's mind by the contemplation of so irresistible a revolution, which has advanced for centuries in spite of such amazing obstacles, and which is still proceeding in the midst of the ruins it has made."

Tocqueville wished democracy well, because he saw no future alternative to that form of government. If time does not remain to make a choice between it and other forms of government, "let us at least endeavour to make the best of that which is allotted to us; and let us so inquire into its good and its evil propensities as to be able to foster the former and repress the latter to the utmost."

He judged the success of democracy up until his own time to be limited, at best. ". . . [It] may be asked what we have adopted in the place of those institutions, those ideas, and those customs of our forefathers which we have abandoned." In Tocqueville's estimation, Europe had abandoned what was best and even good in the old order, without having developed what the new one had to offer: "We have . . . abandoned whatever advantages the old state of things afforded, without receiving any compensation from our present condition; we have destroyed an aristocracy, and we seem inclined to survey its ruins with complacency, and to fix our abode in the midst of them." Furthermore, the deplorable social and political situation was matched by the intellectual one:

Where are we, then? The religionists are the enemies of liberty, and the friends of liberty attack religion; the high-minded and the noble advocate subjection, and the meanest and most servile minds preach independence; honest and enlightened citizens are opposed to all progress, whilst men without patriotism and without principles are the apostles of civilization and of intelligence. Has such been the fate of the centuries which have preceded our own? and has man always inhabited a world like the present, where nothing is linked together, where virtue is without genius, and genius without honor; where the love of order is confounded with a taste for oppression, and the holy rites of freedom with a contempt of law; where the light thrown by conscience on human actions is dim, and where nothing seems to be any longer forbidden or allowed, honorable or shameful, false or true?

No nobler question has been put in all of modern literature; self-evidently, Toqueville's concerns are as relevant to the democratic world of today as they were to that of the early nineteenth century. Though he does not attempt to answer himself, the thought doubtless occurred to Tocqueville, as a devout Christian, that all ages have *not* been like "ours," that the confusion and disconnection of modern society are the result of the revolution—inspired by the scientific worldview as much as by the democratic one—against the historic faith of the West, and thus against the structure of reality itself. (The possibility raises a further question: whether democracy might be incompatible with the natural order of society?)

One way or another, such was the anguish of soul in which Toqueville approached his subject: as a traveler, an investigator, and a writer. ("The best lack all conviction," William Butler Yeats writes a century later, "while the worst are full of passionate intensity.") He did not operate from predetermined conclusions, nor with the intention of writing a panegyric to democracy and the democratic spirit. "Whoever should imagine that I have intended to write a panegyric will perceive that such was not my design; nor has it been my object to advocate any form of government in particular, for I am of opinion that absolute excellence is rarely to be found in any legislation; I have not even affected to discuss whether the social revolution, which I believe to be irresistible, is advantageous or prejudicial to mankind." Similarly, Tocqueville never expected that a likeness in social conditions between France and the United States would result in identical political institutions, or an identical political life. ("I am far from supposing that [the Americans] have chosen the only form of government which a democracy may adopt.") His purpose was not to discover in America a blueprint for a democratic society that could be imposed on his native land, but quite simply "to discover the evils and advantages which [democracy] produces."

What he found there often disturbed or dismayed him, while frequently commanding his respect:

The first thing that strikes the observer is an innumerable multitude of men, all equal and all alike incessantly endeavoring to procure the petty and paltry pleasures with which they glut their lives. . . . It is not impossible to conceive the surpassing liberty which the Americans enjoy; some idea may likewise be formed of the extreme equality which subsists amongst them, but the political activity which pervades the United States must be seen in order to be understood. It is impossible to spend more efforts in the pursuit of enjoyment. . . . [A]n American cannot converse, but he can discuss; and when he attempts to talk he falls into a dissertation. He speaks to you as if he was addressing a meeting; and if he should chance to warm in the course of discussion, he will say, "Gentlemen," to the person with whom he is conversing . . . I am persuaded that, if ever a despotic government is established in America, it will find it more difficult to surmount the habits which free institutions have engendered than to conquer the attachment of the citizens to freedom.

Yet, Toqueville never expected despotism, if ever it arrived in America, to establish itself through the agency of a de facto aristocracy, or what in later generations has been called a plutocracy, or a criminal gang seeking personal power. Rather, he thought it might arise from a tendency natural to democracy itself, what he termed "democratic despotism": the analysis of which, in Russell Kirk's judgment, is Tocqueville's "supreme achievement as a political theorist, a sociologist, a liberal, and a conservative." By "democratic despotism," Tocqueville meant a tyranny of mediocrity, imposed by the democratic mass and realized by central government through legally enforced standardization and uniformity.

"I think, then," he wrote,

that the species of oppression by which democratic nations are menaced is unlike anything that ever before existed in the world. . . . [T]he old words *despotism* and *tyranny* are inappropriate; the thing itself is new. . . . Above this race of men stands an immense and tutelary power, which takes upon itself alone to secure their gratifications and to watch over their fate. That power is absolute, minute, regular, provident, and mild. It would be like the authority of a parent if, like that authority, its object was to prepare men for manhood; but it seeks, on the contrary, to keep them in perpetual childhood; it is well content that the people should rejoice, provided that they think of nothing but rejoicing.

Democracy is dead: Long live democracy! Not even the form but only the name has been retained, the substance having been washed clean away and popular government replaced by an oligarchy—beneficent or not, depending on how the oligarchs themselves understand the word. Thus, in America the trajectory runs from Jeffersonian republicanism, through Jacksonian democracy, to James Burnham's managerial state, and even to George Orwell's *1984.*

Democracy is teleologically self-destructive. This is owing in part to its tendency to destroy the particularism on which it depends (only centralization, Tocqueville insists, is safe from revolution), and also on account of its susceptibility to a uniform mediocrity in individual men, in society, and in the particular men whom the mediocre mass elects, or suffers, to lead it. For this inescapable dilemma at the heart of the democratic conundrum, Tocqueville had no solution, offering only a provisional answer that recalls Jefferson's admonition to eternal vigilance as the price of democratic liberty. For democracy to work, even in the short run, he believed, men must be given rights to exercise in order that they may respect rights, and faith in God so that they may understand them. Furthermore, their elected representatives must have a just appreciation of democracy's limitations and dangers, as well as of its possibilities and benefits:

We must first understand what the purport of society and the aim of government is to be. If it be your intention to confer a certain elevation upon the human mind, and to teach it to regard the things of this world with generous feelings, to inspire men with a scorn of mere temporal advantage, to give birth to living convictions, and to keep alive the spirit of honorable devotedness; if you hold it to be a good thing to refine the habits, to embellish the manners, to cultivate the arts of a nation, and to promote the love of poetry, of beauty, and of renown; if you would constitute a people not unfitted to act with power upon all other nations, nor unprepared for those high enterprises which, whatever be the result of its efforts, will leave a name forever famous in time—if you believe such to be the principal object of society, you must avoid the government of democracy, which would be a very uncertain guide to the aim you have in view.

But if you hold it to be expedient to divert the moral and intellectual activity of man to the production of comfort, and to the acquirement of the necessities of life; if a clear understanding be more profitable to man than genius; if your object be not to stimulate the virtues of heroism, but to create habits of peace; if you had rather witness vices than crimes and are content to meet with fewer noble deeds, provided offences be diminished in the same proportion; if, instead of living in the midst of a brilliant state of society, you are contented to have prosperity all around you; if, in short, you are of the opinion that the principal object of government is not to confer the greatest possible share of power and of glory upon the body of the nation, but to ensure the greatest degree of enjoyment and the least degree of misery to each of the individuals who compose it—if such be your desires, you can have no surer means of satisfying them than by equalizing the conditions of men, and establishing democratic institutions.

Though he never declares a personal preference between democracy and what Churchill referred to as the "other" sorts of government, one may guess where the heart of this aristocratic French lawyer lies. Alexis de Tocqueville, however, never less realistic than he was fastidious, and perceiving that history had set itself against his predilections, faced the future he foresaw in a spirit of piety, and the hope that piety engenders, rather than with cynicism.

"I cannot . . . believe that the Creator made man to leave him in an endless struggle with the intellectual miseries which surround us: God desires a calmer and a more certain future to the communities of Europe; I am unacquainted with His designs, but I shall not cease to believe in them because I cannot fathom them, and I had rather mistrust my own capacity than His justice."

20

THE MANAGERIAL REVOLUTION: WHAT IS HAPPENING IN THE WORLD

by James Burnham

1941

The most important works of James Burnham (1909–1987) are *The Machiavellians: Defenders of Freedom, Suicide of the West: An Essay on the Meaning and Destiny of Liberalism*, and *The Managerial Revolution: What Is Happening in the World*. The last of these was read with great interest by—among many others—George Orwell, who borrowed from it the author's prediction that three superstates would arise to rule the world between them for purposes of his own in *1984*. Since its original publication, only months before the United States went to war with Germany and Japan, *The Managerial Revolution* has been recognized, on both the Right and the Left, as a prophetic and seminal work. Today, it enjoys the status of a classic one.

The book's thesis is straightforward enough (some critics, at the time and since, have thought *too* straightforward). Its plausibility was at once recognized, and while many of its brave predictions (such as that capitalism would be finished within a generation, or perhaps the next) have proved either incomplete or false, nevertheless Burnham's vision in its broad outlines has been substantially realized sixty years later. It may be summarized as follows:

Those people (and in 1941 they amounted to nearly every thoughtful observer of the times) who assume that the future belongs either to capitalism or to socialism are wrong in postulating two possible alternatives only. There is a third choice, to which Burnham assigns the term "managerialism." The managerial revolution, he insists, is already occurring in the West, and it will prevail. Socialism (i.e., public ownership of the means of production, by which ownership enjoys sole access to those means) has proved itself unworkable in the Soviet Union and elsewhere; capitalism is manifestly incapable of meeting the challenges and resolving the problems posed by industrial society. It is the managers of industrial corporations, freed from their capitalist masters and from the constraints of the necessity for profit, who alone possess the skills to manage an increasingly state-owned economy; even as an ever more economically involved state relies more heavily on bureaucrats (at the expense of the posturing politicians) to direct it. The result amounts to an historical probability (Burnham insists on this, even though he describes his thesis as a "theory"): In an age in which modern societies are forced to become efficiency machines in the struggle for survival against one another, the future belongs to the managerial class, which alone is indispensable to it.

In an early chapter, "The World We Live In," Burnham describes how modern capitalist society has been characterized not only by "a typical mode of economy," but by a typical mode of political organization as well. Just as, under capitalism, production is aimed at profit, so, under liberal parliamentary government, governance is directed toward permitting capitalists to operate with as few handicaps as possible imposed by the state. As the political institutions of feudalism were gradually displaced by the institutions of aggrandizing sovereign states concurrently with the replacement of a feudal economy by capitalism, so the political institutions of capitalism will be displaced by those of the emergent managerial state, reflecting the development of managerialism's economic outline. In fact, Burnham argues, this development is already in train, as the decline of parliamentary authority in the European "democracies" since World War I suggests.

In "The Theory of the Permanence of Capitalism," Burnham explains with a wryness that never quite becomes sarcasm why the capitalist system is no more immune than the feudal one was to the processes of time and decay. He cites, among other reasons for the impending collapse of capitalism, its inability to solve the problem of mass unemployment; the recurring economic crises that plague it; the high volume of public and private debt it incurs; unshakeable agricultural depression; the end of exploitive colonialism; capitalism's inability to realize its own technological possibilities; and the impotence of bourgeois and capitalist ideology. In the chapter "The Theory of the Proletarian Socialist Revolution," Burnham explodes in its turn the Marxist myth of the coming classless society and the abolition of the state. "[I]t is clear," he says, "that in no important respect has the theory that socialism is coming been justified; every Russian development runs counter to what that theory leads us . . . to expect." Further chapters take up the theory of the struggle for power, by which emergent elites supplant earlier ones; the identity of the managers (while not the owners of the means of production, they enjoy ownership rights de facto in consequence of having access to those means) contrasted with the new role of the legal owners, who find themselves increasingly distanced from actual production; the shift of the "locus of sovereignty" from political institutions to bureaucratic ones; and the affinity managerial societies have for totalitarian systems.

Throughout the book, Burnham maintains a dispassionate tone, while repeatedly reminding the reader that his argument is descriptive only, not prescriptive or disapproving. We must face facts, he insists, and see the world for what it is and where it is headed. As a prophet, James Burnham strives rather for the detachment of the scientist than the stoicism of the tragedian. In the end, he acknowledges (almost in passing) that the world of the managerial state is not the world he would prefer to inhabit. Yet, *The Managerial Revolution*, in its general effect, belies and overrides its author's dispassion: The book directly inspired, after all, one of the greatest literary nightmares of its time. As for its impact on three generations of readers, no one of them who has had cause to feel ill at ease in the modern world is likely to have closed the volume without telling himself: "I recognize the present in this book, and I deplore it; I see the future, and I fear it."

21

THE EDUCATION OF HENRY ADAMS: AN AUTOBIOGRAPHY

by Henry Adams

1918

As a small boy growing up in Quincy and Boston, Massachusetts, Henry Adams (1838–1918) took for granted that every family included several presidents in its family tree. His great-grandfather was John Adams, the second president of the United States, his grandfather, John Quincy Adams, the sixth president; Charles Francis Adams, his father, was a congressman and later the United States' minister to the court of St. James during (and for some time after) the War Between the States. Himself temperamentally unsuited to a political career, Henry was a newspaper correspondent and private secretary to his father in London, before accepting the editorship of the *North American Review* and an assistant professorship of medieval, European, and American history at Harvard College, at the personal invitation of President Charles W. Eliot. In addition to his *History of the United States of America during the Administrations of Thomas Jefferson and James Madison* in nine volumes, Adams wrote a pair of novels and *Mont-Saint-Michel and Chartres: A Study in Thirteenth-Century Unity,* the companion volume to *The Education of Henry Adams* (originally subtitled *A Study in Twentieth-Century Multiplicity*), which has been described quite simply as the best book ever written by an American.

The bearer of a name that remains to this day synonymous with American history, Henry Adams was the quintessential representative of American civilization in a time when "American" signified New England Yankee Protestant (and "Protestant" signified Unitarian, shading into agnostic). To a degree that Adams recognized with honest precision, he typified the narrow, Puritanical, and limited aspect of the American mind, as well as its learned, liberal (in the broadest meaning of the term), principled, and humane one; the provinciality that was nevertheless part of its cultural strength, its charm, its historical originality. *The Education of Henry Adams* is more than an American classic, it is among the greatest works of American literature, a model of the confessional genre that manages to transcend its own mode. Its success as a work of art is the result of the author's having discovered the exactly appropriate key (key, as in a musical composition) for the work at hand, which gives the book an unfailing artistic poise capable of withstanding the intrusion of the occasional Jamesian passage; the precise, and precisely sustained, point of view belonging to the narrator, who is identified in turn as "the boy," "the private secretary," and, finally, as "Adams." Whatever the merits and demerits of Adams's novels (*Democracy* and *Esther*), *The Education of Henry Adams* is a novelist's autobiography, handling narrative, scene, character, and atmosphere compellingly, and always to superb effect.

The Education is—fittingly, and in the author's words—"a story of education, not of adventure! It is meant to help young men . . . but it is not meant to amuse them." For Henry Adams,

The object of education for [the mind that is capable of being educated] should be the teaching itself how to react with vigor and economy. No doubt the world at large will always lag so far behind the active mind as to make a soft cushion of inertia to drop upon, as it did for Henry Adams; but education should try to lessen the obstacles, diminish the friction, invigorate the energy, and should train minds to react, not at haphazard, but by choice, on the lines of force that attract their world. What one knows is, in youth, of little moment; they know enough who know how to learn. Throughout human history the waste of mind has been appalling, and, as this story is meant to show, society has conspired to promote it. No doubt the teacher is the worst criminal, but the world stands behind him and drags the student from his course. The moral is stentorian. Only the most energetic, the most highly fitted, and the most favored have overcome the friction or the viscosity of inertia, and these were compelled to waste three-fourths of their energy in doing it.

Adams, as a civilized man, regarded his life as one and the same with his education, the exception being the twenty-year period (his mid-thirties to his mid-fifties) in which he put into practice what he had previously made his own. His private, or personal, obstacle in the realization of an education was the fact of his having been born, as an Adams, with an eighteenth-century mind; the public, or historical, stumbling block was that nineteenth-century America, after 1865 especially, "asked for no education and gave none." The problem for Adams was less that America offered no market for educated labor; it was that, in the circumstances, "the more he knew, the less he was educated"—a fact of which society was aware, and of which it was actually inclined to boast.

The new Americans, of whom he was to be one [after his return from London following the war's end], must, whether they were fit or unfit, create a world of their own, a science, a philosophy, a universe, where they had not created a road or even learned to dig their own iron. They had not time for thought; they saw, and could see, nothing beyond their day's work; their attitude to the universe outside them was like that of the deep-sea fish. Above all, they naturally and intensely disliked being told what to do, and how to do it, by men who took their ideas and their methods from the abstract theories of history, philosophy, or theology. They knew enough to know that their world was one of energies quite new.

In this world—"this vast plain of self-content"—the young Adams
felt that

> he could no longer see his own trail; he had become an estray; a
> flotsam or jetsam of wreckage. . . . His world was dead. Not a
> Polish Jew fresh from Warsaw or Cracow—not a furtive Yacoob
> or Ysaac still reeking of the Ghetto, snarling a weird Yiddish to
> the officers of the customs—but had a keener instinct, an in-
> tenser energy, and a freer hand than he—American of Amer-
> icans, with Heaven knew how many Puritans and Patriots behind
> him, and an education that had cost a civil war. He made no
> complaint and found no fault with his time; he was no worse off
> than the Indians or the buffalo who had been ejected from their
> heritage by his own people; but he vehemently insisted that he
> himself was not at fault. The defeat was not due to him, nor yet
> to any superiority of his rivals. He had been unfairly forced out
> of the track, and must get back into it as best he could.

Yet, facing the crisis of secession and the war that ensued, political and military leaders on both sides of the dispute found
(whether they were aware of doing so or not) that "[a]ll the education in the world would have helped nothing." After the war,
when society "dropped every thought of dealing with anything
more than the single fraction called the railway system," education was, if anything, of less use. Adams, as an Adams (one, moreover, who had evolved from Unitarianism to the point of being
tone-deaf to religion) and as a reformer, opposed political corruption and the banking interests, believing that American life
should be organized scientifically, toward the realization of "unity."
This meant that the election to the presidency of Ulysses S. Grant
"shipwrecked" his political career. It was at that point that Henry
Adams, despairing of what he called "the shifting search for the
education he never found," decided while spending a summer in
the Uinta Mountains of Utah Territory with his friend, the geolo-
gist Clarence King, that "no more education was possible" and
that he must therefore "stand the chances" of the world in which
he lived. Or perhaps it was simply that the object of education

was changed. For years, Adams had concerned himself with what the world had stopped caring for; now, he would try to discover "what the mass of man did care for, and why. Religion, politics, statistics, travel had thus far led to nothing."

Henry Adams, who for years had believed "instinctively" in evolution, saw devolution in the descent from President Washington (and the Presidents Adams) to President Grant. After the War Between the States, he had immediately perceived the system of 1789 to have broken down and the old constitutional government grown as antiquated as was government under the Articles of Confederation. The fervent Unionist, who before and during the war had regarded the Confederate leaders as (literally) insane, found himself fully disillusioned by the victorious Union less than a decade after it had succeeded in imposing its will on the Southern States. As a history professor, he felt himself crippled by the fact that, "In essence incoherent and immoral, history had either to be taught as such—or falsified." The Spanish-American War and the Philippines question allowed him, for a time, to see that "the family work of a hundred and fifty years fell at once into the grand perspective of true empire-building;" for the first time in his life, Adams felt "a sense of possible purpose working itself out in history."

The Boer War, however, which he perceived as an insult on the part of England to the legitimacy of national independence established (presumably) by his ancestors, put him off stride again. In the Chicago Exposition of 1893, Adams saw "the first expression of American thought as a unity; one must start there"; the consolidation of the capitalist regime, forced on the country by the banking class with its single gold standard "with all its necessary machinery" was the second. Seven years later, the Great Exposition of 1900 introduced to Henry Adams the dynamo as a symbol of the infinite. "As he grew accustomed to the great gallery of machines, he began to feel the forty-foot dynamos as a moral force, much as the early Christians felt the Cross. The planet itself seemed less impressive, in its old-fashioned, deliberate, annual or daily revolution, than this huge wheel." Adams's experience of the

Exposition, in combination with his contemplation of Mont-Saint-Michel and Chartres on a trip to France, inspired the famous juxtaposition of "the Virgin and the Dynamo" as the two opposite poles of magnetic attraction operating across a span of eight centuries. The insight was of particular attraction for an historian who believed that "the historian's business was to follow the track of the [historical] energy." Less attractive was the reflection, by a man who had devoted his life to "the shifting search for the education he never found," that "[f]orty-five years of study had proved to be quite futile for the pursuit of power; one controlled no more force in 1900 than in 1850, though the amount of force controlled by society had increased enormously."

Adams was faced with the paradox that, while the unity for which he had struggled all his life had always won, unity itself proved insufficient. "The National Government and the national unity had overcome every resistance, and the Darwinian evolutionists were triumphant over the curates; yet the greater the unity and the momentum, the worse became the complexity and the friction. One had in vain bowed one's neck to railways, banks, coporations, trusts, and even to the popular will as far as one could understand it—or even further; the multiplicity of unity had steadily increased, was increasing, and threatened to increase beyond reason." Adams's first conclusion was that modern politics reduces to the struggle, not of men, but of forces; the men themselves become, with every passing year, "more and more creatures of force, massed about central powerhouses." Not men, but the motors that drive men are the combatants in struggles whose motive forces are generated by the motors themselves. In a world in which increasingly impersonal historical processes are subject to ever-greater acceleration, men must discover themselves less and less capable of directing, or even managing, history.

The theory of history imposed by science on the generation born after 1900 was predicated on the recognition that mind exists in a universe created by itself, as a young pearl oyster builds its nacreous shell. "As far as one ventured to interpret actual science," Adams suggested, the mind had thus far adjusted itself by an infinite series of infinitely delicate adjustments forced on it by the infinite motion of an infinite chaos of motion; dragged at one moment into the unknowable and unthinkable, then trying to scramble back within its senses and to bar the chaos out, but always assimilating bits of it, until at last, in 1900, a new avalanche of unknown forces had fallen on it, which required new mental powers to control. If this view was correct, the mind could gain nothing by flight or fight; it must merge in its supersensual multiverse, or succumb to it.

From 1200 to 1900, unity had fragmented steadily into multiplicity to the point where humanity would shortly require a new social mind. At the start of the twentieth century, the Virgin had never been more philosophically compelling for the sexagenarian genius, who nevertheless could not keep himself from asking what purpose Her existence had served, since the world was even more violent and more chaotic than it had been at the time of Her birth. "The stupendous failure of Christianity," Adams laments, "tortured history."

In all the literature of conservatism, there is no more brilliant, instructive, and poignant example of the conservative intelligence separated from religious belief than the mind of Henry Adams as revealed in the great, eponymous *Education*. Allen Tate remarks that Adams's tragedy was that he "never quite understood what he was looking for." What he was looking for—without, indeed, ever finding it—was, of course, religious faith. For an Adams at Henry's stage of descent in the lineage, it was the hardest thing of all to discover.

22

THE MEMOIRS OF A
SUPERFLUOUS MAN

by Albert Jay Nock

1943

It is arguable that Albert Jay Nock (1873–1945) was no true conservative at all but a libertarian, and that his writings (among them *Mr. Jefferson* and *Our Enemy, the State*) make a contribution to libertarian rather than to conservative letters. Even so, no less a conservative than William F. Buckley Jr. has credited *Memoirs of a Superfluous Man* as having been a major influence in his own intellectual and personal formation. Nock worked as editor of *The Freeman,* a short-lived publication in the post–World War I era, and also as an editor for *The New Republic.* He was a contributor as well to many other magazines, among them *The Atlantic, Harper's,* and *The American Mercury* in its palmy days in the 1920s, under the editorship of H. L. Mencken, for whom Nock felt reciprocated admiration.

Like Mencken, Nock affected a skeptical, ironic, amused, and ultimately detached view of human affairs and of humankind itself that scorned indignation, the itch for reform, and any sort of political involvement; like Mencken also, he detested the state (Mencken would have used the word "government") and state interference in society; abhorred democracy and held the mass man in contempt; believed the state had no business meddling in economic affairs, whether in the interests of the plutocracy or of the proletariat; regarded organized religion as fraudulent at best and, at worst, tyrannical; and reserved for himself a cheerful agnosticism concerning man's spiritual nature and the life of the world to come. In fact, Nock as a libertarian and religious freethinker went Mencken one better where the relationship between the sexes is concerned. While Mencken, in some ways the last Victorian, had a thoroughly bourgeois view of marriage and the family, Nock advocated François Rabelais's maxim *"Fay se que vouldras"* ("Do as you wish"), as his rule of sexual morality; disapproved of the marriage contract; and quoted, with relish, a friend who remarked to him, "I tell you, the man who invented the family was an enemy of the human race." Unlike Mencken, who was only a curmudgeon, Nock in certain moods and on certain subjects was a genuine crank, who seems often to have written what it amused him to pretend to believe; where Mencken, writing in the same vein, would have contented himself merely with provocative exaggeration. On the other hand, Nock, like Mencken (or Henry Thoreau, Walt Whitman, Edward Abbey, and Edmund Wilson), represents a peculiarly American dissenting type that, if not properly describable as "conservative," has nevertheless served as an irritant to the liberal mind and an opponent of liberal orthodoxy and the liberal political agenda. What is more, Nock—again like Mencken—had a vision of civilization that, despite its secular foundation, was otherwise sound, complete, and thoroughly traditional.

The Memoirs of a Superfluous Man is indeed an odd book by a very odd person. Though Nock for some years was a clergyman, his book makes no mention of that fact, or of the woman he married or the family he raised. (Nock, in leaving the United States for a stay in Europe, also abandoned his wife. When a close friend asked him, many years later, "Albert, what was your wife like?" he replied, "She was perfect in every respect, so I left her.") *Memoirs* is thus an intellectual autobiography—and sometimes not even that, as it breaks in the second half toward a series of essays on

subjects of distinguishing interest to the author, written increasingly in a somewhat Menckenite style characterized by Mencken's
penchant for sweeping generalizations and opinions unsupported
by detailed example and sustained argument. Nevertheless, it is a
work of exquisite literary prose, whose fundamental arguments
are plainly of a piece with those of a long train of defenders of
Western culture—and the determined foes of its enemies.

   Nock recognized himself, along with the educable few like him
(he called them "the remnant"), as being of a type that is necessarily superfluous in a "civilization" dedicated actively to production,
distribution, and consumption and intellectually to the ideology of
economism:

> Almost the only chance to make myself useful that my country
> ever offered me came when the president of a huge sprawling
> mid-Western state university asked me . . . to go out and be the
> head of his department of English literature. I was no end de-
> lighted by the compliment, but the mere thought of such an
> undertaking made me shiver. I told him I had not the faintest
> idea how to set about it; I should be utterly helpless. All I could
> do would be to point to the university's library and say, There it
> is,—wade in and help yourselves. Like a very gracious man, he
> laughed and said that was just what he would wish me to do;
> but it seemed clear to both of us that I should be eminently a
> superfluous man in the realm of modern pedagogy, so we got
> on no further.

Nock, himself superbly educated in the classical tradition, was
appalled (and equally amused, according to his way) by the revolution that had occurred in American education both in theory
and practice since the late nineteenth century, a development that
interested him sufficiently that he eventually produced a book on
the subject (*A Theory of Education in the U.S.*, published in 1932).
In Nock's view, the mass of mankind is divided into two groups:
the educable (a tiny fraction of the whole) and the merely trainable. The "final end and aim of education," Nock insists, is no
more and no less than "the ability to see things as they are":

In a society essentially neolithic, as ours unquestionably is at the moment . . . there can be no place found for an educable person but such as a trainable person could fill quite as well or even better; he becomes a superfluous man; and the more thoroughly his ability to see things as they are is cultivated, the more his superfluity is enhanced. As the process of general barbarisation goes on, as its speed accelerates, as its calamitous consequences recur with ever-increasing frequency and violence, the educable person can only take shelter against his insensate fellow-beings, as Plato says, like a man crouching behind a wall against a whirlwind.

Nock attributed the destruction of the American educational system to the democratic rage for equality and the democratic intolerance of superiority in every form. Democracy, in combination with economism, was rebarbarizing the West (and indeed the world), destroying a civilization that had been in flower for three centuries. Nock, while claiming to understand the process, saw no possible way of averting it, however: quoting the redoubtable Bishop Butler, he held that "[t]hings and actions are what they are, and the consequences of them will be what they will be."

The historical forces at work had been in train since around 1850, and Nock's classical education allowed him to foresee—so he believed—the inevitable succession of events in accordance with a pattern established as early as the Minoan civilization. Thus, Nock had little or no interest in either World War I or II ("When one has known for forty years precisely how a society's course of rebarbarisation must turn out in the long run, one does not waste one's attention on day-to-day incidents of its progress"), reading no newspapers and hearing few reports. For him, as for Marcus Aurelius, human history was endlessly repetitive, being governed by "three great laws of the type known as 'natural.' " These were Epstean's law (named for a friend who had formulated the general notion), Gresham's law, and the law of diminishing returns. The first holds that *Man tends always to satisfy his needs and desires with the least possible exertion*"; the second that bad money drives out good; the third is self-explanatory. "These three laws

dog the progress of every organisation of mankind's effort. Organised charity, organised labour, organised politics, education,
religion,—look where you will for proof of it, strike into their history at any point of time or place." Taken together, Nock's laws,
when applied to an understanding of human society, amount to
an historical law of entropy, postulating a cyclical view of history
in which nations and civilizations, as well as human institutions
generally, progress so far as human potential allows them to develop—at which point they simply fall apart.

The limits of civilizational development are thus determined
by their human material; and this material, Nock believes, is itself
far more limited than is generally supposed to be the case—by democratic man, especially. Persuaded by an article written by
Ralph Adams Cram for *Harper's*, Nock accepts the eminent architect's *ex scholastic* thesis that the masses of mankind are in fact
not human beings—not "psychically-human"—at all, but rather
pyschical-anthropoids who share the physical but not the mental
attributes of the truly human race. "Consequently," Nock says,
"we have all along been putting expectations upon the masses of
Homo sapiens which they are utterly incapable of meeting." The
limit, then, to the development of human civilization is explained
by the fact that the large majority of any civilization's members
are not fully human. There is no point, as Nock sees it, in trying
to overcome this fact, as it is insuperable; and still less in lament-
ing it, since it is a fixity of nature. The educable minority will
therefore do neither but rather "cultivate their gardens," carrying
on their intellectual and artistic work in the face of impending
catastrophe while bettering human society by the steady improvement of *one*—the only possible method of social progress, so far
as Nock is concerned, available to man.

Clearly, Nock's understanding of history and the nature of humanity, like the arguments by which he sustains that conception,
are wide open to counterattack. His assertion that no man has
ever managed successfully any unit larger than the family (if he
has successfully managed *that*) is plainly at odds with his assumption that the political institutions of the modern age are in decay.
(But from what?) And Christian readers (educable ones, at least)

are likely to protest the relentlessly secular drive behind his book, while recognizing that many of Nock's assertions (e.g., the individual nature of social salvation, the uses of ignorance in the realm of the spirit) are simply Christian orthodoxy and that Nock has merely recast Christian understanding in secular form, by substituting want of intellectual capacity for lack of the spiritual sort to explain man's inability to achieve Heaven on Earth.

Hugh MacLennan writes of Albert Jay Nock that he was "never more consistent in his originality than when he was writing shameless nonsense." On the other hand, Nock was never more consistently himself than when he was mocking bunkum. Nock spent his early childhood in Brooklyn, at a short distance from the Wigwam (the political headquarters of the New York Democratic Party), described by him as "a ramshackle one-story turtle-shaped wooden building," "an evil-looking affair, dirty and disreputable . . . the people who frequented it look[ing] to me even more disreputable than the premises." It was this sad structure, and the visitors attracted by it, that awakened in the young Nock the first stirrings of a political consciousness. It happened during a political campaign in summer, when "in the evenings the Wigwam became a kind of Malebolge, spewing up long columns of drunken loafers who marched and countermarched, some carrying banners and transparencies, and others carrying tin torches that sent out clouds of kerosene-smoke. What first attracted my attention to these obscene performances was the sound of a steam-calliope at the head of a troop of marchers. I took this to mean that a circus-parade was going on, and when I went down there and found there was no circus, I was disappointed and did not care what was taking place."

Nock continues:

Thus my first impression of politics was unfavourable; and my disfavour heightened by subsequently noticing that the people around me always spoke of politics and politicians in a tone of contempt. This was understandable. If all I had casually seen,— the Wigwam and its denizens, the processions of disgusting hoodlums who sweat and stank in the parboiling humidity of

our Indian-summer nights,—if all this was of the essence of
politics, if it was part and parcel of carrying on the country's
government, then obviously a decent person could find no
place in politics, not even the place of an ordinary voter, for the
forces of ignorance, brutality and indecency would outnumber
him ten to one. Nevertheless there was an anomaly here. We
were all supposed to respect our government and its laws, yet
by all accounts those who were charged with the conduct of
government and the making of its laws were most dreadful
swine; indeed, the very conditions of their tenure precluded
their being anything else. For a moment I wondered why this
should be so; but my wonderment almost immediately petered
out, and I did not brood over the rationâle of politics again for
a great many years.

23

THE REVOLT OF THE MASSES

by José Ortega y Gasset

1929

The Revolt of the Masses is a classic work at least as likely to be cited by conservatives as by others, despite the fact of its author having been a political liberal (albeit of the classical school) and antimonarchist who sat in the constituent assembly of the Spanish Second Republic in 1931–1932 and served as deputy for the Province of León and civil governor of Madrid. Greatly disillusioned by his single term in Parliament, he retired from politics thereafter and exiled himself in Argentina and in Europe during the Spanish Civil War (in which he took no side) and the ensuing World War. As a professor, lecturer, essayist, and journal editor, José Ortega y Gasset (1883–1955) enjoyed an international reputation and wrote numerous books on history and politics, philosophy and metaphysics, ethics and aesthetics, epistemology, and art criticism. *The Revolt of the Masses,* of all these books, remains by far the best known.

"There is one fact," it begins,

which, whether for good or ill, is of the utmost importance in the public life of Europe at the present moment. This fact is the accession of the masses to complete social power. As the masses, by definition, neither should nor can direct their own personal existence, and still less rule society in general, this fact means that actually Europe is suffering from the greatest crisis that can afflict peoples, nations, and civilization. Its characteristics and consequences are well known. So also is its name. It is called the rebellion of the masses.

In Ortega's view, society is a "dynamic unity" comprised of "minorities" and "masses." The mass is "the assemblage of persons not specially qualified"; the minority represents "individuals or groups which are specially qualified." Thus, Ortega does not employ the term "masses" in the Marxist sense; rather, the mass for him is simply the average man as a collective. The minority individual stands apart from the mass by virtue of his holding "some desire, idea, or ideal, which of itself excludes the great number." The mass, by contrast, is "all that which sets no value on itself—good or ill—based on specific grounds, but which feels itself 'just like everybody,' and nevertheless is not concerned about it; is, in fact, quite happy to feel itself as one with everybody else." The mass man has no aspirations, makes no demands on himself; the select man demands everything, whether he succeeds in fulfilling his aspirations or not. The distinction between them is not occupational or social, let alone hereditary, but rather cuts straight across class and occupational lines: it identifies classes of men, not men of classes.

There exist, nevertheless, certain operations, activities, and functions in society that by nature are special, hence require special skills and abilities of the kind that only the select man possesses. ("For example: certain pleasures of an artistic and refined character, or again the functions of government and of political judgment in public affairs.") Before the present crisis, qualified minorities exercised these activities: a situation in which the masses acquiesced, understanding their need to acquire equal skills in order successfully to exercise the same functions. Early in the twentieth century, Ortega argues, all this changed. "[T]he mass has decided to advance to the foreground of social life, to occupy the places, to use the instruments and to enjoy the pleasures hitherto reserved to the few. It is evident, for example, that the places [previously reserved to the few] were never intended for the multitude, for their dimensions are too limited, and the crowd is continuously overflowing; thus manifesting to our eyes and in the clearest manner the new phenomenon: the mass, without ceasing to be mass, is supplanting the minorities." A general result is the inflation of democracy into "hyperdemocracy," "in which the mass acts directly, outside the law, imposing its aspirations and its desires by means of material pressure"—the political analogue of the cultural situation, where "the commonplace mind, knowing itself to be commonplace, has the assurance to proclaim the rights of the commonplace and to impose them wherever it will." A more specific one is the rise of mass political movements like Bolshevism and Fascism.

Ortega takes issue with the commonplace diagnosis of decadence in Western civilization. What he calls "the height of the times"—the vitality level of any given period—in the modern era is unusually high, he argues; as one might expect of a society that, besides having open to it a life more spacious than any that had previously existed for mankind, has lost all respect for and consideration of the past, regarding itself as something unique in history and facing a wholly inscrutable future in which anything (or nothing: Francis Fukuyama's "end of history," postulated sixty years later) can happen.

The West, Ortega believes, suffers from the loss of its historic sense of destiny, of which the accession of the masses to public place and responsibility has deprived it. "Such has public power always been when exercised directly by the masses: omnipotent and ephemeral. The mass-man is he whose life lacks any purpose, and simply goes drifting along. Consequently, though his possibilities and his powers be enormous, he constructs nothing. And it is this type of man who decides in our time."

What is this type? He is the product of a new world made possible by democracy, scientific experiment, and industrialism, abandoned to his own devices by the century that created him: "the spoiled child of human history" who regards himself as per-

fect and who, mistaking civilization for a natural force and condition, takes his superabundant life for granted on the assumption
that the entire mechanism runs by itself—unsupported and undirected by anything so undemocratic in principle as a gifted and
hardworking elite of select men, toward whom he displays a radical ingratitude. "The [modern] world is a civilised one, its inhabitant is not." And it is the mass inhabitant and his kind who are
currently running the show, having learned to use the machinery
of civilization while living in the most abysmal ignorance concerning its principles. Absence of principles produces absence of
standards, and absence of standards the absence of culture that is
barbarism—the barbarism that Ortega saw beginning to appear
in the Europe of his time, induced by the "progressive rebellion of
the masses."

Believing civilization to be as spontaneous and self-producing
as Nature, the mass man turns himself into a primitive living in
his own state of nature. He is unable therefore to keep pace with his
own civilization—including its problems, which grow more complex every year, along with civilization itself. "This disproportion
between the complex subtlety of the problems and the minds that
should study them will become greater if a remedy be not found,
and it constitutes the basic tragedy of our civilisation," Ortega
suggests. "By reason of the very fertility and certainty of its formative principles, its production increases in quantity and in subtlety, so as to exceed the receptive powers of normal man." He
adds, tellingly, "Of course, as problems become more complex,
the means of solving them also become more perfect." Here we
detect a positivistic note striking dissonantly on the traditionalist
ear, a warning of the seachange to occur in the book's second
half. Indeed, only several pages on we read that "Europe needs to
preserve its essential liberalism. This is the condition for super-
seding it." The chapter concludes on the overleaf: "There is no
hope for Europe unless its destiny is placed in the hands of men
really 'contemporaneous,' men who feel palpitating beneath them
the whole subsoil of history, who realise the present level of existence, and abhor every archaic and primitive attitude. We have

need of history in its entirety, not to fall back into it, but to see if we can escape from it."

Almost from this point on, Ortega sounds steadily less conservative and more modern-minded, as he builds to a conclusion that amounts to an astonishing anticipation of European unificationist and American universalist doctrine at the turn of the third millennium. While on all sides, he argues, Europeans complain of the outdatedness and inutility of Western institutions—parliament, democracy, capitalism, and so forth—it is not the institutions but the uses that are made of them, and the programs to which they are dedicated, that really are at fault. These, Ortega suggests, give too little scope to the aspirations of Europeans in their circumscribed potentiality as Frenchmen, Englishmen, Germans, Italians, and Spaniards. The nation-state, as he describes it, is not historically definable in terms of race, language, and territory, but rather of an animating and unifying "programme" that gives purpose, coherence, and life to a type of human organization first conceived of by Julius Caesar, who sought by his Gallic campaign to transcend the Roman ideal of the city-state by creating an expansive and—as we say today—diverse nation of the modern type, embracing western Europe from the Italian peninsula to the Atlantic Ocean and freed from a unipolar administrative system fixed remotely in Rome.

"The image of the City, with its tangible materialism, prevented the Romans from 'seeing' that new organisation of the body politic. How could a State be formed by men who did not live in a City?" The Romans could not see how this were possible; or that

> [t]he State is neither consanguinity, nor linguistic unity, nor territorial unity, nor proximity of habitation. It is nothing material, inert, fixed, limited. It is pure dynamism—the will to do something in common—and thanks to this the idea of the State is bound by no physical limits. . . . That is the State. Not a thing, but a movement. Where there is a stoppage of that impulse towards something further on, the State automatically succumbs,

and the unity which previously existed, and seemed to be its
physical foundation—race, language, national frontier—becomes useless; the State breaks up, is dispersed, atomised. . . .
[T]he secret of the national State [is] in its specific inspiration
as a State, in the policy peculiar to itself. . . . [W]e find a radical
intimacy and solidarity between the individual and the public
Power that is unknown to the ancient State. . . . Everyone
forms a part of the State, is a political subject who gives his support to the enterprise. . . . It is not the community of the past
which is traditional, immemorial . . . which confers a title to
this political fellowship, but the community of the future with
its definite plan of action. . . . The capacity for fusion is unlimited. Not only the fusion of one people with another, but what
is still more characteristic of the national State: the fusion of all
social classes within each political body. In proportion as the
nation extends, territorially and ethnically, the internal collabo-
ration becomes more unified. The national State is in its very
roots democratic, in a sense much more decisive than all the
differences in forms of government.

All this looks backward to G.W.F. Hegel's philosophy and forward to the democratic propositionalism of Harry Jaffa and neoconservatism generally in our own time. It is an expression of
elitism rather than conservatism. Surely, no conservative could
have written those lines, which defend and promote every idea
and every tendency in history concerning the nature and function
of the state—in relation to its subjects as well as to other states—
that Augustine, Burke, Kirk, Nisbet, Minogue, and so on opposed. Ortega envisioned the unification of Europe, a project that
he expected would provide the masses with direction and a sense
of purpose external to themselves, while proving to the rest of the
world (in his day, Eurocentrism still enjoyed a degree of intellectual and social respectability) that Europe and the European idea
continue to rule internationally. Ortega would have been content
with "fusing" the European nations, leaving it to the American
globalists of sixty years later to propose melding the entire world
into a single democratic-capitalist system, ruled programatically
in accordance with universalist principles from Washington, D.C.

By contrast, Ortega's indictment of mass man and his mass culture amounts to an expansive restatement of the complaint of the twentieth century's most distinguished cultural and political conservatives: Eliot, Ezra Pound, William Butler Yeats, Waugh, Wyndham Lewis, Irving Babbitt, Faulkner, the Southern Agarians, and Richard Weaver.

Mencken's advice in his review of Theodore Dreiser's novel *An American Tragedy* (Hire your pastor to read the first volume, but don't miss the second) might apply as well to *The Revolt of the Masses*. The first half of this little book represents the classic treatment of the democratic revolution—the principal phenomenon of the modern world—from the antimodern point of view. The second, however wrongheaded, is a striking anticipation of a branch of liberal doctrine laying claim to conservative roots, while having none. One might as well go ahead and read it, too.

24

THE ORDEAL OF CIVILITY: FREUD, MARX, LÉVI-STRAUSS, AND THE JEWISH STRUGGLE WITH MODERNITY

by John Murray Cuddihy

1974

Jews and Jewish culture are commonly assumed to have had a liberalizing, even a radicalizing, influence on Western civilization since the eighteenth century. Yet, it is the Jews who, to a substantial degree, have represented premodern culture in its resistance to revolutionary forces set in motion by modernizing gentile societies whose agendum has been the destruction of traditionalist values and institutions several thousands of years old. This startling paradox, which calls into question received definitions of "liberalism" and "conservativism," and the reciprocal relationship between them, is the subject of this fascinating book by John Murray Cuddihy (1916–), a professor emeritus of sociology at Hunter College.

When *The Ordeal of Civility: Freud, Marx, Lévi-Strauss, and the Jewish Struggle with Modernity* was published over a quarter-century ago, notices were largely confined to literary back alleys where the book was treated with skittish ambivalence by mostly third-string critics. (Though a runner-up for a National Book Award, it was never to my knowledge reviewed by the *New York*

Times.) In *Ordeal,* John Murray Cuddihy did exactly what one prominent sociologist accused him of having done: He wrote a book about civility that is itself most uncivil in the context of contemporary Western discourse. Deliberately tackling what he himself would call a "ritually delicate" subject, Cuddihy produced a deflationary study of modern Jewish thought in the last century-and-a-half. Besides disrupting William Butler Yeats's "ceremony of innocence," he committed what C. S. Lewis calls the "grossest" incivility of "thinking about the man who addresses us instead of thinking about what he says."

Cuddihy's thesis is that Jews and the modern West have been at odds with one another for the past 150 years, as a tribal and essentially premodern people confronted a civilization representing secularized Christianity compounded with a specialized, "dedifferentiated" modernism, and that celebrants of an illusory "Judeo-Christian" civilization have deliberately disguised the schism that has prevented that civilization from ever coalescing. Cuddihy perceives that "a kind of predifferentiated crudeness on the culture system level, and a kind of undifferentiated rudeness on the social system level of behavior, is believed to be—by certain Jews themselves—not only an integral part of what it means to be a Jew, but integral to the *religious* essence of Judaism, and not an accidental result of Exile or of socioeconomic disadvantage." For this reason, "[s]ocialization into modernity is, at best," he concludes, "a difficult matter. It is least difficult, perhaps, for the members of the WASP core culture descended from Calvinist Christianity. They, in a sense, are 'ego-syntonic' to [in harmony with] modernity." Cuddihy proceeds to develop his theory by taking what he describes as an approach consistent with Karl Mannheim's "sociology of knowledge" to argue that the grand ideologies of Marx, Sigmund Freud, and Claude Lévi-Strauss derived their inspiration from the resentments experienced by their founders: members of a pariah minority only lately escaped from the shtetl and hence newcomers to a world that they regard "in dismay, with wonder, anger, and punitive objectivity."

According to Cuddihy, Jewish emancipation, while it bestowed on Jews many of the civic privileges and duties offered by Western

parliamentary democracy, also brought them into violent colli-
sion with the "Protestant Etiquette": that elaborate conglomera-
tion of polite ritual evolved from feudal courtoisie to meet the
exigencies of a complex commercial society where life is not, as in
the ghetto, "with people" but rather "with strangers" who cannot
be accommodated as members of an extended family. "Good
manners" entailed such things as wearing a morning coat and
lemon-colored gloves, telling hurtling strangers in the street, "I
am so sorry—my fault entirely," and serving business rivals tea as
if they were maiden aunts. They were at once superficial and fundamental, at once appurtenances of a civilization and its essence.
And to the assimilating protagonists of coarse authenticity, they
were at best evasive and, at worst, hypocritical. Even more, they
were foreign and unnatural.

Nevertheless, many assimilating Jews in the vanguard of emancipation mastered this etiquette—only to discover themselves in
an uncomfortable situation. On the one hand, they revered their
people and the roots from which they sprang; on the other, they
felt shame and distaste for the ghetto and bourgeois Jew alike. It
is, Cuddihy believes, "this recoil from the vulgarity of their own
Jewish community, in which we find the covert root of the social
and intellectual creativity of the Diaspora intellectuals." And because "[t]o accept the achievement of Western modernization at
its own self-estimation would have been to downgrade themselves," these intellectuals turned theodicy into ideology, at once
explaining the Jewish condition and apologizing for it: a sleight of
hand accomplished by universalizing the Jewish plight. ("Beneath
it all, we—you—are all Jews.")

"In 'scientific' socialism as in 'scientific' psychoanalysis," as
Cuddihy puts it, "the normative and the cognitive are conflated."
Thus, Freud considered politeness to be the anti-Semitism of the
middle classes; his "id" was in fact the crude, unruly "Yid" in
Everyman, and psychoanalysis "a compromise strategy for living-
the-diaspora" by which his assimilating bourgeois Jewish patients
were able to keep up "polite" appearances by day, giving the id-
Yid full rein only during the fifty-minute hour. Thus, Marx considered civility to be repression, and a disguise by which the

greedy operations of a capitalist society might be cloaked by civic-minded obeisances. In his "Essay on the Jews," he attacks such self-serving ideologies by exposing the hypocritical contradictions implicit in the behavior of the only group with which he was thoroughly familiar, although to his mind all men secretly fit the Jewish stereotype. And thus, Lévi-Strauss, unable to stomach the "insult" paid to Jewish history by the celebrators of the modernizing West, rejects Western history with his declaration that "to reach reality we must first repudiate experience."

"The clear tendency of [Cuddihy's] historical exposition," a contemporary Jewish commentator writes, "is to represent Jewish social thought as inherently meretricious, disruptive, vindictive." A patrician Protestant scholar found Cuddihy guilty of "dismissing [the ideas of Freud and Marx] as impolite products of Jewish resentment." That Cuddihy does indeed root both Marx's and Freud's systems in "resentment," and that he does in fact believe that their intellectual descendants and elaborators (and perverters) have exercised a frequently pernicious influence on the West, are beyond contention; yet, there seems no particular evidence that he has talked himself into "dismissing" them. And while the first-mentioned critic refers suspiciously to Cuddihy's "ostensibly descriptive terms," other readers have accepted those terms as warmly descriptive; "the author prefer[ing] the coarseness which reveals to the courtesy that conceals fundamental disagreements," as one of them noted.

Cuddihy, indeed—three-fourths of the way through his book and deciding, perhaps, that he has been incivil long enough—leaves off speaking about the Jews exclusively and begins talking about everyone else. At the start, he notes that his study is "in the end, only methodologically Judeocentric"; now, he insists that "[a]ll of us, any of us, are only relatively modern, be we Irish, Jewish, German, black, whatever." "The almost continuous immigration of Jews into Western Europe and Anglo-America from the culturally 'backward' areas of the pale has brought it about that they have lived a revolutionary situation of the 20th-century type [i.e., an ethnic clash between modern and early modern, or premodern, cultures] from the 19th century up to our day." Like the "great unassimilated Jews of the West" whose thought he has been dissecting, Cuddihy universalizes his theory of modern Jewish history by extending it to the history, not only of Third World peoples encountering the modernizers of the West, but that of the modernizers themselves.

Most likely, Cuddihy underwent his own ordeal of civility in writing this book. Although he might have consoled himself simply by reflecting that good manners in society are not to be confused, ever, with good manners in print, he concludes *The Ordeal of Civility* by extending a gracious hand. He quotes Dietrich Bonhoeffer, whose *Arkandisziplin* served to "manage" "the differentiation of modernity"—"Why do I decide on expression of thoroughly penultimate human solidarity?"—and observes, "[m]odernity, child of Protestant Christianity, 'acts back' on its parent, secularizing it out of sight, offended by the unsightliness of its own visibility. . . . [T]he *ius divinum* self-destructs; a new *ius civile* is all in all."

This statement raises the question whether modernity is superior to premodern life or not; therefore, whether assimilating to it is a good thing, or a bad one. But that is a subject for another book.

25

GOD AND MAN AT YALE

by William F. Buckley, Jr.

1951

In 1951 appeared a book by a vigorous and (some thought) brash young man, then twenty-six years old, which shocked and appalled Yale University, the Northeast establishment, and American liberalism (in that order). Indeed, there was cause for alarm. *God and Man at Yale,* by William F. Buckley, Jr. (1925–), was not American conservatism's Ninety-five Theses, nor its Bastille, nor even its *Common Sense.* Neither did it represent the beginning of the modern conservative movement in America, which in fact is traceable from the 1930s: the Liberty League, Martin Dies's House Committee to Investigate Un-American Activities, and the America First Committee. Yet, Buckley and his book did shape American conservatism from the post–World War II era up until, roughly, President Ronald Reagan's first administration.

In this period, the principle concern of mainstream conservatives was communist aggression abroad, communist subversion at home, and "creeping socialism" in the American economy: What became known as social conservatism did not move to a forward position in their thought until the late 1960s. Buckley (who had himself done a brief stint with the Central Intelligence Agency) was widely recognized as one of the country's preeminent intellectual Cold Warriors when he founded *National Review,* four years after the publication of *God and Man at Yale.* Nevertheless, the subject of Buckley's first book was (ostensibly, anyway) far more parochial than the continuing War of the Worlds.

Inspired by the author's experiences as a Yale undergraduate, and based substantially on ideas and arguments worked up for the editorials Buckley wrote during his yearlong editorship of the *Yale Daily News, God and Man at Yale* is as much a personal testament as it is an institutional one. Even so, the book's treatment of Yale is synecdochal, never losing sight or sense of the American system of higher education as a whole. William Buckley's subject (as the alert reader recognizes all too painfully upon finishing the book) is bigger than communism, bigger than the Soviet Union, bigger than the Cold War. It is the future of a beleaguered civilization that, absent the threat of Soviet missiles and tanks, would remain imperiled nonetheless by an Americanized version of communist ideology.

President A. Whitney Griswold, confirmed as the sixteenth president of Yale University in October 1950, stated the matter to Buckley's complete satisfaction: "What happens at Yale and the small company of American, British and European universities that share a historic role with her will determine the whole course of education in those countries during the next half century; and it is not too much to expect that the character of their political and social institutions will reflect the character of their schools and universities." Only fifteen years after *God and Man at Yale,* barbarism revolted against civilization at the University of California at Berkeley; two years after that, the barbarians rose against Columbia in the spring of 1968, and the long train of similar uprisings (including at Yale) ensued. Thirty-plus years later, the United States—indeed, the Western world—has reaped the whirlwind with a culture that looks like Columbia. Invasion and occupation by the Red Army could never have accomplished half as much. Thus, William F. Buckley, Jr., at the outset of a long and various career, set his finger firmly on the agency that within the next half-century was to devastate Western civilization.

From the vantage of more than fifty years, *God and Man at Yale* (published originally by the Henry Regnery Company in Chicago, on which so many conservative authors depended for publication in the 1950s, 1960s, and 1970s) stands forward as an undoubted classic. Written in the American-Appollonian style, it exhibits something of Mencken's rakish offhandedness, and of Belloc's British dash. In 198 pages, plus appendices, the book makes its case in a direct and economical matter as follows:

Yale is a private university; therefore, reponsibility for her governance devolves constitutionally on her alumni (broadly speaking, Christian individualists)—not on her administration (mainly capitalist Christian gentlemen, who, unfortunately, are disposed to tolerate agnostic and atheistic collectivists on the faculty and to condone secular collectivism and agnosticism in the curriculum, where they go mostly unchallenged). The university, founded by Christians and individualists, has historically subscribed to a traditional "value orthodoxy" at odds with her present commitment to "laissez-faire education" and the shibboleth of "academic freedom," tantamount to institutional acquiescence in moral relativism and social collectivism. Yale still subscribes to orthodoxy; but hypocritically, by lip service, or simply in the sense that the university maintains limits within which faculty members (and students) must restrict their opinions if they expect to be tolerated by the Yale community. These limits, latitudinarian as they may be, nevertheless are "prescribed by [social and intellectual] expediency, not principle"—prescribed, that is, by none other than the reigning *liberal* orthodoxy, which runs wholly counter to the traditionalist orthodoxy officially espoused by Yale! For this reason, it is necessary *not* that limits be set to the Yale curriculum, to free speech, and to academic freedom in its other forms (since, manifestly, limits already exist); rather, the existing limits should be *narrowed* to conform with Yale's stated historical mission, described by President Charles Seymour as "the upraising of spiritual leaders."

It is the duty of every responsible person, Buckley argues, to embrace those values he believes reflect truth, or come closest to reflecting it. Contrary to liberal sentimentalism, truth does not always conquer error in the arena, nor does it prevail in the marketplace; believers in truth must champion it by "promulgat[ing] it on every level and at every opportunity." Maintaining a commitment to truth by insistence on value orthodoxy need not (as critics of orthodoxy charge) promote intellectual inflexibility and an imperviousness to new ideas and understanding; neither must it produce credulous students unfit to think for themselves and fearful of skepticism as a first step toward conviction. "We betray our trust," President Seymour continues, "if we fail to explore the various ways in which the youth who come to us may learn to appreciate spiritual values, whether by the example of our own lives or through the cogency of our philosophical arguments. The simple and direct way is through the maintenance and upbuilding of the Christian religion as a vital part of university life." Buckley asks: Has Yale betrayed that trust? His regretful conclusion is, yes, it has. If the modern university is to honor its ancient mission, it must impose what the American academic community calls "censorship." Academic freedom, Buckley argues, is a valid concept solely in respect of the researcher; it should not be stretched to apply to the university professor's role as a *teacher*. Thus, "[f]reedom is in no way violated by an educational overseer's insistence that the teacher he employs hold a given set of values," commensurate with the nature and purpose of the institution that hired him.

The youthful author anticipated a firestorm following the release of *God and Man at Yale*; in the event, he was not disappointed. Yale, finding itself accused of hypocrisy by an alumnus, chose to take the whole thing personally. American liberals, aghast at discovering that questions they thought had been closed for years (and forever), responded furiously; the academic community, despoiled of its covering vestments, was outraged. In attacking collectivism, secularism, academic freedom, and the autonomy of "professionals" in private university administration from the supporting alumni, whose generous gifts funded their institution's survival, William Buckley had affronted and assaulted all that modern liberals held dear, all that they were ready to live (if not to die) for. *God and Man at Yale* was savaged from one end of the United States to the other. The author was described as "a twisted young man"; his book as "a series of fanatically emotional attacks on a few professors who dare to approach religion and politics objectively." (In a long introduction to the twenty-fifth anniversary of *God and Man at Yale,* Buckley provides a comprehensive account of its critical reception.) It sold well, however, establishing a career that has been a scourge of liberalism for decades.

(Needless to add, the questions raised by *God and Man at Yale* never have been accorded, in more than half a century, anything remotely like the answers they invited—and deserved.)

26

SINGLE ISSUES: ESSAYS ON THE CRUCIAL SOCIAL QUESTIONS

by Joseph Sobran

1983

Essayists, more still than poets and novelists, are born, not made. It is relatively easy to fake a poem or a novel, but a faked essay is always seen for exactly what it is: another journalistic or academic article. From the beginning of his career in the early 1970s, Joseph Sobran (1946–) has been acknowledged as a natural—a master of the essayist's craft, in whose hands one of the oldest and most distinguished of literary forms achieves the compression, grace, and intensity of poetry.

Raised in Ypsilanti, Michigan, where he attended Michigan State University, Sobran was introduced to William F. Buckley Jr. in the green room adjacent to the university auditorium, where Buckley was scheduled to deliver a speech. Their meeting led to Sobran's appointment as an editor at *National Review,* where he was a dominating intellectual and artistic presence until the early 1990s, when a disagreement on editorial policy resulted in his dismissal from the magazine. As a nationally syndicated columnist, the author of the monthly bulletin *Sobran's,* and a popular speaker and lecturer, Sobran has established himself nevertheless as an admired and respected presence on what remains of the American Right. All fifteen essays included in *Single Issues: Essays on the Crucial Social Questions* are reprinted from the *Human Life Review,* to which he was a regular contributor for nearly twenty years under the editorship of James P. McFadden, the founding editor.

It was McFadden's genius to recognize how the "single" (or seemingly isolated and disconnected) issue of legalized abortion in fact connects with every other moral and political issue of the time, as a gigantic oak tree growing at the center of a garden is connected to every other tree and plant within the same garden: Dig it up, and the intertwined roots drag every other living thing up and along with it. And it was the genius of Joseph Sobran to demonstrate the truth of McFadden's insight by discovering, elucidating, and dramatizing, by his rhetorical eloquence and wit, all of those perceived interconnections. Sceptics, however friendly, doubted for years McFadden's (or anyone's) ability to develop the anti-abortion argument sufficiently to fill a substantial quarterly magazine devoted solely to the subject. Thirty years later, the *Human Life Review* continues to publish, having survived James McFadden himself. Similarly, Sobran for nearly twenty years spun out essay after essay on a wide variety of topics—pornography, gay rights, the decay of the family, fatherhood, irreligion, sex education, and secular humanism—each one of which, no matter how far from the subject of abortion it seemed to have found its inspiration, returned in the end to the tonic for its resolution. As Sobran himself puts it in his foreword, "I have always marvelled at the charge that the anti-abortion movement is engaged in 'single-issue politics.' To meet the charge head-on, why not? What single issue lies nearer the heart of civilization? . . . The debate about abortion is really the kind of debate America shies away from: a debate about what man is, and about what society should be."

Joseph Sobran has been described, admiringly, as a counterpuncher. He is that, but not intrinsically, and certainly not exclusively. A counterpuncher is essentially a debator, taking every advantage, fair or not, of his adversary's logical and rhetorical fumbles. The debater ordinarily cares nothing for his opponent's arguments and ideas, but merely for their exploitable weaknesses. He does not, in other words, take opposing positions seriously. What makes Sobran a deadly critic of liberal thought is his willingness to pay liberal ideas the compliment of giving them his close attention in respect of their premises, assumptions, and motivations; the logical structure by which they are developed and expressed; how they are formed (and deformed) by the moral and political aims of the people who hold them; and how they reflect on the character of those people. We discover in his essays the moral, sympathetic, and imaginative powers of the novelist, and also his psychological insight. With his uncanny ability to assume the liberal's nature by an extraordinary act of the imaginative intellect, Sobran is a convincing anatomist of the liberal personality, as well as of the liberal mind.

The most important of Sobran's many accomplishments as a social critic is to have demonstrated the ontologically false, metaphysically incomplete, self-contradictory, solipsistic, self-serving, self-deluding, and finally illogical nature of an ideology that considers itself the last word in intellectual and moral sophistication, objectivity, power, and enlightenment. "I have found," he says in his foreword, "that the abortion issue has so many ramifications that it can't possibly remain isolated. Time and again when I thought everything there was to say had been said, new and vital considerations came to the fore." This is because the way liberals think about and defend abortion is also the way in which they think about man's control of nature and his own destiny; the secular society versus the pious one; sexual morality and gay rights; freedom of speech and the role of the media in society; the nature and function of public education; public welfare; the power of taxation; the expanding claims of the state; the encroachment of the public domain into private life; and centralization versus the federal principle. "All these issues converge in the abortion issue. . . . Those of us who oppose abortion, morally and legally, are trying to keep alive the very idea of piety—man's subordination to creation and the Creator—at a time when we are being seduced with false promises of power over creation, society, each other." "Power"—the first and preeminent temptation, roaming the modern world like a ravenous beast in search of countless victims to devour—comprehends it all.

The handmaiden of power is moral, intellectual, and rhetorical dishonesty of the sort George Orwell was so good at identifying and exposing in the 1930s and 1940s—and now, in a later generation, Joseph Sobran. A few instances of the writer ("Crucial Issue Politics") in full bay:

"It is vital to keep things straight. Opposing abortion is 'single-issue politics.' Favoring abortion isn't. [National Abortion Rights Action League] people, who keep sending out form letters accusing their opponents of firebombing clinics, are manifestly well-rounded human beings—*fully* human, as they might say."

"It is still less than a decade since the Supreme Court imposed its view on—or rather, 'expanded the constitutional right to privacy' to include terminating a pregnancy. Only the *anti*-abortion side would 'impose its views' on everyone else. They, not the judiciary, are 'divisive.' When a majority of the Supreme Court contradicts the Western moral tradition and the laws of 50 states into the bargain, anything other than instant unanimity of assent indicates that a divisive spirit is abroad. And so, alas, it is."

"Abortion violates every decent human instinct—so much so that its indecency must be clothed in euphemism. Its champions try to enlist compassion with an endless parade of hard cases, and to invoke snobbery by sneering at their opponents. Beyond that, they have tried to rule out, on precedural grounds, the very instincts that work against them: opposition to abortion, they say, is 'religious,' *ergo* inadmissible in the political process."

"The rhetoric of abortion is all about assuming responsibility. The reality of abortion is the evasion of responsibility. *Spina bifida,* poverty, hydrocephalus, and other afflictions have very little to do with it, *pace* Mike Wallace."

"What is strange—at least at first sight—is that this callousness about the unborn child should occur in a society where we are forever hectored to show 'compassion' for others. Even as enlightened voices sternly urge us to take responsibility for unseen strangers, they soothingly release us from responsibility to our own children. . . . To put it simply, we are required to love, and provide for, our neighbor, and our neighbor's neighbor, and our neighbor's neighbor's neighbor; but not our sons and daughters. This has quite literally given a new meaning to the word 'compassion,' which now means a strangely politicized form of love; a highly unnatural love, at the expense of more natural kinds. The duties of the taxpayer begin to look more absolute than those of the parent."

"To me, at any rate, it seems clear that there are now two warring views among us as to whether the state or the family should be the formative social principle in America."

"In keeping with its general deviousness, the pro-abortion side fears recognition that abortion is a *crucial* issue, one of those issues that define the very nature of society. And it condemns that recognition as obsessive—'single-issue politics'—to prevent the general public from realizing the stakes."

Societies, like individuals, which are forever spreading about the words "love," "compassion," "justice," and "honesty" like cheap currency are infallibly those societies from which the realities these words signify are most absent. Joseph Sobran is one of our own society's unwelcome prophets, come to judgment; a role he has been filling for more than a quarter-century now with wit, learning, and an intellectual integrity that yields to nothing, and to no one.

27

THE QUEST FOR COMMUNITY: A STUDY IN THE ETHICS OF ORDER AND FREEDOM

by Robert Nisbet

1953

This classic work by Robert Nisbet (1913–1996), published first in 1953, debuted in a world hostile (following the sobering experience of the Great Depression and the triumphant one of World War II) to any but the nationalist idea of community. By 1962, when a subsequent edition of the book appeared (under the title *Community and Power*), Daniel Riesman's *The Lonely Crowd* was famous and the concept of alienation, which is central also to *The Quest for Community: A Study in the Ethics of Order and Freedom*, had been widely popularized. By 1969, when *Quest* saw its third edition (back to the original title, now), "community" had joined "alienation" as a cliché of Left and New Left cultural discourse. Yet by 1990, the date of *The Quest for Community*'s latest republication, "alienation" had largely ceased to be a popular concern in America and in Europe, while "community" was no longer an aspiration, nor even a matter of social or intellectual interest—except when prefaced by the adjective "global."

Nearly a decade and a half later, after the economic bubble of the 1990s, the further homogenization of Western societies, the advanced deconstruction of national cultures, the relentless war against education and the intellect, and the intensified commitment to sensation at the expense of thought, there is still less interest in the idea of community—indeed, in most ideas at all. Ours are, quite literally, mindless times. Also, they are insensitive times, incapable, it seems, of registering the absence of community from mass commerical society and of responding in a human way to that absence. It has become almost a truism, for those alike who deplore the fact and those who welcome it, that human beings can adapt to *anything*. And at the start of the twenty-first century, it looks very much as if the several most recent generations of Americans have adapted quite nicely to a denatured and dehumanized world created by corporate capitalism and undirected technique, mass transportation, mass realty development, mass democracy, and mass society. After half a century, *The Quest for Community*, though plainly recognizable as a classic, is also an eclipsed one—for now anyway. This is not to say that its time will not come round again—and rather sooner, perhaps, than later. The inherent restlessness of human nature more often draws us back to old ideas (often in fashionable dress) than it leads us forward to new ones (if, indeed, there are such).

"This book," Robert Nisbet writes in his "Preface to the First Edition," "deals with political power—more specifically, with the impact of certain conceptions of political power upon social organization in modern Western society." Chief among these effects, he goes on to say, is the Western world's preoccupation with the idea of community—"community lost and community to be gained." Many possible explanations for this preoccupation have been set forward:

But I have chosen to deal with the *political* causes of the manifold alienations that lie behind the contemporary quest for community. . . . I believe that the single greatest influence upon social organization in the modern West has been the developing concentration of function and power of the sovereign political State. To regard the State as simply a legal relationship, as a mere superstructure of power, is profoundly delusive. The real

significance of the modern state is inseparable from its successive penetrations of man's economic, religious, kinship, and
local allegiances, and its revolutionary dislocations of established centers of function and authority. These, I believe, are
the pentrations and dislocations that form the most illuminat-
ing perspective for the twentieth-century's obsessive quest for
moral certainty and social community and that make so difficult present-day problems of freedom and democracy.

Nisbet holds that the modern nation-state, originating approx-
imately three centuries ago, destroyed the medieval forms of community from which it arose. Nisbet does not lament those forms
in themselves, nor (like the economist Wilhelm Röpke) does he
wish to see them re-created. Rather, his argument is that any political system large and strong enough to destroy smaller forms of
community is capable equally of preventing the establishment of
the new communal forms, forms appropriate to contemporary
life, seeking growth in its stygian shadow. For the modern West,
with its peoples in anxious search of communities to which both
function and authority have been restored, Leviathan (for the last
three hundred years the preeminent reality of Western government) acquires, for Nisbet, a particularly menacing aspect. "That
combination of search for community and existing political
power seems to me . . . a very dangerous combination . . . [since]
the expansion of power feeds on the quest for community."
Indeed, Nisbet argues, power comes to resemble community—in
cataclysmic periods such as the twentieth century, especially.
Here lies the "essential tragedy" of the quest for community:
"Too often [it] has been through channels of power and revolution which have proved destructive of the prime sources of [the]
human community" it seeks to rediscover and re-create.
   Alienation (which Nisbet defines as "the state of mind that can
find a social order remote, incomprehensible, or fraudulent; beyond real hope or desire; inviting apathy, boredom, or even hostility") in his estimation is one of the primary formative forces
behind the present age. And alienation has been substantially induced and aggravated by the surrender of function by traditional

communitarian institutions—family, church, parish, school, and local and state government—to the national state and also by the replacement of multiple social authorities by power. ("Power I conceive as something external and based on force. Authority . . . is rooted in the statuses, functions, and allegiances which are the components of any association.") Freedom, Nisbet explains, exists in "the interstices of authority." Power gains control when the system of interlinked authorities collapses. The modern ideology of power has not only worked indirectly to exploit whatever weaknesses inhere in these links, it has made it its business aggressively to dissolve and smash them:

> It is the ideology of power, I believe, that has had the most to do in the history of modern society with the general reduction of social differences and conflicts, the leveling and blurring of social authorities, and the gradual filling of the interstices within which creativeness and freedom thrive. It is power of this type— not merely absolute but often bland, providential, minute, and sealing—that has reduced so many of the social and cultural frictions that cultural advancement has depended upon, historically; that even intellectual energy depends upon. And it is power in this same sense that has destroyed or weakened many of the established contexts of function and natural authority— and, by its existence, choked off the emergence of new contexts and thus created a great deal of the sense of alienation that dominates contemporary man.

What is more, the modern obsession with centralized power, organized and subordinated to a positively military model, has reached beyond the national level: It has not spared the intermediary institutions themselves—churches, universities, and business corporations—which have taken for their organizational model the paramilitary one embodied by the power-minded central state. In result, "It would be hard indeed to say that centralized power over human life and aspiration, and all the administrative techniques that go with it, is more dangerous in the larger areas of national government than it is in the relatively small institutional areas."

In *The Quest for Community,* Robert Nisbet at once echoes ideas expressed in an immediately previous classic (Hannah Arendt's *The Origins of Totalitarianism,* published in 1951, makes a related argument regarding the importance of intermediary institutions to free societies) and anticipates those incorporated in another appearing just ten years later. Kenneth R. Minogue, in *The Liberal Mind* (1962), ratifies Nisbet's insight that liberalism's founders universalized the moral and psychological components of a specific society to describe the makeup of abstracted individuals removed from any social context at all. ("Despite," Nisbet writes, "the rationalist [liberal] faith in natural economic harmonies, the real roots of economic stability lay in groups and associations that were not essentially economic at all. . . . [T]here never has been a time when a successful economic system has rested upon purely individualistic drives or upon the impersonal relationship so prized by rationalists. There are always, in fact, associations and incentives nourished by the non-economic process of kinship, religion, and various other forms of social relationships.") The most important, as well as, perhaps, the most original, chapter in the book is "The Political Community," in which Nisbet (while noting that both the modern state and the ideology of power are the result, not of the "worship of naked power," but rather of the attempt to realize the salvation of man on earth), argues that, still and all, "[o]f . . . the subtle alchemies of thought performed by Rousseau and by the guiding spirits of the revolution [and of their nineteenth-century democratic successors], the subtlest and most potent was the conversion of absolute power into the illusion of mass freedom."

While a centralist polity and collectivism have been regarded for more than a century and a half as no less than an historical inevitability, Nisbet believes otherwise, while conceding the difficulties in overcoming belief itself. Planning, at the local as well as the national level, he thinks indispensable (whether conservatives like it or not) in a technological, democratic, and densely populated world. "What is needed," he adds, "is planning that contents itself with the setting of human life, not human life itself." Accordingly, he proposes what he calls "a new *laissez-faire*" whose aim is not the release into freedom of "economic atoms in a supposed legal void," but the freeing up of the autonomous groups and associations of which society formerly was composed.

That *The Quest for Community* speaks to the pathologies of the present time is confirmed by the fact that ours is as deaf to its arguments as it is insensible of the social and political evils the book condemns. A Nisbet revival in the next decade or two could be one of a number of signs that human nature, which in the short run may indeed appear infinitely malleable and adaptable (or nearly so), in the long run is as unwilling to be altered as it is incapable of fundamental alteration.

Part IV
ECONOMICS

28

RERUM NOVARUM

by Pope Leo XIII

1891

The Roman Catholic Church, under attack from and besieged by the forces of liberalism throughout the nineteenth century, never was backward in recognizing many of the social and political ills and injustices that liberalism desired to remedy. On May 15, 1891, Pope Leo XIII (1810–1903) issued the famous Encyclical Letter *Rerum Novarum* (*On the Condition of Workers*), in which the Church addressed what was called in those days "the social question," arising from the spread of materialist philosophies, scientism, industrialization, urbanization, and extreme economic inequality. In his encyclical, Leo XIII restated doctrines regarding the rights and responsibilities alike of property and the reciprocal relationship between employer and employed that had been part of the magisterium (or teaching authority) for many centuries. Thus, it is owing to the authority, force, and timing of this document, rather than to the novelty of its arguments, that *Rerum Novarum* was immediately recognized, by non-Catholics as well as by the faithful, as a template for economic and social justice in the modern industrial world.

"The momentous nature of the questions involved in [the contemporary social conflict]," Leo wrote, is

evident from the fact that it keeps men's minds in anxious ex-
pectation, occupying the talents of the learned, the discussions
of the wise and experienced, the assemblies of the people, the
judgment of lawmakers, and the deliberations of rulers, so that
now no topic more strongly holds men's interests. . . . Therefore, Venerable Brethren . . . We have thought it advisable, following Our custom on other occasions when We issued to you
the Encyclicals "On Political Power," "On Human Liberty,"
"On the Christian Constitutions of States," and others of similar nature, which seemed opportune to refute erroneous opinions, that We ought to do the same now, and for the same reasons,
"On the Condition of Workers."

Paradoxically, *Rerum Novarum,* after condemning "devouring
usury" and the consolidation of the productive power in the
hands of "a very few rich and exceedingly rich men" who have
"laid a yoke almost of slavery on the unnumbered masses of non-
owning workers," proceeds to attack, not capitalism and capitalists, but socialism and socialists, who deliberately incite the poor's
envy of the rich and the abolition of private property, thus injur-
ing the very people—the workers—whom they profess to help.
Private property, Leo insists, is effectively an absolute right, since
"nature confers on man the right to possess things privately as his
own." Moreover, the Pope propounds a Christian labor theory of
value that recalls the Marxian version, even as it supports opposite economic conclusions. Because "man expends his mental energy and his bodily strength in procuring the goods of nature, by
this very act he appropriates that part of physical nature to himself which he has cultivated. On it he leaves impressed, as it were,
a kind of image of his person, so that it must be altogether just
that he should posses that part as his very own and that no one in
any way should be permitted to violate his right." Leo defends the
right of family ownership through the father, the transmission of
inheritance to children, and social inequality: "a condition of human

existence must be borne with, namely, that in civil society the lowest cannot be made equal to the highest. Socialists, of course, agitate the contrary, but all struggling against nature is in vain. . . . It is a capital evil with respect to the question We are discussing to take for granted that the one class of society is of itself hostile to the other, as if nature had set rich and poor against each other to fight fiercely in implacable war. This is so abhorrent to reason and truth that the exact opposite is true"; rather, the classes are intended to agree harmoniously with each other, as the various parts of the body do.

"Private ownership," the Pontiff concludes, "must be preserved inviolate." But, "the just ownership of money is distinct from the just use of money." A most important duty of an employer is to pay every one of his workers what is due him in justice, so that he may frugally devote the surplus, however small, to the accretion of more wealth to himself. Beyond that, though nobody is obliged to assist others from the fund he requires to support himself and his family, and to maintain his social station ("to live unbecomingly"), still, "when the demands of necessity and propriety have been met, it is a duty to give to the poor out of that which remains." In this way, through charity on the one hand and gratitude on the other, the classes may eventually be united, not in friendship only, but (if they obey Christian teaching) brotherly love itself. "Such is the economy of duties and rights according to Christian philosophy. Would it not seem that all conflict would soon cease wherever this economy were to prevail in civil society?"

Private property, the family, and (to a certain extent) civil society all should be immune from interference by the state. When, however, injustices related to these institutions occur, the state may properly intervene to protect offended persons and classes by insisting that their rights be recognized and observed. This, because "the State is bound by the very law of its office to serve the common interest," from which its sovereignty, in all its parts, derives; thus, for the state to look out for one part of society while neglecting the others would be an absurdity, and a crime. "Therefore . . . it is within the competence of the rulers of the State that, as they benefit other groups [from which they themselves are drawn], they also improve in particular the condition of the workers. . . . And the richer the benefits which come from this general providence on the part of the State, the less necessary it will be to experiment with other measures for the well-being of the workers," from whose labor the wealth of nations originates. On the other hand, the state has a further and reciprocal duty to keep the masses "within the bounds of their moral obligations" by intervening to put "restraint upon . . . disturbers, [and] protect the morals of workers from their corrupting arts," while protecting the owners from spoliation. "[P]rivate property ought to be safeguarded by the sovereign power of the State and through the bulwark of its laws." Riot and labor strikes constitute an offense against the peace of the state and the public, and so the state is entitled—indeed, it is obligated—to intervene against these evils, as much as against exploitation of labor by the employer class.

In respect of the worker, the state is duty-bound to protect, first, the good of his soul (by ensuring that he is granted cessation from his labor to worship on Sundays and on Holy Days of Obligation) and, second, his bodily health (the physical exertion demanded of him should neither exceed his bodily capability nor be destructive of his health). Beyond that, it has a duty to insist that the laborer receive a living wage, since "to preserve one's life is a duty common to all individuals, and to neglect this duty is a crime." A fair wage will not only allow working-class families a comfortable existence, it will enable them to save money and acquire property, including of the landed sort—thus reducing inequality of wealth and encouraging, in time, "one class to become neighbor to the other." Yet, "these advantages," Leo warns, "can be attained only if private wealth is not drained away by crushing taxes of every kind. For since the right of possessing goods privately has been conferred not by man's law, but by nature, public authority cannot abolish it, but can only control its exercise and bring it into conformity with the commonweal. Public authority therefore would act unjustly and inhumanly, if in the name of taxes it should appropriate from the property of private individuals more than is equitable."

Finally, the Pope urges the importance of charitable and mutual aid associations established by employers, workers, and beneficent persons (Catholics especially); all manner of private associations; and Church societies. (He adds, pointedly, "We see the road being closed to Catholic associations, which are law-abiding and in every respect useful, at the very time when it is being decreed that most assuredly men are permitted by law to form associations, and at the very time when this freedom is being lavishly granted in actual fact to men urging courses of conduct pernicious to religion and the State.") By way of summary, Leo concludes, "let this be laid down as a general and constant law: Workers' associations ought to be so constituted and so governed as to furnish the most suitable and most convenient means to attain the object proposed, which consists in this, that the individual members of the association secure, so far as possible, an increase in the goods of body, of soul, and of prosperity."

It might be objected that the Pope's vision of a just society in which harmony prevails between the classes is dependent on the moral reform of society, and so begs the question; the Western world at the end of the nineteenth century having become manifestly less Christian than more so. In fact, Leo acknowleges the predicate on which the encyclical is based: For his vision to be effective, "First and foremost Christian morals must be re-established, without which even the weapons of prudence, which are considered especially effective, will be of no avail, to secure well-being."

Perhaps for this reason, *Rerum Novarum* has been criticized for being too general in concept and statement, an unrealistic response to dire reality. Yet, Leo XIII did not intend his encyclical as a blueprint for institutional reform. Rather, he meant it as an act of moral encouragement of industrialism's victims, rich and poor alike; also, more important, as a reminder to the world that no social system, however unjust and deformed, justifies the abrogation of the natural law as a means to reforming or replacing

184 ECONOMICS

it. Human society is by its nature organic and hierarchical in its organization: It may not licitly be leveled, therefore, nor inorganicized through petrifaction. Prescriptions for various social ills, more often than not more pestilential still than the diseases they were intended to alleviate or cure, in fact need not be so. *Rerum Novarum* shows why they must not be, as well.

29

THE SERVILE STATE

by Hilaire Belloc

1912

Hilaire Belloc (1870–1953), the son of a Frenchman and an Englishwoman who converted to her husband's Catholic faith before she met him, had a binational upbringing. As a boy, he attended the Oratory School, presided over by John Henry Cardinal Newman, near Birmingham, and summered at La Celle Saint Cloud outside Paris. In his youth, Belloc volunteered for military service in the French army, but returned to England, where he won a First in History at Balliol College at Oxford. Believing that he had a better chance of pursuing a successful literary and political career in England than in France, he made the deliberate choice to remain in England, where he married an American from California, Elodie Hogan. Already, Belloc had fallen under the influence of the aged Henry Edward Cardinal Manning, an ultramontanist (defender of the Pope) and advocate for the poor and the working classes. As Belloc's biographer, Joseph Pearce, writes, "For the impressionable youth, whose own background was rooted in the philosophy of the Church and in the politics of the French Revolution, the combination of traditionalism and radicalism that Manning preached was a potent one." "Old Thunder" maintained that combination in balance for the rest of his life, until his death at age eighty-three.

Belloc was a foremost example in the twentieth century of what used to be called "a man of parts." He wrote "nonsense" (only it was not nonsensical) cautionary poetry for children, "serious" poetry for adults that has lived, novels, travelogues, history, historical biography, and political tracts and books. Besides his literary work, he got himself elected twice to the House of Commons, hiked across the American West and later from Paris to Rome, and sailed his own seagoing boat, the *Nona*. Of his hundred-odd books, *The Path to Rome*, *The Cruise of the Nona*, and *The Servile State* (the most often referenced and certainly the easiest to come by) are best known today.

The Servile State is a classic illustration of the graded distinctions between "conservatives," who so often content themselves with defending present institutions and arrangements, and "Rightists" or traditionalists, who insist on past ones—insist, that is, on being "radical." Belloc's small book, first published in 1912, is the most concise statement ever written of the principles of what he and his friend and colleague, G. K. Chesterton, called "distributism," defined by Belloc as "the wider distribution of property until that institution shall become the mark of the whole state, and until free citizens are normally found to be possessors of capital or land, or both." (While the name, "destributism," is Belloc's invention, the concept itself had been explicitly stated by Pope Leo XIII in his Encyclical Letter of 1891, *Rerum Novarum.*)

Such a distribution, Belloc argues, began to be made in Europe during the Dark Ages, as the gradual dissolution of the universal pagan institution of slavery was effected by the gradual extension of the Catholic faith over the Roman and barbarian West alike. The system consolidated itself in the Middle Ages, the serfs emerging from their servile status to acquire property and a degree (often a considerable degree) of personal freedom from their lords, who shared with them the fruits of their labor. It was eroded, however, and eventually ruined through forces encouraged by the Reformation—in England in particular, where the

Crown, unable to retain its hold on the monastic lands confiscated by Henry VIII, lost them to the great Protestant families who from that time on used their wealth to subordinate the monarchy to themselves, through Parliament. Wealth in lands meant wealth in capital; and by the eighteenth century, when England had become a thoroughgoing capitalist society, the land *and* the capital of the realm were overwhelmingly in the hands of a very small percentage of the population. Since England was at the time the model for European industrialization, the continental powers imitated the pattern England set for them, insofar as their own institutions permitted them to do so. The "problem" of capitalism, Belloc insists, was not caused by the Industrial Revolution, but by preexisting economic and social arrangements developed over a period of four centuries. Had capital been held by guilds in this time of explosive industrialization, as was the case in the Middle Ages, the capitalists would not have been needed to finance the expensive plants and machinery required. The consolidation of the capitalist system, reenforced and facilitated by the attenuation of the historic Catholic faith, allowed for the reintroduction of the old pagan slavery in modern form. "That arrangement of society," Belloc explains, "in which so considerable a number of the families and individuals are constrained by positive law to labor for the advantage of other families and individuals as to stamp the whole community with the mark of such labor we call the servile state."

Belloc and the other distributists perceived a third way (other than slavery) between capitalism and "collectivism," much as James Burnham (writing thirty years after Belloc) rejected the false choice between capitalism and socialism by positing managerialism as the probable future. Like Burnham, Belloc believes capitalism to be inherently an unstable system, though for different (if perhaps related) reasons. The first strain, he suggests, is the moral one: A fatal contradiction exists "between the realities of capitalist society and the moral base of our laws and traditions." The second he thinks is political: "capitalism, proving almost as unstable to the owners as to the nonowners, is tending toward stability by losing its essential character of political freedom. No better proof of the instability of capitalism as a system could be desired."

If capitalism is finally unworkable, so, Belloc argues, is socialism, for the reason that the two are simply modified versions of one and the same system. You could socialize capitalism while retaining its essentials by the simple expedient of promoting a deal between capitalist and proletarian by which the second would agree to the appropriation of the labor surplus by the first, in return for the guarantee of a living wage and employment security made by the first to the second. Belloc is against socialism—for the reason that such an arrangement *amounts to* the servile state! (In his last chapter, "The Servile State Has Begun," he offers a persuasive argument why the minimum wage concept is a servile one.) Socialism—Belloc calls it collectivism—is neverthless a program far less disruptive to the existing plan of society than distributism (or proprietarianism), which explains why reform in the early twentieth century was proceeding in that direction, pushed by dogmatic and pragmatic socialists *and* concerned capitalists, all of them able to agree on the necessity for resorting to the path of least resistance. It is also, of course, the explanation for why distributism never succeeded, though scholars of the period have pointed out that the movement was substantially a casualty of the better-funded, better-connected, and better-publicized Fabianism of Sidney and Beatrice Webb, George Bernard Shaw, and other reformist programs popular at the time.

In any case, Belloc as a Catholic and Chesterton as a Catholic fellow traveler (he was received at last into the Church in 1922, fourteen years before his death) considered socialism a heresy and as much an economic and social evil as capitalism—a view that precluded their embracing it in any form whatsoever. Their vision was rather of an England restored to its former happy estate under which every Englishman was freeborn, and every freeborn Englishman the possessor of *some* property both in land and in capital, free to sell or withhold his labor as he saw fit.

There was, of course, a quixotic aspect, fully recognized by Belloc, to the distributist plan. In his conclusion, he predicts that servile status will be restored in "North Germany" and in Great

Britain. But he adds immediately, "My conviction that the reestablishment of servile status is actually upon us does not lead me to any meager and mechanical prophecy of what the future of Europe shall be. The force of which I have been speaking is not the only force in the field. There is a complex knot of forces underlying any nation once Christian; a smoldering of the old fires."

A pessimist might have concluded instead with the prophecy that Europe, rather than refuse the servile state, would in time adapt or even reject outright "the moral basis of our laws and civilization" that is so fundamentally at odds with it. Ninety years after Hilaire Belloc wrote his book, there is a persuasive case to be made that that exactly is what has come to pass in Western civilization, in whole as well as in part.

30

THE ROAD TO SERFDOM

by Friederich A. Hayek

1944

Published first in wartime England, *The Road to Serfdom* describes what Jean-François Revel in the 1970s called "the totalitarian temptation" that, in the future that Friederich A. Hayek (1899–1992) foresaw, would follow surely from the ensuing peace. In 2003, Irving Kristol, a godfather of neoconservatism, wrote in *The Weekly Standard* (the house Republican organ edited by his son William) that neoconservatives have no fear that the modern welfare state might be the *via dolorosa* Hayek warned against in his classic exposition. So far as his claim to represent *any* strain of conservatism is concerned, Kristol could scarcely have damned himself more persuasively.

Months after *The Road to Serfdom* appeared in England, it was released in the first American edition by the University of Chicago Press. To the surprise of the author, the book's reception in the United States differed considerably from the attention it had received in Great Britain, where "The Socialists of All Parties" to whom Hayek had dedicated the work took its arguments seriously, and in the spirit in which they were offered. By contrast (as

Hayek notes in his foreword to a second English edition, following ten years after the first), "In America the kind of people to whom this book was mainly addressed seemed to have rejected it out of hand as a malicious and disingenuous attack on their finest ideals; they appear never to have paused to examine its argument. The language used and the emotion shown in some of the more adverse criticism the book received were indeed rather extraordinary." Certainly, the central thesis of *The Road to Freedom*—that the Allied powers, in the name of freedom, were hell bent on following their Axis enemies into that modern form of serfdom known as collectivism—infuriated many American readers. The first three American publishers to consider the book all rejected it, one of them protesting that *The Road to Serfdom* was "unfit for publication by a reputable house." The author himself attributed the discrepancy less to differences in national temperament than to "a difference of intellectual situation." Whereas, he suggested, in England and Europe the ideals he criticized were long familiar ones that had already been tried and proved failures in application, in the United States they were "still fresh and more virulent"—and finally untried. "What to most Europeans had in some measure become *vieux jeux* was to the American radicals still the glimmering hope of a better world which they had embraced and nourished during the recent years of the Great Depression." However that may be, it is hard to imagine a principled conservative today who would not find in *The Road to Serfdom* confirmation of his gravest suspicions in respect of the pretensions of the modern social-democratic state with its commitment to "freedom" and of a refurbished conservatism—however "realistic" and "enlightened"—that fails to challenge those pretensions. And it seems hardly too much to say that, in *The Road to Serfdom,* no conservative should discover an exceptionable idea by this exemplar of humane classical liberalism (saving, perhaps, in the last chapter, where Hayek muses on the desirability of an international federation charged with the task of keeping international peace).

Friederich Hayek was an exponent of the Austrian school of economics, founded by Ludwig von Mises in the 1920s, which

functioned as the chief free-market rival of the Keynesian school
until the 1940s, when Mises's theory of capital and of the business cycle and his hostility to central planning were eclipsed by
the opposition until 1974—the year Hayek shared the Nobel
Prize in Economic Science with the Swedish economist Gunnar
Myrdal. An expatriate from his native Vienna, Hayek, at work at
the London School of Economics, considered *The Road to Serfdom*
a dutiful distraction from his theoretical writing (his collected
works are extant in nineteen volumes); a burden undertaken, he
explains, to counter "a peculiar and serious feature of the discussions of problems of future economic policy at the present time,
of which the public is scarcely sufficiently aware." Yet, it is for this
immensely readable and popular little book that Friedrich A.
Hayek is largely known today.

The Road to Serfdom argues that the evil intellectual, social, and
political policies represented by the enemy powers, Germany and
Italy, represent not a barbaric departure from the Western tradition but a logical consequence of what, in the twentieth century,
that tradition has become in *all* the countries of the West, Great
Britain and the United States included. "Few," Hayek suggests,
"are ready to recognize that the rise of facism and naziism was
not a reaction against the socialist trends of the preceeding period
but a necessary outcome of those tendencies. . . . [I]f we take the
people whose views influence developments, they are now in
the democracies all socialists." In result,

> [i]t is necessary now to state the unpalatable truth that it is
> Germany whose fate we are in some danger of repeating. . . .
> There exists now in [Britain and America] certainly the same
> determination that the organization of the nation which has
> been achieved for purposes of defense shall be retained for the
> purposes of creation. There is the same contempt for nineteenth-
> century liberalism, the same spurious "realism" and even cyni-
> cism, the same fatalistic acceptance of "inevitable trends." And
> at least nine out of every ten of the lessons which our most vo-
> ciferous reformers are so anxious we should learn from this war
> are precisely the lessons which the Germans did learn from the

last war and which have done much to produce the Nazi system.

Those lessons teach the superiority of the collectivism demanded by socialism over the individualism honored by Old Liberalism. In the twentieth century, individualism came to be viewed as synonymous with egotism and selfishness. Yet, it is an essential feature of the Western tradition, rooted in the moral philosophy of classical antiquity and of Christianity, and developed during the Renaissance into the coherent cultural pattern we know as "Western civilization." Individualism, as the West has understood the concept for centuries, comprehends "the respect for the individual *qua* man, that is, the recognition of his own views and tastes as supreme in his own sphere, however narrowly that may be circumscribed, and the belief that it is desirable that men should develop their own individual gifts and bents." "Freedom" and "liberty" having become, through dishonest and cynical abuse, suspect terms, Hayek suggests "tolerance" as "the only word which still preserves the full meaning of the principle which during the whole of this period was in the ascendant and which only in recent times has again been in decline, to disappear completely with the rise of the totalitarian state."

That individualism should have been brought into such contemptuous disrepute, Hayek believes, is more than a tragedy, it is the catastrophe of our time and in some sense the catastrophe of history, which up until the advent of the totalitarian impulse had indeed made "progress"; collectivism, as individualism's mortal adversary, being the enemy of economic welfare, humane government, objective truth, and morality alike. With Wilhelm Röpke, his fellow in the Austrian School, Hayek recognizes that classical liberalism was in substantial degree a victim of its own success. "What had been an inspiring promise seemed no longer enough, the rate of progress far too slow; and the principles which had made this progress possible in the past came to be regarded more as obstacles to speedier progress, impatiently to be brushed away, than as the conditions for the preservation and development of what had already been achieved." More broadly, this reaction against individualism is part of modern man's revolt against the impersonal forces that shape societies and drive the destinies of individuals in ways that he was formerly prepared to accept, however unwillingly. And yet, mere human determination cannot make of collectivism anything more than an impossible dream, far beyond realization by the finite capacities of man—a fact that in no way diminishes, but rather increases, the threat it poses against civilization.

Hayek considers the fundamental principle of individualist society to be "that in the ordering of our affairs we should make as much use as possible of the spontaneous forces of society, and resort as little as possible to coercion." This for him was a pragmatic precept, as well as a moral one; man being a creature whose active and moral natures conform with and complement one another. Seduced by an infinitely expansive vision of "freedom," and more recently by the Faustian "passion for conscious control of everything," the intelligentsia since the late nineteenth century had confidently followed the supposed Road to Freedom, blissfully unaware that they trod the High Road to Servitude in the form of a planned society—the opposite of the liberal society that, as they saw it, had no plan at all. Hayek understands that the dispute between modern planners and the opponents of planning is not whether foresight and systematic thinking should be employed in planning common affairs, but whether the social authority should content itself with creating conditions in which individuals might themselves plan successfully within their self-allotted purviews, in preference to employing central direction and organization for the purpose of producing a consciously created blueprint. "It is of the utmost importance to the argument of this book," he warns, "for the reader to keep in mind that the planning against which all our criticism is directed is solely the planning against competition—the planning which is to be substituted for competition." (Röpke argued the same.)

Hayek denies that modern technological development somehow makes planning "inevitable" and observes rather that "there is a great deal in [it] which makes infinitely more dangerous the power a planning authority would possess." Planning is perilous to democracy, he asserts, since it assumes the existence in democratic societies of an "all-inclusive scale of values" that democracies do not in fact exhibit. "It is not difficult to see," he adds, "what must be the consequences when a democracy embarks upon a course of planning which in its execution requires more agreement than in fact exists. . . . It is [therefore] the price of democracy that the possibilities of conscious control are restricted to fields where true agreement exists and that in some fields things must be left to chance."

The truth of this profound insight proves to have been as lost on subsequent generations as it was on Hayek's own. It is precisely to the modern refusal to leave some things to chance that we owe the displacement of formal law—or justice—by substantive law ("affirmative action" being a salient example in our time), resulting in the suspension of the Rule of Law; our toleration of a political system in which, as John Stuart Mill wrote more than a century and a half ago, "a handful of human beings . . . weigh everybody in the balance, and give more to one and less than another at their sole pleasure and judgment"; and the fatal fashion among Western leaders, now as in Hayek's day, of "extolling security at the expense of freedom." Similarly, the relentless approach to collectivism—from which, since World War II, there has been no sustained deviation—guarantees that democracy becomes more and more a kakistocracy (rule by the worst) for the very simple and obvious reason that "[j]ust as the democratic statesman who sets out to plan economic life will soon be confronted with the alternative of either assuming dictatorial powers or abandoning his plans, so the totalitarian dictator would soon have to choose between disregard of ordinary morals and failure. It is for this reason that the unscrupulous and uninhibited are likely to be more successful in a society tending toward totalitarianism." ("This makes," Hayek adds, "collectivist morals so different from what we have known of morals that we find it difficult to discover any principle in them, which they nevertheless possess.") Finally, the advance of collectivism entails and encourages hatred of and contempt for truth and the human intellect, since "collectivist thought . . . while it starts out to make reason supreme, ends by destroying reason because it misconceives the process on which the growth of reason depends."

In spite of his loathing for collectivism generally and the totalitarian state in particular, unlike so many American and British "conservatives" of the present day, Hayek was no "idolator" (as Norman Podhoretz, another neoconservative godfather, describes himself) of democracy, of which he pointedly refuses to make a "fetish." "It cannot be said of democracy," he says, "as Lord Acton said of liberty, that it . . . 'is itself the highest political end.' . . . Democracy is essentially a means, a utilitarian device for safeguarding internal peace and individual freedom. As such it is by no means infallible or certain." And it is uncertain primarily on account of the popular delusion that no limit exists to the powers of the legislator and that "so long as all actions of the state are duly authorized by legislation, the Rule of Law will be preserved." Acting under this delusion, the people, by investing the state with unlimited powers, may make legal—in the juridical sense—the most arbitrary rule, "and in this way a democracy may set up the most complete despotism imaginable."

No writer on twentieth-century politics has done more than Friederich Hayek to identify the Faustian impulse underlying modern political history or to reveal the secret agendum, disguised by the rhetoric of "freedom" and driven by "the passion for conscious control of everything," that is the quest for omnipotence—added, inevitably, to the claim of omniscience.

31

THE SOCIAL CRISIS OF OUR TIME

by Wilhelm Röpke

1950

Wilhelm Röpke (1899–1966), though raised in his native Nuremberg, spent much of his life in Switzerland, a country he loved and came to regard as a model for the other countries of the West. He wrote his masterpiece, *The Social Crisis of Our Time,* in Geneva, but it was in Nuremberg that Röpke received the Willibald Pirckheimer Award in 1962. "For Röpke," the citation notes, "the measure of the economy is man. The measure of man is his relationship to God." It is precisely on account of his peculiar orientation that Röpke has never enjoyed the professional prestige accorded to others of his fellow economists such as Ludwig von Mises, Friederich A. Hayek, and Milton Friedman; yet, it was Röpke who, in his unostentatious way and through the intermediary of his pupil Ludwig Erhardt, indirectly created the economic plan that returned Germany to prosperity after World War II.

In his foreword to the 1992 edition of *The Social Crisis of Our Time,* Russell Kirk recounts an anecdote that is as revealing as it is amusing. Geneva, during the war, made small plots of land available to its citizens for the private production of vegetables to

augment the meager food supply. Röpke, who heartily approved
of the city government's action, exhibited the plots to Herr
Doktor Von Mises on the occasion of the famous economist's visit
to Geneva. "Mises shook his head sadly: 'A very inefficient way of
producing foodstuffs!' 'But perhaps a very efficient way of producing human happiness,' Röpke told him."

The Social Crisis of Our Time, in which Röpke propounds his
"Third Way," is not exactly an economic treatise; rather, it is an
essay in social and historical criticism. The Third Way (as between
modern capitalism and socialism, or collectivism) is the attempt
to restore "economic humanism" to the economy of the West
and to Western civilization that, Röpke believes, suffer from "the
cult of the colossal" created by eighteenth- and early nineteenth-
century ideas and their actualization in the hundred-year period
between the 1840s and World War II. Overly elaborated and
overly extended, classical liberalism as it is embodied in the political and economic systems of modern Europe and North
America is a perversion of its original self. "There has been a
great deal of confusion," William Campbell says, "on the concept
of the 'Third Way' "—no matter that Röpke, who distinguished
himself from most economists by being a fine prose stylist, is
never less than straightforward in expressing his ideas. "It is not
what economists would call a 'mixed economy' or a soft socialism
in contrast to the hardness of collectivism and laissez-faire. In
essence it is an attempt to socially nurture the ethic and spirit of
the bourgeoisie." (The last sentence suggests a congruence between Wilhelm Röpke's understanding of the "crisis" of his age—
the dehumanization of the economy—and an insight of the
historian John Lukacs, who has argued for half a century now that
the modern world ended with the collapse and disappearance of
the bourgeoisie in 1914.) Enlargement in government and consolidation in the economy in the twentieth century, Röpke
thought, destroyed social equilibrium, created intellectual and
moral decay, and extended the proletarization of the lower classes
to the middle, upper, intellectual, and artistic ones as well. Admittedly, capitalism was responsible for the creation of the original proletariat. Socialism, however, which is no alternative to

capitalism but simply the capitalist system in a later stage of development, is busy creating the phenomenon of mass man—the proletariat universalized and internationalized. The result, Röpke foresaw, was social, economic, and political collapse—and, after that, an end to liberty, individual rights, and personal identity.

Röpke's indictment of the modern condition and his proposed remedies reflect in part the thinking of the English distributists, Hilaire Belloc and G. K. Chesterton; though, oddly, he refers only in passing to distributism in a book rife with historic, philosophical, theological, literary, and poetic allusion. Belloc's argument (in *The Servile State*) that egregious economic inequality is the product, not of capitalism per se but of economic consolidation in England in the seventeenth and eighteenth centuries, finds an echo in *The Social Crisis of Our Time,* where Röpke extends Belloc's argument by locating the origins of inequality in the feudal and absolutist systems of premodern Europe, with which Chesterton and Belloc were largely in sympathy. Unlike the distributists, whose acceptance of a market economy and a liberal political system seems grudging by comparison, Röpke believed ardently in both institutions as sound in their fundamental principles, arguing that they had been corrupted, deformed, and degenerated over the previous century to the point where their original nature and shape were scarcely recognizable. Liberal government and a free economy, he thought, work from the bottom up only, never from the top down. Once the first was decentralized and the second deconsolidated, Röpke suggests, the "crisis of our time" could resolve itself through the transformation of society, which, by rediscovering reverence, respect for authority and a vertical social structure, manners, and a respect for truth, would reestablish social and political stability founded on the guarantee of individual and personal rights.

The immediate crisis, as Röpke perceived it, lay in the fact of parliamentary democracy and market capitalism having so compromised themselves, and in the process forfeited so much credibility, that Western publics, unable to imagine an alternative between democratic capitalism and socialism, would demand—and get—a collectivist system burdened by all of the problems of democracy and socialism that, owing to its genetic identity with them, it would be unable to resolve. The time was fast approaching, Röpke believed, when such a choice would be forced, and he very much feared it would be made in favor of a collectivist solution that would extinguish civilization.

Wilhelm Röpke's fears mark him as a pessimist. In his hopes, however, he was an optimist—"a cheerful and manly social thinker," Kirk calls him. In this respect, *The Social Crisis of Our Time* reflects the guarded optimism many leading conservatives— including Kirk himself and even that somber realist James Burn- ham—felt around the middle of the twentieth century. History (they permitted themselves to guess) had finally turned against the Left, which in the century's first half had discredited itself in so monstrous a way that the people had to—they *must*—throw their weight against it. In part, this optimism was an expression of that unexpected but fundamental faith in human nature charac- teristic of true conservativism—the faith that comes from the conviction of mankind made in the image of God and having His spirit breathed into it. "When not abandoning themselves," Röpke writes, "to the ecstasy of mass intoxication, people know after all very well what is healthy and not healthy, what is strong and what decadent, what is just and what unjust, what is legitimate and what against the law, what is in keeping with the nature of man and what is not." Nearly four decades after Röpke's death, mass consumerism, generated by consumer capitalism organized on the global scale, has accomplished the proletarization of the world to a degree that soft collectivism never managed to achieve.

While Röpke never advocated a "mixed economy," his under- standing of what constitutes an unmixed one is considerably more flexible than that of most free-market economists. For him, a free economy is one in which government refrains from intrud- ing on the fundamental and defining principles of the free mar- ket. ". . . Outside the sphere of self-sufficiency [as practiced by artisans, peasants, and so on]," he writes,

> we have only the choice between monopoly and collectivism on the one hand and competition on the other. . . . There is a

world of difference between the competitive principle and the frequently perverted form of competition as it is practiced today. . . . [T]he economic order of a free society is a market economy based on the division of labor. Competition, therefore, is only one of the pillars on which such an order rests, while the other is self-sufficiency. We are, therefore, free to modify the competitive character of the economy in full harmony with the principles of our economic order, by enlarging the sphere of marketless self-sufficiency. . . .

It is a permanent job of economic policy, Röpke insists, to determine the rules of economic life and enforce them in accordance with the economic constitution; what is more, that policy must itself be created by strong government, in which Röpke (like Alexander Hamilton) was a believer. The great reform he advocated was the creation of the "Third Way," which would be "neither laissez-faire nor . . . intervention for preservation (obstructive intervention) but [rather] intervention for adjustment (constructive intervention) . . ." For Röpke, state management of individual enterprises, including entire branches of production, by which government acted in the capacity of producer or merchant, was not incompatible with a competitive economic policy; nor were public works projects, inaugurated by the state in times of depression.

It must be clear that, if Wilhelm Röpke fell short of making his a household name among twentieth-century economists, the reason lies in his having been what professional and mass men alike suspect above all else: neither the one thing nor the other, but an unsettling admixture. Röpke, despite his virtuosity as an economist, was not only more than an economist: The part of him that was more was the higher part as well, because its subject was the higher truth, as unprofessional as that makes him appear today.

"Economic freedom," Röpke argues, "belongs . . . to the total picture of a society which is diametrically opposed to collectivism. While this social order is necessarily based on economic freedom, other factors are also essential. . . . It is . . . a form of society whose arbiters are not the proletarians—with or without white collars—not the vassals of a new industrial feudalism . . . but men who . . . depend on no one but themselves."

What Ivy League economist, whether of the free-market or mixed-market type, ever thinks such ideas, or even thinks to care about them? How many of the intellectual proletarians in white collars whose dream and ambition is socialism (from what they perceive to be their own class interests, not those of the proletariat) could actually *understand* them, or the humane Western vision they represent?

32

THE COLD WAR AND THE INCOME TAX: A PROTEST

by Edmund Wilson

1963

Candidly identifying himself as "a former Leftist," the author of this subversive little right-wing book explains why he "should be making so much fuss about state control, in particular state control as it is exercised by the income tax." The reason, Edmund Wilson (1895–1972) claims, is that socialism and state socialism are simply not the same things. One cannot, he goes on to explain,

> assume that there is anything in common between, on the one hand, the programs of the old American socialists and, on the other, the measures of nationalization . . . which have actually been put into practice in the course of the New Deal and of subsequent administrations. Norman Thomas and the early Max Eastman as well as Eugene Debs were imagining an extension of democracy which would get the big "capitalist" off the wage-slave's neck and restore the American community to the realization of something like Walt Whitman's vision of a robust fraternal race exploring and cultivating and building and enjoying the country's resources. . . . But our giant bureaucracies

in Washington have shown as little of this once much-advertised American spirit as any government of a Communist state.

Wilson was arguably the greatest literary historian and critic in America in the twentieth century. In both capacities, this intensely curious and engaged writer cut a wide swath intellectually; the body of his work is as much concerned with social history and contemporary social, political, and even economic matters as with literature. His two most important books are probably *Axel's Castle: A Study in the Imaginative Literature of 1870–1930* and *To the Finland Station: A Study in the Writing and Acting of History,* the second of which traces the development of Marxism from its intellectual inceptions to its violent political application by Lenin in the midst of World War I. (Though Wilson indeed was self-consciously a socialist during the period of its composition, *To the Finland Station* is sufficiently balanced and professional to have been distributed abroad by the U.S. Department of State, both in English and Italian translations.) In the early part of his career, he worked for *The New Republic;* later on, he was a fixture at *The New Yorker.* The compleat man of letters, Wilson in the course of a long, industrious, and essentially Spartan life produced books some of which were more or less independent of his journalism, others collections of previously printed journalistic pieces. (Late in life and in career, he was working on three books simultaneously, moving from one desk to the next as the day— and he—progressed.)

The Cold War and the Income Tax: A Protest was inspired by Wilson's prolonged ordeal (two tax lawyers spent five years getting his account settled) at the hands of the Internal Revenue Service, owing to Wilson's failure, from a combination of negligence and ignorance, to file income tax returns between the years 1946 and 1955. (Wilson claimed to have had no idea how heavy the U.S. income tax burden had grown, nor understood that failure to file had been made a serious offense: facts, he acknowledged, that seemed hard to explain in the case of a man who had worked for decades for journals devoted to commentary on pub-

lic affairs.) The IRS agents placed liens and levies on his sources
of income and on his houses that left him "strapped for nearly a
year" and put Wilson himself on a kind of allowance: demanding
that he submit a monthly itemized account of every cent he spent
for living expenses and then complaining that too much money
went for liquor, and that the tax criminal—a man with "no place
to lay his head," as one agent expressed it—ought not to have
bought a $6 mat for his dog. Gumshoes uncovered his leftist
opinions; also his four marriages, which the IRS apparently considered un-American.

There is a liberal tradition in American social and political
thought that deserves to be thought of as in some sense conservative, if only because it *is* traditional, in a distinctively American
way that is both entirely honorable and requiring of no apologies.
Edmund Wilson belonged to this tradition; so did Edward Abbey.
Rather recently, an appellation has been invented to identify such
people: "Old Believer" nicely distinguishes them from the newer
type of liberal, as well as from conservatives of the mainstream variety.

Wilson, like every Old Believer, was an individualist and a republican (lowercase) who neither asked anything of government
nor was prepared to take anything from it without an argument,
or, if necessary, a fight. Descended from a well-off and relatively
distinguished Middle Atlantic family, himself a graduate of Princeton, where he was an intimate of Scott Fitzgerald, Wilson had the
Old American civilization in his bones in spite of his considerable
familiarity with European culture, with which he was also entirely
at ease. As a representative of the American aristocracy, Wilson
possessed the aristocrat's assertive independence of mind, as well
as his self-confidence and fastidiousness. Despite a democratic
streak that showed strongly in his predilection for social slum-
ming (with working-class women particularly) as well as in his
politics in youth and middle age, Wilson had no tolerance either
for the upstart proletariat or the presumptuous political bureau-
cracy that governed hypocritically in its name.

Wilson's complaint extends beyond personal pique and offended

individualism to include a swollen and distorted social, bureaucratic, and political order that had no precedent, legitimacy, or
sanction in the history of the old American republic:

> I have always thought myself patriotic and have been in the
> habit in the past of favorably contrasting the United States with
> Europe and the Soviet Union; but our country has become
> today a huge blundering power unit controlled more and more
> by bureaucracies whose rule is making it more and more diffi-
> cult to carry on the tradition of American individualism; and
> since I can accept neither this power unit's aims nor the meth-
> ods it employs to finance them, I have finally come to feel that
> this country, whether or not I continue to live in it, is no longer
> any place for me.

For Wilson, an original delinquency due to negligence had hard-
ened into a deliberate refusal based on principle. Now, he resented every cent imposed on him by way of debt and penalty and
was resolved to avoid future taxation by earning so little income
that he would come in below the lowest taxable income bracket.

In Wilson's mind, the U.S. government had deliberately in-
stilled in the American public two types of "officially propagated
fear": fear of the Soviet Union and fear of the income tax. "These
two terrors have been adjusted so as to complement one another
and thus to keep the citizen of our free society under the strain of
a double pressure from which he finds himself unable to escape."
Anticipating the paleoconservative argument as yet two or three
decades in future, he understood the American government's
pretensions as "leader of the free world" to be no more than a dishonest cover for "the instinctive compulsion to power," at home
as well as abroad, that had earned the United States its present
image as a "homicidal and menacing" nation fed and increased
by taxes paid by its submissive citizens and their representatives
in Washington, despite the fact of their suffering impositions far
more oppressive and dangerous than those their ancestors had refused to endure under King George III. In a passage as prophetic
as it is descriptive, Wilson writes:

[T]he United States, for all its so much advertized comforts, is today an uncomfortable place. It is idle for our "leaders" and "liberals" to talk about the necessity for Americans to recover their old idealism, to consecrate themselves again to their mission of liberation. Our national mission, if our budget proves anything, has taken on colossal dimensions, but in its interference in foreign countries and its support of oppressive regimes, it has hardly been a liberating mission, and the kind of idealism involved is becoming insane and intolerant in the manner of the John Birch Society.

In result, the average American citizen has become discouraged and confused, while "the accomplished, the intelligent, the well-informed" are subject to self-imposed inhibitions suggested by the spirit of political correctness.

The fact that America in the "liberal" Age of Kennedy bears striking affinities with America in the "conservative" Age of George Bush II suggests less how early the realities of today's America came to be formed than it does the degree to which conservatism as a program for practical political action has been appropriated by liberalism under another name, and to so great an extent that the real thing has simply ceased to exist. As for Edmund Wilson himself: What conservative with a cultural memory would not prefer a "socialist" of his kind to the type of "conservative" dominant in the "conservative" movement today?

Part V
THE PROPHETIC ARTIST

33

THE WASTE LAND

by T. S. Eliot

1922

It is permissible to question the greatness, and even the value, of a poem whose meaning no one can agree on eight decades after its publication (though the "waste land" of the title is commonly understood to represent modern civilization); which was substantially revised by a second poet of high reputation to the extent that the entire plan and structure were altered; and whose final form seems to have been a matter almost of indifference to the author.

For a Dead White Male, Thomas Stearns Eliot (1888–1965) has not fared badly in literary reputation since his death nearly forty years ago. Eliot considered himself the twentieth-century successor to Virgil and Dante Alighieri, a generous self-assessment that few critics in his own time or since have felt confident in challenging, although an adverse reaction to his work among his artistic peers in his own generation (notably G. K. Chesterson, William Carlos Williams, and W. H. Auden) was almost immediate. How long this critical admiration, or timidity, will persist is uncertain. The corrosive smog of political correctness so far has

spared few literary monuments that the common perennial sol-
vents—literary jealousy and envy and artistic fashion—have
proved unable to destroy. Eliot has much going for him today, to
keep him going: poetic genius, originality, erudition, wit, and a
magisterial presence. He also has his liabilities, including incomprehensibility, poetic aridity, donnish pedantry, and more than a
touch of the sterile modern intellectualism he himself despised in
other people. (Regarding Eliot, Raymond Chandler once wrote,
privately and with Eliot's play *The Cocktail Party* in mind, "I long
ago made up my mind that subtlety was not a dimension of thinking but merely a technique, and not a particularly difficult technique at that.") Here and there in his work, there even seem
grounds for suspicion that T. S. Eliot, though no artistic faker or
mountebank, at times engaged in fakery and mountebankism—a
suspicion that is scarcely allayed by the poet's self-deprecating
reference to the "remarkable exposition of bogus scholarship"
displayed in the notes he appended to the *The Waste Land* in order
to pad out the poem to plausible book length.

Most probably, Eliot owes his continuing respect to the remarkable quality of his poetic line, which succeeds in making the
reactionary modernism of the early twentieth century sound
strangely contemporary and iconoclastic in the nihilistic post-
modernism of the twenty-first; to the investment the academic
and critical establishments have made in him and his work; and to
that same splendid incomprehensibility, that regal impenetrabil-
ity, that defies deconstruction as much as it does exposition.
(Nobody wants to argue with what the thunder said.) "Wagner is
better than he sounds," George Bernard Shaw remarks. There are
poems, perhaps, in which T. S. Eliot is better than he reads; others
in which he is worse than he sounds. For nearly a century, *The
Waste Land* has frustrated and displeased many readers who,
however, have never succeeded in forgetting the experience.

T. S. Eliot was born and raised in St. Louis, Missouri, and educated at Harvard College, where he studied under Irving
Babbitt, the New Humanist critic. Later, he attended the Sor-
bonne and Oxford. The outbreak of war in 1914 stranded him in
England, where he became, by degrees, an expatriate and finally,

in 1927, a subject of the Crown. In London, Eliot took a job in the Colonial and Foreign Department at Lloyd's Bank, wrote poetry, and became acquainted with Ezra Pound, who arranged for his early mature work to be published. His first book of poems was *Prufrock and Other Observations,* published in London in 1917; it was followed in 1920 by *Poems* and, two years later, by *The Waste Land*: Eliot's longest and most ambitious work to date, considered by many critics to be his best. Certainly it was his most influential: Edmund Wilson called the poem "[t]he great knockout up to date," as a generation of undergraduate students and young writers and artists embraced *The Waste Land* as being at once the defining example of, and also the inspiration for, the postwar sensibility. Ernest Hemingway's novel, *The Sun Also Rises,* may be read to some extent as a pastiche of *The Waste Land,* while Evelyn Waugh has Anthony Blanche, in *Brideshead Revisited,* declaim the poem through the open window of his rooms at college. And Waugh took as the epigraph for another novel, *A Handful of Dust,* the famous lines from Part I of *The Waste Land,* from which Waugh also took his title:

> I will show you something different from either
> Your shadow at morning striding behind you
> Or your shadow at evening rising to meet you;
> I will show you fear in a handful of dust.

Whether contemporary enthusiasm for *The Waste Land* was the result of a widespread misreading of the poem or simply a misunderstanding of the poet's intent is uncertain. Eliot, like Pound, *was* striving toward a modern aesthetic, a modern way of sight and of expression. Yet, both men, though aesthetic revolutionaries, were political, social, and even intellectual reactionaries: Pound became a Fascist, Eliot a Tory, a monarchist, and an Anglo-Catholic. The apparently schizophrenic combination is explained and reconciled by the fact of both poets having been revolutionary elitists, whose aim (like Richard Wagner's in music) was to rescue art and intellect from the vulgar masses and an unserious, shallow bourgeoisie—eager for easy intellectual access and hungry for instant emotional gratification—and restore it to its earlier aristocratic purview. This was the modernist project, and it explains why, almost to a man, the salient figures of literary modernism—Eliot, Pound, Wyndham Lewis, Waugh, Faulkner, Allen Tate, Andrew Lytle, and so on—were reactionary, in art and in politics.

The Waste Land has alternatively been read as a personal document; as an impressionistic view of civilization in decline and headed for collapse; as an expression of cultural malaise; as an elaborate literary game; and countless other things. What Eliot intended is difficult to say, because he never said. Also, because Ezra Pound, to whom Eliot showed a draft of the poem, cut so much of the original text and shaped the remainder so considerably as to alter the original scheme—and thus the "meaning" and subject of the work—entirely, while imposing on it an order of his own. (Pound, indeed, once referred to the work as a series of poems.) According to one of Eliot's biographers (Peter Ackroyd), *The Waste Land* "embodies an attempt to create meaning which fails." Perhaps on account of the title, however (as well as the poetry that Eliot went on to write), the poem seems generally associated in readers' minds with the cultural and spiritual waste land that is modern life, modern society, the modern world. (Given the use they made of it in their own work, this surely was the interpretation accepted by Hemingway and Waugh.)

Ironically, there is a sense in which T. S. Eliot, together with James Joyce, may be considered as anticipating the late twentieth-century movement known as Deconstructionism. Ackroyd attributes Eliot's enthusiasm for *Ulysses*—his favorite novel—to its author's having "created a world which exists only in, and through, the multiple uses of language—through voices, through parodies of style . . . Joyce had had an historical consciousness of language and thus of the relativity of any one 'style.' The whole course of Eliot's development would lead him to share such a consciousness. His early philosophical investigations had been concerned with the primacy of 'interpretation' and the irrecoverability of any original 'meaning' which is being interpreted." Thus, as Ackroyd points out, Eliot, "a thoroughgoing sceptic and relativist as he himself claimed to be," concluded *The Waste Land* with a layering of lines by Dante, Thomas Kyd, Gérard de Nerval, the *Pervegilium Veneris,* and Sanskrit. Conrad Aiken, reviewing Eliot's poem across the water for *The New Republic,* was of the opinion that it succeeded "by virtue of its incoherence, not of its plan; by virtue of its ambiguities, not its explanations." Pound most likely agreed with him.

Whatever the "meaning" of *The Waste Land,* the poem's publication was one of the major cultural events of the century—an event, moreover, that, unlike Igor Stravinsky's *Le Sacre du Printemps* (which Eliot accorded his own standing ovation after a performance), was never acclaimed by the Left, while rapidly assuming the character of an icon for intellectually discerning traditionalists and reactionaries. A good test of suspected poetic humbuggery is the poet's ability to restate, in clear and direct prose, ideas he had previously presented, through a glass darkly, in verse. Time and again in the course of his career, T. S. Eliot, as a critic and essayist, met this test and passed it with flying colors; it is his prose writings (in particular the essays gathered up in *The Idea of a Christian Society* and *Notes toward a Definition of Culture*), as much as or more than his poetry, his Anglicanism, his royalism, his learning, and his austerely correct personal demeanor that established his reputation, fairly early on, as a man of the Right.

Most important, ultimately, is the fact that Eliot, as a poetic innovator, sought to work within and to extend the Western tradition of rationalism as opposed to irrationalism, beauty to ugliness, consonance to dissonance, style to carelessness and vulgarity, symmetry to asymmetry, erudition to ignorance, Christian faith to impiety:

> After the torchlight red on sweaty faces
> After the frosty silence in the gardens
> After the agony in stony places
> The shouting and the crying
> Prison and palace and reverberation
> Of thunder of spring over distant mountains

He who was living is now dead
We who were living are now dying
With a little patience

Who knows, or cares finally, what a passage from a Mozart sonata *means* (except that nothing in this world could be more beautiful and more civilized)?

34

THE SUN ALSO RISES

by Ernest Hemingway

1926

Ernest Hemingway (1899–1961), despite attacks made on him by the New York critics in the 1930s for his "reactionary" uninterest in politics and his "adolescent" passion for hunting, prizefighting, and bullfighting, certainly was never in his own estimation any sort of "conservative," political or otherwise. (He did convert to Roman Catholicism in the late 1920s in order to marry his Catholic second wife, Pauline Pfeiffer, but did not remain a practicing Catholic for long.) *For Whom the Bell Tolls,* his novelistic treatment of the Spanish Civil War, was written to refute New York's charge and get the critics off his back. Despite its fame, the book is far from being vintage Hemingway, owing to an unconvincing quality that is directly attributable to the author's fundamental apoliticism and lack of sophistication (as well as real interest) in the world of politics, whether of the Left *or* the Right. A great artist, he possessed a natural immunity to ideological infection while remaining susceptible to nostalgia for the old rural America, whose destruction helps explain his becoming an expatriate in his twenties and also his deep affection for Spain—a conservative society, socially and culturally speaking, even before General Franco came to power. Whether this suggests basically conservative instincts or not, Ernest Hemingway is nevertheless a good example of the artist who—unintentionally or incidentally—produces a work of art profoundly conservative in both its nature and in its implications. It is likely no coincidence that Hemingway's first, and by far his best, novel is (with the possible exception of *The Old Man and the Sea,* an also great work praised by Evelyn Waugh for its piety) the most "conservative" of his books in its vision of the fate of Western man, doomed—and damned—within the perverted milieu he has created for himself.

The Sun Also Rises is a prose pastiche of T. S. Eliot's *The Waste Land,* with which the young Hemingway, like every serious literary artist of his generation, was well familiar. By a sad irony suggestive of the author's ambivalence toward his material, Hemingway dedicated his royalties from *The Sun Also Rises* to the support of his first wife, Hadley Richardson, and their son Bumby after he had divorced her to marry Pauline.

"One generation passeth away, and another generation cometh; but the earth abideth forever. . . . The sun also ariseth, and the sun goeth down, and hasteth to the place where he arose." Ernest Hemingway chose this passage from Ecclesiastes for an epigraph to his book. "You are all a lost generation," Gertrude Stein said. And Hemingway took her saying as a second epigraph.

The Sun Also Rises is without "plot," its story linear and simple. The first-person narrator, Jake Barnes, is a young American expatriate employed as a journalist in Paris who, like the author, served as a driver in the ambulance corps on the Italian Front during the Great War; the other principal characters also belong to the American and British expatriate community. Jake is in love with Lady Brett Ashley, an alcoholic English aristocrat by marriage "built with curves like the hull of a racing yacht," and she, in her way, with him. Jake supposes she wants what she knows she can't have. His war wound has removed from him the implement of love, while sparing the seat of all desiring. ("You, a foreigner . . . have given more than your life," the Italian liaison colonel tells him.) Brett, though married, is trying to obtain a divorce in order to marry Mike Campbell, a wealthy, inane, and also alcoholic Scot. In the meanwhile, she is pursuing her unconsummatable relationship with Jake and accompanying homosexuals to cafés after breaking off a fling with Jake's acquaintance Robert Cohen. Cohen, who is the scion of one of the richest Jewish families in New York and a Princeton graduate with literary pretensions, is unsatisfactorily involved with a culturally ambitious paramour named Frances, who has determined to marry him after having discovered she is losing her looks. Bill Gorton, a successful American writer, turns up drunk from Budapest and continues his drinking binge with Jake in Paris. Jake and Bill and Robert Cohen motor from Bayonne across the border into Spain, after agreeing to meet Brett and Mike in Pamplona. Jake, who has just learned from Brett about her affair with Cohen, is fiercely jealous, and Cohen is ungentlemanly enough to rub it in. Convinced that Brett has stayed over with Mike on the way to Pamplona in order to have an assignation with himself in San Sebastian, Cohen insists on awaiting the couple in town while Jake and Bill take a bus to Burguete to fish the Irati River for five days; the two of them delighting in the high mountain country and in the river and in their expatriate status, their release from the American commercial culture with its naïveté, democratic sentimentality, and false piety. In Pamplona again, they meet up with Cohen and Brett and Mike at the Hotel Montoya, where the bullfighters all stay. They attend the unloading of the bulls before the fiesta, and Mike Campbell picks a fight with Robert Cohen; afterward, the party meets for supper. "It was like certain dinners I remember from the war. There was much wine, an ignored tension, and a feeling of things coming that you could not prevent happening. Under the wine I lost the disgusted feeling and was happy. It seemed they were all such nice people." Watching the *corrida*, Brett falls in love with one of the *toreros*, Pedro Romero, nineteen years old. Partly to spite Cohen, partly in the spirit of voyeur, Jake brings her together with Romero, with whom she disappears. Later, Brett, broke in a seedy hotel in Madrid, summons Jake by telegraph to rescue her after she has dismissed her adolescent lover, who wished to marry her. "It isn't the sort of thing one does," she explains.

Insisting that she will not "let herself be the sort of bitch that ruins children," Brett adds, "You know, it makes one feel rather good deciding not to be a bitch." Instead, she will go back to Mike Campbell. "He's so damned nice and he's so awful. He's my sort of thing." After leaving the restaurant where Jake has taken her to lunch, they climb into a taxi.

> The driver started up the street. I settled back. Brett moved close to me. We sat close against each other. I put my arm around her and she rested against me comfortably. It was very hot and bright, and the houses looked sharply white. We turned out onto the Gran Via.
>
> "Oh, Jake," Brett said, "we could have had such a damned good time together."
>
> Ahead was a mounted policeman in khaki directing traffic. He raised his baton. The car slowed suddenly pressing Brett against me.
>
> "Yes," I said. "Isn't it pretty to think so?"

Hemingway's mother complained to Ernest after the publication of *The Sun Also Rises* that the ladies in her reading group in Oak Park, Illinois, thought the novel's characters to be not nice people. Jake Barnes, the self-described "technical Catholic," would have agreed with them. *The Sun Also Rises* is a dramatization of moral nihilism, not an endorsement of it. When Brett remarks to him that not being a bitch is "sort of what we have instead of God," Jake corrects her: "Some people have God. . . . Quite a lot." Jake himself, though he still goes to Confession, nevertheless seems not to be one of them, though clearly he would like to be. He might really *be* in the confessional, when he admits, "I did not care what it was all about. . . . Maybe if you found out how to live in it you learned from that what it was all about." Jake Barnes, like Hemingway himself, is a peculiarly American existentialist; one for whom existentialist philosophy is not an expression of intellectual and moral pride but rather a cry of despair and desolation, and a plea for help in some form or another. He is forever in contempt, not of God, but of himself.

In Paris, Jake has had his vision of Eliot's Waste Land, the modern city, which is to say, Hell; in rural France and Spain, he finds a promise of Heaven. Only, it is a promise he is unable to realize. As with nearly all of Hemingway's work, the characters in *The Sun Also Rises* (the mutilated Jake excepted) enjoy every blessing life has to offer—money, good looks, the love of the opposite sex, good food, good drink, sports, adventure, foreign travel, intellectual and social sophistication, and the intelligence to make the most of these—yet they have hold on absolutely nothing. "Our nada who art in nada, nada be thy name." ("A Clean, Well-lighted Place.") Theirs is the condition of people living out a seductive illusion on a tightrope walk above the bottomless chasm that waits to receive them below. Jake knows, or rather feels, this; possibly Brett does also. But he perceives no means of exit from his condition, while failing to discover any consolation (including, in his case, sexual gratification) that would make that condition bearable (including "pretty" speculations on what might have been).

Hemingway, dismissed by a recent critic as a "hunter-writer," is frequently faulted as an insufficiently intellectual artist who chose going to war over going to college and spent most of his life with men of action and adventurers rather than with fellow writers. A careful reading of *The Sun Also Rises* (and other of his books) gives the lie to this notion. Beneath the pellucid, almost plain prose and the simple, straightforward narrative line, lie subtle structures of meaning that seem nearly inexhaustible. Like all modernist writers, Hemingway shows without telling, includes without explaining. The technique is not, in the opprobrious academic sense of the term, "subtle." Rather it is stunningly effective for sophisticated, careful, and appreciative readers. For example: The critic J. O. Tate notes how the route, traveled by Jake Barnes and Bill Gorton, from Paris south to Pamplona is not only the same followed by pilgrims on their way to medieval Europe's most famous shrine, Santiago de Compostello, it is the invasion route taken by Charlemagne on his way to attack the Moors and drive them from southern Spain, across the Mediterranean to Africa. (Approaching Burguete, Jake points out for Bill the monastery of Roncevalles, recalling the battle of Roncevaux where Roland lost his life and inspired the great poem that became the even greater legend.) And, at the end of the Barnes party's trip, is the bullfight; a ritual nearly as old as the Mediterranean world itself. Thus Jake, in flight from the modern horror that is Paris, retraces in reverse the whole of European history, as far back as early Crete. No mere "hunter-writer" could have conceived of such a plan, much less have executed it with the consummate poise and delicacy with which Hemingway executes this bit of literary virtuosity.

Ernest Hemingway, if not a prophet, was at least a visionary. *The Sun Also Rises,* his second and best novel written when the author was twenty-six years old, is also his greatest and most complete vision of the terror, confusion, and chaos that the modern project has created.

35

A HANDFUL OF DUST

by Evelyn Waugh

1934

The release of the film version of *Brideshead Revisited* a decade or so ago makes that novel the most popular, as well as the best known, of Evelyn Waugh's books. The fact remains that *Brideshead* is not vintage Waugh, largely for its plummy quality amounting almost to sentimentality that is uncharacteristic of the author working at the top of his form.

Evelyn Waugh (1903–1966), the son of a London publisher and brother of a best-selling novelist whose own books failed to survive even the lilies of the field, came down from Oxford with a vague ambition to become a cabinet maker and woodworker. He published a biography of Dante Gabriel Rossetti, the Pre-Raphaelite, before discovering his vocation in the writing of his first novel, *Decline and Fall*—a madcap story inspired by his experience teaching at a boys' school in North Wales. The book, which received small attention from the reviewers, was followed by a succession of wildly wicked comic masterpieces: *Vile Bodies, Black Mischief, Scoop,* and *Put Out More Flags.* Between the second and third of these comes a contextually anomalous novel that in retrospect can be seen to anticipate the "serious" fiction to which Waugh turned in the second half of his career, while retaining the mordantly satirical humor and nearly surrealistic storyline and atmosphere of the early period. *A Handful of Dust* is a fulcrum novel, on which the author's art can be seen to balance. Also, it is Waugh's masterpiece, a distillation of his finest qualities as a literary artist, social observer, and prophet.

Evelyn Waugh in his choice of subject and in his modernist technique was a writer for his time; in intellect and sensibility, however, he was a total misfit, at sword's point with the modern world. It was his good fortune to be not so much misunderstood by the "bright young things" of the 1920s and 1930s who bought his (socially as well as intellectually) sophisticated books, as not to be understood at all. Waugh is so skillful and amusing a writer that it is very easy to satisfy oneself with the icing, while ignoring the cake altogether. It is true also that Waugh was highly reticent about what he was really up to in his fiction, never deigning to "explain" his work to his public or to the critics—as, of course, it is always a mistake for an artist to do. For Waugh, to write novels was to create "small systems of independent order" as a means of holding chaos at bay. A monarchist who disdained to vote on the ground that no candidate for Parliament was sufficiently reactionary to suit his principles, a convert to Catholicism whose ideal century was the thirteenth, and a defiant social snob who hobnobbed with, and married into, the English aristocracy, though of bourgeois origins himself, Evelyn Waugh became something of a figure of condescending amusement in England, following the end of World War II and the beginning of the "Century of the Common Man." None of this gainsays the truth: Waugh, who saw the world and saw it plainly, put his comic genius in service to the most serious purpose, which was no less than a metaphysical, political, and social critique of the modern world. Appropriately, the title of his finest book is taken from T. S. Eliot's *The Waste Land,* which also supplies the epigraph:

> I will show you something different from either
> Your shadow at morning striding behind you

Or your shadow at evening rising to meet you;
I will show you fear in a handful of dust.

A Handful of Dust is the story of Tony Last (Waugh is always wonderfully apt in naming his characters), a well-bred Englishman who lives with his beautiful aristocratic wife and their young son John Andrew on Hetton estate at an easy distance from London. Tony, who is of independent means, devotes his life to the estate and to the neighboring village where he acts the part of squire, involving himself in local affairs and serving as vestryman at the Anglican church. He has, as he thinks, a developed sense of place and of history, of family and country. Waugh deftly leads us to perceive, though, that Tony's sense of the past is nostalgic and sentimental rather than living and realistic. (He has naïvely and even tastelessly named the bedrooms in his house after the Arthurian legend: "Guinevere," "Lancelot," and so forth.) Tony Last, we understand, despite his breeding and cultivation is the modern Everyman who has lost contact with the tradition he venerates and believes he is upholding, without ever grasping its meaning and essence.

Tony's comfortable, complacent life is wrecked when Brenda Last begins an affair with John Beaver, a feckless and unattractive young man (his unlikeliness as a lover is precisely what causes Brenda to take him for one) who spends his days sitting at home by the telephone waiting for some society hostess to invite him to make up a couple at a luncheon or supper party. (John's mother is a busy interior decorator who specializes in renovating fine old London townhouses in chrome and sheepskin. " '[N]o one [was hurt] I am thankful to say,' said Mrs. Beaver, 'except two housemaids who lost their heads and jumped through a glass roof into the paved court. They were in no danger. The fire never properly reached the bedrooms I am afraid. Still they are bound to need doing up, everything black with smoke and drenched with water and luckily they had that old-fashioned sort of extinguisher that ruins *everything*. One really cannot complain.' ") When the news is broken to her that "John" has been killed in a riding accident, Brenda inadvertently expresses the relief she feels that the victim is her son, not her paramour. She leaves her husband for John Beaver after the funeral and demands a divorce from him. In order to protect Lady Brenda's good name, her family's solicitor prevails on Tony to let himself be taken in an "infidelity" in a Brighton hotel. Shadowed by "detectives," he arrives in the company of an employee of London's most elegant and unobtrusive brothel and her eight-year-old daughter, who share the "adulterer's" bed between them. Later, when Lady Brenda's brother demands a divorce settlement that would require the sale of Hetton to make up the amount, Tony at last puts his foot down politely and joins Dr. Messinger, a new acquaintance, on an archaeological expedition to Brazil in search of a "City," fabled among the natives, which Tony imagines as "Gothic in character, all vanes and pinnacles, gargoyles, battlements, groining and tracery, pavilions and terraces, a transfigured Hetton." On the voyage out, he strikes up a shipboard friendship with a charming and wistful Creole girl returning from her convent school in Paris to Trinidad to be suitably married. Tony and Dr. Messinger debark at Georgetown, British Guiana, and head at once for the interior, where they are abandoned by their native guides and proceed alone on their journey down a tributary of the Amazon. Tony is stricken with a tropical fever; delirious, he imagines Brenda is in the boat with them. (From interspersed flashbacks to London, we learn that she and John Beaver have tired of one another, and Brenda has paid a visit to Tony's solicitor to inquire if she is made a beneficiary in his will.) Dr. Messinger leaves Tony stretched in his hammock to search out help downstream and is drowned in a falls. Tony, delirious again with fever, is discovered and rescued by the eccentric Mr. Todd. (Waugh gave his novel two endings: this one—left deliberately incomplete for the first-time reader's benefit—and a "realistic" but also less striking and effective alternative, supplied to please the more prosaic-minded critics.)

A Handful of Dust is a powerful restatement of Waugh's overriding novelistic theme: the vulnerability of civilization to a resurgence of the barbarism from which it developed slowly over the ages at the cost of immeasurable travail. Twentieth-century intellectual fashion held that the two deserve to be viewed as equal alternative "preferences." In fact, the relativistic spirit that so regards them is rebarbarizing civilization to produce a culture that will make precivilization seem innocent by comparison. Barbarism versus civilization was not, for Waugh, a racial issue—he wrote a short story about black explorers a millennium hence landing in Darkest Britain to convert the repaganized Britons, painted blue with wode—but a matter of faith, will, and fortitude. (Not even Evelyn Waugh could have imagined that less than forty years after his death, human flesh would be sold in the Africanized streets of London, along with chimpanzee and bushrat meat.) The satire cuts most deeply, the prophetic vision penetrates furthest, perhaps, in "English Gothic—II," where Waugh deftly renders a social world in which maintaining appearances is everything—and appearances finally count for nothing (everyone sees the moral reality of adultery, divorce, and thievery plainly, accepts it unquestioningly, and expects Tony to accept it also by selling Hetton in order to allow Beaver to marry Brenda and maintain her in accustomed luxury). The dramatic power and poignancy of the chapter obviously derive from the trauma Waugh experienced in his first marriage, which ended in divorce after his wife cuckolded him with a mutual friend and left a lifelong impression on him. The black savages in Brazil, Waugh is saying, are not—any longer—morally or even culturally superior to the white heathens and neopagans in England.

Artistically, Evelyn Waugh has affinities with the reactionary literary pessimists of his time, though not necessarily those of his own generation (Eliot and Pound and their circle), and what Gertrude Stein called the Lost Generation (Hemingway, Fitzgerald), old enough to have experienced the horrors of the Great War that effectively wrecked Western civilization. In other respects, however, he stands apart from these writers by virtue of his religious faith (excepting Eliot) and his social sophistication (excepting Fitzgerald). Waugh was a deeply unhappy man: an alcoholic, glutton, and insomniac whose detestable behavior was deliberately incorporated into a personal as well as a professional identity. Like many people, he loathed in others and in the world around him what he identified and despised in himself, and made his art from the tension between opposing tendencies. (The problem with *Brideshead Revisited* is really that, in writing the book, Waugh felt too comfortable and at home with his material.) For Evelyn Waugh, these were civilization versus barbarism, order versus chaos, God's Church versus the Devil.

In response to a friend who had temerariously inquired how he could reconcile notorious personal conduct with pious Christian belief, Waugh replied that, without his faith, he would scarcely be human at all. His tone was airy, as if his answer were the most obvious thing in the world.

36

THE NAPOLEON OF NOTTING HILL

by G. K. Chesterton

1904

Gilbert Keith Chesterton (1874–1936), though not widely read today, was among the greatest of twentieth-century British writers—"a colossal genius," George Bernard Shaw, his friend and intellectual sparring partner, called him. It might be added that he was one of the most unusual also, were it not for the fact that the great British writers in the twentieth century were nearly all of them unusual, for uniqueness of personality and viewpoint as well as for literary scope and versatility.

Chesterton, best known today for his chronicles of the adventures of Father Brown, the clerical amateur sleuth, and for his major apologetic works *The Outline of Sanity, Everlasting Man,* and *Orthodoxy* (written twenty-five years before he was received at last into the Roman Catholic Church), was thirty years old when *The Napoleon of Notting Hill* was brought out in 1904. The first of his many novels, it was preceded by two volumes of poetry, two collections of essays, and two biographies (one of Robert Browning, the other of the painter G. F. Watts). Besides the popular

Father Brown stories from which the author derived a significant portion of his income in later years (Father Brown was something of a literary hit in the United States as well as in Britain), *The Man Who Was Thursday* (1908) is of all Chesterton's novels the most familiar to modern audiences, to whom *The Napoleon of Notting Hill* is almost unknown.

British literature in the twentieth century, as far forward as World War II, was strangely dominated by reactionaries protesting against an age profoundly radical in its assumptions and attitudes, including those embraced by self-avowed "conservatives" and "practical" or "commonsense" people. (The same is not true, or not true to the same extent, of American literature in the same period.) These writers, though related by a set of fundamental assumptions of their own in respect of the wrongheadedness and inadequacy of the modern world, nevertheless did not comprise a single social bloc or literary school. Rather, they formed a number of overlapping circles defined less by social identity and interest than by intellectual assurance and artistic inclination. G. K. Chesterton, like Hilaire Belloc a working journalist as well as a novelist and poet all of his career, belonged to a cadre of almost militantly assertive Catholic lay writers who wrote not only as defenders of the Faith, but as advocates of the premodern European societies the Faith had inspired and shaped. Thus, the emergence of what Shaw dubbed the "Chesterbelloc:" the four-legged beast with two heads, each of them poetical as well as polemical, one predominantly romantic, the other essentially Roman in its realism and practicality; both committed finally to the same end, which amounted to an encompassing program for restoring the mental, emotional, and social sanity opposed and nearly destroyed by an ever-more centralized and dehumanized world.

Chesterton, in his first novel, displays the whimsicality, flight of fancy, poetic purple, and splendid disregard of the laws of probability that give this (and all the later fiction) the quality and feel of a fairy tale for intelligent adults. The story came to him (he wrote in his posthumously published autobiography) while he wandered in North Kensington, telling myself stories of feudal sallies and sieges in the manner of Walter Scott, and vaguely trying to apply them to the wilderness of bricks and mortar around me. I felt that London was already too large and loose a thing to be a city in the sense of a citadel. It seemed to me even larger and looser than the British Empire. And something irrationally arrested and pleased my eye about the look of one small block of little lighted shops, and I amused myself with the supposition that these alone were to be preserved and defended, like a hamlet in the desert.

So *The Napoleon of Notting Hill* was conceived as a dramatization of the modern antimodern proposition that "Small Is Beautiful"—in the political context, the equivalent of the term "community control."

The novel's wildly implausible story succeeds on its own charm, as well as on the author's wit, his total lack of artistic self-conciousness, the outrageous quality of his imagination, and his intellectual irrepressibility. Chesterton's interest as a fiction writer was essentially the presentation of the literary essay in imaginative guise, not the realization of the aesthetic possibilities inherent in the novel as a unique art form. His concern was always with the dramatization of an idea, rather than the idea of a dramatization. As with so many fine novels, *The Napoleon of Notting Hill* manages to achieve the status of great writing, while not necessarily amounting to great fiction.

The setting is London in the year 1984 (which may or may not have suggested to George Orwell one of the most famous dates in literary history). Eighty years forward from the time Chesterton wrote, the streets of London are still lit by gas lamps, Londoners dressed in frock coats get about town in hansom cabs, and the airplane is not even imagined. This complete absence of technological projection reflects no imaginative dearth on the part of the author, but rather his good-humored contempt for such technological futurists as Jules Verne, H. G. Wells, and all the "clever" men of the time who believed that the future could be learned by extrapolating present trends into the coming decades; Chesterton's uninterest in science; and his prophetic vision of a New

World Order in which every independent nation has been agglomerated into a single global state from which local and national customs and cultures have been expunged. "Very few words," the narrator begins,

> are needed to explain why London, a hundred years hence . . .
> was very like it was in those enviable days when I was still
> alive. . . . The reason can be stated in one sentence. The people
> had lost faith in revolutions. All revolutions are doctrinal—such
> as the French one, or the one that introduced Christianity. For
> it stands to common sense that you cannot upset all existing
> things, customs, and compromises, unless you believe in some
> thing outside them, something positive and divine. Now, Eng
> land, during this century, lost all belief in this. It believed in a
> thing called Evolution. And it said, "All theoretic changes have
> ended in blood and ennui. If we change, we must change slowly
> and safely, as the animals do. Nature's revolutions are the only
> successful ones. There has been no conservative reaction in
> favor of tails.

And so, "Things that were not much thought of dropped out of sight. Things that had not often happened did not happen at all." The police force has shrunk "almost to a point," since the people do not believe anything is to be gained by getting rid of it entirely. "Democracy was dead; for no one minded the governing class governing. England was now practically a despotism, but not an hereditary one. Some one in the official class was made King. No one cared how: no one cared who. He was merely an universal secretary."

In this careless way, a government clerk named Auberon Quin is selected king, to the horror of his fellow clerks and the routine approbation of his new subjects. Quin (modeled by Chesterton on Max Beerbohm) is a cynic, "a dangerous man" who "cares for nothing but a joke" and believes that "a sense of humour, a weird and delicate sense of humour, is the new religion of mankind!" As Quin explains to an outraged Minister of State, "I am an English gentleman with different tastes [than Herbert Spencer]. He liked philosophy. I like art. He liked writing books on the nature of human society. I like to see the Lord Chamberlain walking in front of me with a piece of paper pinned to his coat-tails."

Mingling with his people one evening, King Auberon is accosted on the streets of Notting Hill (the neighborhood where Chesterton was born and raised) by a small boy wearing a paper cocked hat who strikes him in the waistcoat with a wooden sword and announces, " 'I'm the King of the Castle.' " Being a kind-hearted man "and very fond of children, like all people who are fond of the ridiculous," Quin is in the act of congratulating the boy on his patriotic defense of his neighborhood, when he is struck by "perhaps the noblest of all my conceptions": A Charter of the Cities, reviving "the arrogance of the old medieval cities applied to our glorious suburbs." Thus, Clapham shall have its city guard, Wimbledon its city wall, Surbiton a tolling bell to raise its citizens, West Hampstead its military banner. The King establishes a Council of Provosts and designs uniforms and coats-of-arms for the various London municipalities, decrees that heralds shall accompany the Lord High Provosts wherever they go, and that city guards and walls surrounding the cities be established and built. His subjects, mildly amused at first by the "Great Proclamation of the Charter of the Free Cities," are horrified to learn that King Auberon takes his mad scheme seriously. Various business interests wish to lay a road through Notting Hill, which will require the demolition of old streets and buildings. The king, already inclined to veto the plan, has his mind made up for him by the dramatic appearance of Adam Wayne, the Lord High Provost of Notting Hill, who drops on one knee before him to proffer his sword to his liege. Staggered by delight and appreciation of what he takes to be a brother artist and cynic, Auberon is finally overwhelmed by the realization that Wayne is deadly serious and astounded to discover that Wayne is the same small boy who, ten years before, struck at him with a wooden sword in Notting Hill—thus unwittingly setting in train the madcap scheme for the Charter of the Cities! " 'My God in Heaven!' he said; 'is it possible that there is within the four seas of Britain a man who takes

Notting Hill seriously?' 'And my God in Heaven!' said Wayne passionately; 'is it possible that there is within the four seas of Britain a man who does not take it seriously?' "

Even the king cannot muster sufficient frivolity to side openly with Adam Wayne in his quixotic dispute with the burgers of Notting Hill. Nevertheless, his sympathies are with the Lord High Provost as he raises an army drawn from among the urchins of greater London and led by the shopkeepers and tradesmen of Pump Street to fight the developers and their armies, drawn from the neighboring Cities of Bayswater and South Kensington. In his self-assumed role of war correspondent, Auberon files a single lengthy dispatch in which he describes in flights of poesy the concluding battle of the war, when Wayne captures Notting Hill's Waterworks Tower and forces the terms of surrender by threatening to flood the entire valley under 50,000 tons of water. As General Buck commanding the vanquished force has understood for some time, however, Wayne's victory and his own defeat were actually accomplished long before. Given the conditions prevailing in the soporific, conformist England of 1984, the military atmosphere of Notting Hill, pervaded as it is with martial enthusiasm and the zest for combat, is " 'Adam Wayne's atmosphere. It's the atmosphere which you and I thought had vanished from an educated world forever. . . . This old thing—this fighting, has come back. It has come back suddenly and taken us by surprise.' " And with it awakened local pride and loyalty, an appreciation of local custom and culture, the fierce insistence on independence and self-determination, the willingness to revolt against despotism and the constraints of a forcible and unnatural unity. As a result of King Auberon's "immense joke" and Adam Wayne's madly serious response to it, the humane Old World has arisen like the Phoenix from the dreariness of the inhuman new one.

Ten years after the battle of the Waterworks Tower, the City of Notting Hill has developed imperial tendencies in its relations with the neighboring cities, who form a military alliance to resist it. Adam Wayne remonstrates with his people:

"Is it altogether impossible [he demands] to make a thing good without it immediately insisting on being wicked? The glory of

Notting Hill in having achieved its independence, has been enough for me to dream of for many years. . . . Is it really not enough for you, who have had so many other affairs to excite and distract you? Notting Hill is a nation. Why should it condescend to be a mere Empire? You wish to pull down the statue of General Wilson, which the men of Bayswater have so rightly erected. . . . Fools! Who erected that statue? Did Bayswater erect it? No. Notting Hill erected it. Do you not see that it is the glory of our achievement that we have infected the other cities with the idealism of Notting Hill? It is we who have created not only our own side, but both sides of this controversy. O too humble fools, why should you wish to destroy your enemies? You have done something more to them. You have created your enemies."

In the ensuing battle, Notting Hill is destroyed. At dawn the following day, King Auberon and Wayne are discovered alone amid the ruins of the ancient oak tree Wayne has uprooted in defeat. Auberon makes his confession to the former Lord High Provost: "Wayne, it was done as a joke." To which Wayne replies by thanking the king for the great good his joke has wrought for the world. " 'When dark and dreary days come,' " he adds, " 'you and I are necessary, the pure fanatic, the pure satirist. We have between us remedied a great wrong. We have lifted modern cities into that poetry which every one who knows mankind knows to be immeasurably more common than the commonplace. . . . Auberon Quin, we have been too long separated; . . . let us start our wanderings over the world. For we are its two essentials. Come, it is already day.' "

37

BRAVE NEW WORLD

by Aldous Huxley

1931

At the time when he wrote *Brave New World* (in four months, in 1931), its author was toying with an idea amusing to him: that human beings enjoy free will so that they may choose between insanity and lunacy. Aldous Huxley (1894–1963), like the ruling class he imagined for his novel, though he was not insane, seems himself not to have been completely sane, either.

The great-grandson of Thomas Arnold, the famed headmaster of the Rugby School, grandnephew of the poet Matthew Arnold, and grandson of Thomas Henry Huxley, the distinguished biologist, evolutionist, and essayist, Huxley was a scion of the English ruling class (though not of the English aristocracy) and died an example of the degenerate condition to which, by the end of his lifetime, that class had fallen. Born in 1894, he moved with his family to the United States in 1937 and the following year settled in Hollywood, where he became a scriptwriter and drug guru in anticipation of Timothy Leary, his more crazed and less responsible successor. Huxley wrote forty-seven books, of which the best are *Point Counterpoint, Brave New World, Crome Yellow,* and *After*

Many a Summer Dies the Swan. Many of his later works deal with the beneficial and useful properties of drugs, with which Huxley experimented under close supervision; his last novel, *Island,* published a year before his death on November 22, 1963, centers on the quest for a nonintoxicating, nonstupefying equivalent of soma, the pacifying drug by which the Alphas control the lower orders in the World State in *Brave New World* (and a direct prevision of Prozac). In respect of religion, Huxley was entirely unorthodox, as *The Perennial Philosophy*—a volume comprised of annotated texts on mystical and religious practices as a means to achieving sanity—demonstrates. Ironically, though not entirely unsurprisingly, the creator of one of the most famous humanity-denying dystopias in literature spent the second half of his life in a futile attempt at escaping his human self.

The facts remain that the *Brave New World* imagined by Huxley *is* a dystopia in the eyes of its inventor, and that his prophetic vision is uncannily accurate. As Huxley himself understood, seventeen years after the novel's publication, *Brave New World,* not Orwell's *1984,* foretold the future. In George Orwell's Stalinist dystopia, the rulers control the ruled by force, with punishment following on the commitment of antisocial acts. In Huxley's therapeutic one, punishment is mostly obviated or averted by biological and behavioral conditioning, by which the slaves are brought to love both their slavery and the induced infantilism that has dehumanized them. From the vantage point of the late 1940s, Huxley saw therapeutic totalitarianism approaching by leaps and bounds; from the perspective of the beginning of the twenty-first century, four decades after his death, we can see the horror actually upon us in the form of the calculated proletarianization of the Western publics by a collaborative effort between big government, big business, and the entertainment industry to infantilize the populace in the interests of creating a docile and obedient citizenry, a captive, suggestible consumer market, and a passively receptive mass audience. (Political correctness and lowest-common-denominator culture are really about nothing else.) And so the inanities parroted by the citizens of the World State ("everyone belongs to everyone else"), and the "feelies" that are all special-effect and no coherent or intelligent story, are instantly recognizable today, as are the regime's disdain and fear of history, which is carefully rewritten when not strictly suppressed. "Great is the truth," Huxley writes in his foreword to the 1956 edition, "but still greater, from a practical point of view, is silence about the truth." The president of Harvard University couldn't say it better today, nor act more effectively on that maxim.

Brave New World (the phrase is Miranda's in Shakespeare's play *The Tempest*: "How beauteous mankind is! O brave new world that has such people in it!") takes place in the year 632 After Ford (inventor of standardized mass production and author of the "beautiful and inspired saying, 'History is bunk' ") and 491 years after the beginning of the Nine Years' War that, together with the great Economic Collapse that followed the hostilities, confronted humanity with the choice between World Control and destruction. In the interest of social stability—"the primal and the ultimate need," as the Controller, Mustapha Mond, puts it—individual stability has been assured almost 100 percent by eliminating strong feeling and emotion in all their forms from individual and social life. Motherhood, monogamy, and romance have been removed from human experience, along with pain, disease, and the ravages of old age. A caste system has been developed, under which all men and women are guaranteed "physico-chemically equal," by means of in vitro fertilization and the careful manipulation of embryos within the bottles from which they are "decanted" at term to produce a range of social classes, from Alpha Pluses through Epsilon semimorons. ("Mother" and "father" are regarded as smutty words from the revolting, viviparous past.) As with Englishmen in the England of Belloc and Chesterton, the inhabitants of the World State are mostly propertyless. Unlike them, they are employed (to the State's own ends, of course), well-housed, well-fed, and paid a sufficient wage to bear comfortably the burden of "the conscription of consumption" and indulge in infantile pasttimes like Obstacle Golf and Centrifugal Bumble-puppy. Education consists of hypnopaedia, or sleep teaching (Elementary Sex, Elementary Class Consciousness; hatred of nature, hatred of books), and erotic play beginning in preadolescence. Marriage, of course, is outlawed and "going steady" frowned on, promiscuity being strictly the rule and encouraged (as well as made practical in a nonviviparous society) by state issues of contraceptives, carried by adult men and women at all times in Malthusian Belts. No one is ever supposed to be "alone." All the old religions have been banished and replaced by the nontranscendental, secular religion recognizing Our Ford, in whose name all the crosses have had their tops cut off to become T's; Ford's Day is observed; and Community Sings and Solidarity Services held. For the preservation of their order, finally, the rulers of the World State employ hardly any physical constraints whatsoever. "'In the end,' said Mustapha Mond, 'the Controllers realized that force was no good. The slower but infinitely surer method of ectogenesis, neo-Pavlovian conditioning and hypnopaedia.'"

Huxley has been criticized for caring more for ideas than for the development of his characters and his story, and indeed *Brave New World* is, really, more an animated essay than a proper novel. There is cleverness—even brilliance—here, along with learning and foresightedness; but nothing like Evelyn Waugh's accomplished artistry as a satiric novelist, his ability to conjure a living, independent, and convincing world from surrealistic materials. (Huxley violates time and again the first rule of novel writing, which is "Show, don't tell.") In this respect as in many others, the book compares poorly with, for example, Jonathan Swift's *Gulliver's Travels*: Its antecedents are not to be found in modern fiction, perhaps, but rather in the stiff and artificial genre of the eighteenth-century travel novel, where the author employs disingenuous accounts of the mores and manners of foreign societies for the purpose of criticizing by implication the customs of his own country (as Montesquieu did in his *Persian Letters*). One can reasonably argue that Huxley ought not to be faulted for failing to make plausibly human characters out of dehumanized semiautomatons. To this objection, the response must be that the aesthetic risk was the novelist's to take and he took it; also that the awakening characters who rebel against the system, like the Savage from New Mexico who stands opposed to it, are scarcely better realized than the hopelessly conditioned and conformist ones.

The dialogue is banal and underdeveloped, the Ford conceit silly and implausible (a World Controller would find better material at hand for popular divinization than a crabbed and dessicated Yankee inventor). The names, too, seem obvious and unfunny ("Lenina," "Bernard Marx," "Mustapha Mond," "Dr. Wells," "Benito Hoover," "Morgana Rothschild," "Herbert Bakunin," "Sarojini Engels," "Joanna Diesel," "Darwin Bonaparte") before we realize that Huxley is lumping plutocratic captalism, communism, scientism, and even anarchism together as forerunners of his Brave New World, which he rather cleverly offers to the scrutiny of the socialistic H. G. Wells and the reactionary T. S. Eliot (from whose *The Waste Land* the Controller derives his surname). Capitalism and communism, the author is telling us, are simply two halves of the same walnut, alike expressions of the modern materialist philosophy.

It is always a mistake, however, to read a book for what it is not and never was intended to be. Huxley's tale of a "Savage" (the Shakespeare-reading offspring of two citizens of the World State, born by mischance on a Savage reservation in central New Mexico and discovered at Acoma by a mildly rebellious young man and his conformist sex partner) who is transported along with his obscenely fat and aged natural "m——r" to the "civilized" England that inevitably destroys him, functions as a solid and compelling thesis for this classic work. Aldous Huxley's prophetic vision foretells a world in which absolute power and total control by a preternaturally energized and single-minded elite have been finally achieved by means of scientific technique employed in the reconciliation of its own superhuman aspirations with the subhuman yearning of the people for "happiness"—that is, for total security, material surfeit, ceaseless entertainment, and a life of physical and mental ease. The Alphas' agendum matches precisely that of the economic and political globalists of both the "right" and "left" today, who trust to "technology," the socialized propaganda of mass education and the infantilism of mass entertainment, "silence about the truth," and the demoralizing effects of capitalist consumerism to realize their inhuman and impious goals on a universal scale.

38

ONE DAY IN THE LIFE OF IVAN DENISOVICH

by Aleksandr Solzhenitsyn

1962

It is an interesting moral and aesthetic question whether a great book is necessarily the work of a great man—whether, to turn the statement about, only a great man can write a great book. One way or another, only a great man (and artist) could have written this magnificent small novel about an innocent Russian peasant, drafted into the Red Army during World War II and later sentenced as a "spy" to twenty-five years at forced labor in a "Special" Soviet camp in Siberia.

Aleksandr Solzhenitsyn (1918–), descended from Cossacks, was himself arrested while serving as captain in the same army in February 1945 by the counterintelligence agency of the armed forces of the Soviet Union and charged with the crime of having referred to Joseph Stalin in unflattering terms in a private letter. For this offense, he received eight years in the labor camps and three in exile. After his rehabilitation in 1956, while teaching mathematics and having already begun to write, he became ill with cancer, from which he recovered after undergoing treatment in a Soviet hospital where he found his inspiration for another

novel, *The Cancer Ward. One Day in the Life of Ivan Denisovich,*
based on his own prison experience, was an immediate success in
the Soviet Union and abroad after it appeared in *Novy Mir,* the
Soviet-era literary periodical, in 1962. Following Nikita Khrushchev's disgrace in 1964, however, the author became a marked
man, harassed by the authorities for his candid criticism of the
Soviet regime's repressive policies and forced to publish his novels (*The First Circle,* etc.) and stories through *samizdat* (the Soviet
literary underground) and abroad. In 1970, Solzhenitsyn was
awarded the Nobel Prize for Literature. Fearful of being denied
reentry to his native country, he refused to travel to Stockholm to
receive his prize. Four years later, following the publication in 1973
of volume one of *The Gulag Archipelago*—a nonfiction trilogy
about the extensive Soviet prison camp system—he was again arrested, charged with treason against the Soviet Union, stripped of
his Soviet citizenship, and sent into exile by the government in
Moscow. After *Lenin in Zurich* appeared in 1975, Solzhenitsyn
came to the United States and bought a house in Cavendish,
Vermont, where he lived as a recluse of sorts, restless and home-
sick for his native land. In a rare public appearance, he delivered
a commencement address at Harvard College in which he dealt
as frankly with what he perceived to be the faults of his adoptive
country as he had earlier with those of the Soviet Union.
"Conservatives" in particular were horrified to learn that the great
Russian literary patriot felt nothing but scorn for consumer capitalism and capitalist democracy, secularism, and what he dismissed with fine hauteur as "intolerable music"—icon and symbol
of modern Western culture. Russian Orthodox in his religion and
czarist in his politics, Solzhenitsyn favors a humanely authoritarian state informed by orthodox Christianity. While Mikhail Gor-
bachev's glasnost hardly reflected either of these, Solzhenitsyn
accepted the official restoration of his citizenship in 1990 and returned, four years later, to Mother Russia, where he has been
nearly as loud in his condemnation of Boris Yeltsin and Vladimir
Putin as he had been of Khrushchev and Leonid Brezhnev.

One Day in the Life of Ivan Denisovich is as simple in structure
and method as its title suggests: From reveille to lights out, it de-

tails the experience of Ivan Denisovich Shukhov—a former Red Army soldier and prisoner of war who, after serving years in a lumber camp prison for "espionage" following his escape from behind the German lines, has been transferred to a "Special" camp for politicals, where both the discipline and the conditions of existence are more rigorous still. The novel, a record of human endurance and resilience, is still more a testimony to the essential unmalleability of human nature by a political system whose professed raison d' être is to alter not only human behavior but humanity itself. Shukhov is not a hero, but he could, given time and grace, become a saint like Aloyshka, the Baptist prisoner in his gang. Captivity, brutal servitude, degradation, ill health, malnutrition, exhaustion, the hopelessness of his situation—none of these things, alone or together, is capable of extinguishing his charity for his fellow prisoners; his conscientiousness and pride in work well done, no matter if it is performed at gunpoint and without benefit to himself; his patient acceptance, not of his personal fate alone but of the human condition; and his ability to find contentment, and even pleasure, in whatever life sends him.

All the same, Shukhov knows how to play the game: He has learned the ropes in camp, knows how to fend for himself and to look out for his best interest, often at the expense of some prisoner less experienced—or simply less agile and skilled at finagling an extra ration of gruel, or ingratiating himself with prisoners from better-off circumstances on the "outside" who regularly receive parcels containing luxury items from home. But such behavior makes him only the more human in an environment created, deliberately and in cold blood, by an ideological government dedicated to crushing free enterprise and bourgeois "selfishness" and replacing them with a communist economic system and an abstract moral code based on the slogan "each according to his needs."

Shukhov, of course, is not the only unregenerate kulak in camp: The entire place runs on a system based on accommodation, bribery, self-interest, a pecking order closely akin to class arrangements "outside" (and certainly to the governing political one), and the spirit of "might makes right" and "nature red in tooth

and claw." The law and practice of the camp, in context, are positively refreshing as human nature, though vilely repressed, asserts
itself endlessly, re-creating in this artificial Siberian hellhole a fac-
simile, however degraded, of the normal human patterns "outside."

Finally, *Ivan Denisovich* is about what a man can make of his
life, even the worst life, whether he chooses that life or doesn't.
At the end of the novel (and of the short winter day), Aloyshka
expresses horror at the idea that Shukhov would pray to God
for his freedom. " 'You musn't pray for that. . . . What d'you
want your freedom for? What faith you have will be choked in
thorns. Rejoice that you are in prison. Here you can think of
your soul.' " God is not the first but the last thing that cannot be
obliterated by the regimen of the camps. Shukhov, observing him
and seeing that his friend truly *is* happy to be in prison, protests:
" 'Look, Aloyshka . . . it's all right for you. It was Christ told you
to come here, and you are glad because of Him. But why am *I*
here? Because they didn't get ready for war like they should've in
forty-one? Was that *my* fault?' "

Shukhov is not against God, in Whom he believes. " 'But what
I don't believe in is Heaven and Hell. . . . That's the thing I can't
take.' " Given his circumstances, his doubt is understandable. As
for freedom, "He didn't know any longer himself whether he
wanted [it] or not. At first he'd wanted it very much and every day
he added up how long he still had to go. But then he got fed up
with this. And as time went on he understood that they might let
you out but they never let you home. And he didn't really know
where he'd be better off. At home or in here."

Read in one way, Ivan Denisovitch Shukhov's reflections are
those of a spirit that has finally been broken. Read in another,
they suggest a soul that has just begun to live. One way or the
other, at the end of a day in which he'd had a lot of luck—escaped
the cooler, cadged an extra bowl of mush, felt good making a
brick wall, bought a little tobacco from the Latvian—"Shukhov
went to sleep, and he was very happy."

39

THE BEAR

by William Faulkner

1942

Flannery O'Connor, describing William Faulkner (1897–1962) as the Dixie Limited of Southern literature in the twentieth century, excused the fact of her having read so little of his work by explaining with a change of metaphor, "I keep clear of [him] so my own little boat won't get swamped." O'Connor was being overly modest, of course. Still, it is true that Faulkner is the cyclonic literary phenomenon of Southern letters, from Jamestown to the dawning of the twenty-first century.

He wrote many novels, not all of them great, a few (*Mosquitoes, Pylon, The Mansion*) quite bad ones. The major works (*The Sound and the Fury, Absalom! Absalom!, Sanctuary, The Wild Palms, The Hamlet, The Unvanquished,* and *The Bear,* a novella), plus a double handful at least of the stories, rank nevertheless among the great literary achievements in the English language in spite of their being not to everyone's taste, in the author's time as since. Raymond Chandler, himself a genius, thought Faulkner "overrated," while Ernest Hemingway (Faulkner's literary rival) dismissed the later work as being all "sauce." Their reservations had chiefly to do with style. Chandler wrote a racy prose that was an admixture of classicism and twentieth-century American slang; Hemingway's stoic simplicity followed directly from his credo that what a writer leaves out is more important than what he puts in. Faulkner, by contrast, was a rhetorician who seems to have left little out that came into his mind while he was in the throes of creation. No artist can have it all: He must make aesthetic choices that preclude other choices, and what Faulkner's most characteristic work loses in clarity and restraint it makes up for in sweep and grandeur.

That deliberate choice *was* involved is shown by many of the short stories, where Faulkner writes as clearly and straightforwardly as Hemingway ever wrote. *The Bear* combines both styles, parts 1 to 3 and 5 being composed in Appollonian prose, while part 4 ranks with *The Sound and the Fury* and *Absalom! Absalom!* for its experimental impressionism, indirection, and opacity. Yet, Faulkner is not really so difficult as he looks or sounds. Perhaps the final critical word to be said in regard to Faulkner's technique is that, for Faulkner, it produced (more often than not) stupendous results. For his countless imitators, on the other hand, it has proved an artistic siren song, for the reason that its eccentric experimentalism—or experimental eccentricity—is rather obviously insusceptible of further development by another writer. Faulkner's method has always been a literary dead end, then—for everyone but William Faulkner. Evelyn Waugh intuited something of this when he wrote that Faulkner had originality and nothing else. But Waugh, who was not well read in—or particularly sympathetic to—the American literary tradition from which Faulkner arose, was hardly the man to appreciate his work.

Faulkner's high modernist style and aesthetic might seem theoretically at odds with his subject matter, which is the rural South from the Civil War era to the mid-twentieth century. Like every major artist, Faulkner evinces an obsessive concern with recurring themes: His are loss, endurance, and the past, which for him was reality's chronological dimension. ("The past is never dead. It's not even past.") It has been noted that the greatest writers of the twentieth century were reactionaries. William Faulkner deplored a world that seemed to him inhuman to the degree that it was manmade, man-dominated, and man-centered. It was Faulkner's luck, therefore, that his native Mississippi, until well into his own manhood, remained sufficiently continuous with the premodern setting for his fiction that he had mostly to observe, rather than to imagine reconstructively. The cultural overlap in time, combined with the exuberant oral tradition to which Faulkner had been exposed as a boy, was an invaluable aid to the artistic realization of the fictional Yoknapatawpha County, Mississippi, from what Sherwood Anderson called "the postage-stamp" sized territory the novelist received as his birthright.

For many years, Faulkner helped make up a party that went to hunt deer in the Big Bottom of the Tallahatchie River. Each November, the men loaded the horse-drawn wagons with the canvas tents, the bedding, the guns, the food, the whiskey, and the dogs, and drove out from Oxford to their wilderness camp. History has it that Bill Faulkner did little hunting but much camp sitting with his pipe, his idled rifle, and a bottle of Jack Daniel's ("it never lets you down"), listening to the older men's stories of hunts long ago, before the timber companies began logging the ancient forest, building roads, laying track, leveling the primeval forests, and killing the game. From this material, Faulkner created *The Bear*—once described as the greatest hunting story ever written, in the way that *The Old Man and the Sea* is the greatest fish story, or *Tristan and Isolde* the greatest love tale.

Faulkner frequently shows to best effect in the short story or the novella—his natural form—where focus and architecture are not a problem for him, unlike in the novels. In his most experimental work (e.g., *The Sound and the Fury*), he employs interior monologue—the Joycean "stream of consciousness"—as his narrative vehicle. Elsewhere, he characteristically merges the authorial overvoice with third-person narrative informed by a modified interior consciousness to a degree that gives the author great technical and emotional flexibility, allowing him to enjoy the advantages of both these techniques in point of view. This is the narrative style in which most of *The Bear* is told, excepting part 4 (as infamous in the memory of college graduates as the loftier passages in Thomas Wolfe's *Look Homeward, Angel*). Faulkner's ambition was to put the entire world into a single sentence, and in *The Bear* he comes as close as he would ever get to its fulfillment: Sixteen hundred words and more, bracketed between an upper-case letter and an endstop, extend across six pages of Malcolm Cowley's *The Portable Faulkner*, with two pages of parenthetical material inserted at the middle.

The Bear is set in 1883: eighteen years after Appomattox and six after the end of Reconstruction, when the postwar industrialization of the South is already under way. The Mississippi wilderness is being cleared and settled by the white men and their former black slaves, pushing in together upon the wilderness inhabited up until then by red men (the Chickasaw), and the commercial logging companies have begun their assault on the primeval forests. Isaac McCaslin, sixteen years old, has been hunting with Major de Spain's camp since he was ten:

> For six years now he had been a man's hunter. For six years now he had heard the best of all talking. It was of the wilderness, the big woods, bigger and older than any recorded document—of white man fatuous enough to believe he had bought any fragment of it, of Indian ruthless enough to pretend that any fragment of it had been his to convey; bigger than Major de Spain and the scrap he pretended to, knowing better; older than Thomas Sutpen of whom Major de Spain had it and who knew better; older even than old Ikkemotubbe, the Chickasaw chief, of whom old Sutpen had had it and who knew better in his turn. It was of the men, not white nor black nor red, but men, hunters, with the will and hardihood to endure and the humility and skill to survive, and the dogs and the bear and the deer juxtaposed and reliefed against it, ordered and compelled by and within the wilderness in the ancient and unremitting contest according to the ancient and immitigable rules which voided all regrets and brooked no quarter.

Already, at ten, the boy Ike has "inherited then, without ever having seen it," the great old bear with one trap-lamed foot whose territory extends for a hundred square miles across which he has earned a name for himself, "a definite designation like a living man," by the mayhem he has committed, the grown pigs and even calves he has carried off to devour like an ogre in the woods. Old Ben, his ursine nature apart, is "not malevolent but just big, too big" for the dogs and horses and men and guns and bullets that try to take him every year: "too big for the very country which was its constricting scope . . . that doomed wilderness whose edges were being constantly and punily gnawed at by men with plows and axes who feared it because it was wilderness." For all its size, however, the bear is no "mortal beast but an anachronism indomitable and invincible out of an old, dead time, a phantom, epitome and apotheosis of the old, wild life." To the young boy, watching the wagons depart for the bottom while he was yet too young to take part in the hunt, Major de Spain and General Compson and McCaslin Edmonds and Sam Fathers and Boon Hogganbeck "were going not to hunt bear and deer but to keep yearly rendezvous with the bear which they did not even intend to kill." Now, for six years, he has been a part of the hunt, and the rendezvous.

Sam Fathers, Ike's "spirit's father"—born of a black slave and a Chickasaw chief—has trained the boy in the wilderness to the point where his woodsman's skills exceed those of General Compson and of his cousin, Cass McCaslin. Beginning with Ike's first hunt, the old man has set up a series of encounters between the child and the bear, whom Ike sights at close range one summer only after he has left behind him in camp not just his rifle, but his compass and watch as well. Each November, the hounds scent the bear, but are unable to bay it. "Too big," Sam tells the boy. "We ain't got the dog yet. But maybe some day." When a predator kills a colt belonging to Major de Spain, de Spain suspects that Old Ben is responsible. Sam, knowing better, baits the killer and captures an enormous dog as tall as a calf, with yellow eyes and colored a gun-barrel blue, whom he manages to train without actually taming him. "He's the dog that's going to stop Old Ben and hold him," Boon Hogganbeck ("the violent, insensitive, hard-faced man with his touch of remote Indian blood and the mind almost of a child" and who as Sam's huntsman has adopted the animal to the point of sleeping with him) tells McCaslin. "We've already named him. His name is Lion."

The boy understands that he should hate Lion, the designated killer of the mythic creature that has haunted his mind for almost the whole of his life. With the splitmindedness he shares with Sam Fathers, however, he takes part in the chase that ends with Lion baying his quarry against a tree, before Old Ben catches the dog in both arms, "almost loverlike." As the old bear rakes Lion's belly with his front claws, Boon leaps upon its back and stabs it from behind through the heart. "For an instant they almost resembled a piece of statuary: the clinging dog, the bear, the man astride its back, working and probing the buried blade." Carrying the man and the dog together, the great bear takes "two or three steps toward the woods on its hind feet as a man would have and crashed down. It didn't collapse, crumple. It fell all of a piece, as a tree falls, so that all three of them, man, dog and bear, seemed to bounce once." Boon wraps the dying Lion in his coat, as the boy spots Sam Fathers lying face down in the trampled mud.

In *The Bear,* Faulkner neatly pairs character and theme, and as neatly offsets those pairs. Boon Hogganbeck and Lion represent the destructive force of impersonal nature, Sam Fathers and Old Ben nature's primevally conscious element, under assault by a commerical-industrial civilization incapable of apprehending, or even suspecting, that this element exists. The death of Old Ben entails Sam Fathers's death, as he would have known it must: In arranging for Old Ben's end in the jaws of the great blue dog, he was actually willing his own in a final defiant gesture on behalf of the wilderness the two of them embody and represent.

As is characteristic with Faulkner, his theme is in some degree blurred by the burden of part 4, which is that the institution of slavery has brought a curse upon the land itself. The introduction of the slavery issue into that of the despoliation of nature is confusing for several reasons. First, the Chickasaw themselves owned black slaves, acquired from the white men, as acknowledged by another Faulkner story, "Red Leaves." Second, slavery, far from being an invention of the American South, is an ancient institution throughout the world and human history: the invention of tribal and agricultural societies rather than industrial-capitalist ones, which extirpated it almost as soon as they had the power to do so.

Appropriately, therefore, Faulkner returns to the tonic at the end of his story, which closes with Ike McCaslin, now eighteen years old, making a visit to the site of Sam Fathers's and Lion's graves, where Old Ben's paw is also interred. He just misses stepping on a six-foot rattlesnake, whom he hails as "Grandfather," and discovers Boon Hogganbeck—the primitive who can kill a bear literally with his bare hands but is unable to hit anything with a modern rifle—sitting impotently beneath a gum tree full of squirrels, banging on his disassembled gun. Ike, who had invited Major de Spain to accompany him to the graves, was perplexed when the Major begged off. Now, viewing the recently expanded logging town called Hoke's squatting in the doomed wilderness, he understands why and knows that "after this time he himself, who had to see it one other time, would return no more."

Where William Faulkner's great story ends imaginatively, the Southern Agrarians take up its prophetic plaint theoretically, to consider the possibility of a livable future constructed from the reality of the living past.

40

DESERT SOLITAIRE: A SEASON IN THE WILDERNESS

by Edward Abbey

1968

Hidden away in one or another of Edward Abbey's books, temporarily misplaced in memory like some desert gnomon or secret spring, is an admonition to this effect: The hell with keeping it the way it is—let's keep it the way it *was*.

Abbey (1927–1989) is an excellent example of a writer who, though not a philosophical or political "conservative", nevertheless had deeply conservative instincts that found their developed expression in one or more works that clearly belong within the American conservative tradition. Abbey, a self-described liberal who found sport in baiting liberals and being attacked by them in turn, was really an Old Believer: a cracker-barrel liberal, Don't-Tread-On-Me individualist, across-the-board dissenter, defiant desert rat, and all-round American eccentric of a type most commonly associated with the nineteenth century. (He has frequently been compared to his hero Henry Thoreau, another nineteenth-century "liberal" who, were he to wake beneath a tree by Walden Pond after a century and a half of sleep and wander into Concord in search of conversation, would scandalize the good liberals in the vicinity of greater Boston.)

Edward Abbey did not, like Evelyn Waugh or Henry Adams, look back to thirteenth-century Europe for a vision of Heaven on Earth. There is reason for suspecting, however, that he might have preferred it to twentieth-century America, whose vast expanses of still substantially unspoiled deserts and mountains offered the lingering possibility that alone made life in the industrial superstate tolerable. (As etymology suggests, radicalism and conservatism are not incompatible with one another.) A fiercely eloquent critic and implacable enemy of industrial capitalism and technological industrialism, of mass democracy and mass man, and the modern project as a whole, Abbey is finally a tragic figure—a man of natural piety unwittingly corrupted by the impious and ignorant spirit, the shallow philosophy, of the age he despised; too honest to take more than poetry from the pantheism with which he flirted, too proud to accept so much as poetry from truth itself. Though his most famous novel, *The Monkey Wrench Gang* (about would-be ecoterrorists plotting to blow up Glen Canyon Dam at the head of Lake Powell on the Colorado River), directly inspired the founding of the radical environmentalist group Earth First!, the urban Leftists who took over the organization soon came to regard Abbey as "racist" for his anti-immigration views, while he, in turn, distanced himself from Earth First! Following his death, aged sixty-two, in March 1989, his body was transported by prearrangement 150 miles from Tucson into the Cabeza Prieta Wilderness west of Ajo, Arizona, and buried (quite illegally) in his sleeping bag by his father-in-law and three closest friends at a secret desert place. He wished his carcass to metamorphose as a tree, Abbey wrote before he died, having instructed the interment party to pile "lots of rocks" on his grave to keep the coyotes out.

Abbey thought of himself as preeminently a novelist, and indeed he wrote and published many works of fiction. These are not by any standard (excepting perhaps the author's) his best work, owing partly to an adolescent streak (in the romantic department especially) and a programatic political schema (e.g., *The Monkey*

Wrench Gang and its posthumously published sequel, *Hayduke Lives!*). As his most recent biographer, James M. Cahalan, argues, Abbey is best understood as an autobiographer: This explains why most of his fictional characters are unconvincing, and why the narrative essays, or nonfiction stories, are his best and most distinctive work. In this category, *Desert Solitaire: A Season in the Wilderness* represents Abbey's sole book-length effort (the other nonfiction volumes are collections of rewritten magazine pieces, many of them jewels of their sort), as well as, perhaps, his finest.

Despite its subtitle, *Desert Solitaire* recounts not one but two seasons in the wilderness, elided and framed by a single spring and winter in the interest of narrative and dramatic form. In the late 1950s, its author took a job as a seasonal park ranger in Arches National Monument near the old uranium town of Moab in southeast Utah. "Why I went there," he explains, "no longer matters; what I found there is the subject of this book."

The little tin house on wheels that housed Ed Abbey during his career at Arches was long ago removed from its setting among the sandstone arches and monoliths, beside the "private" juniper tree with its "one dead claw reaching at the sky." A friend of literature rescued the trailer for posterity after the U.S. Park Service was through with it and towed it into Moab, whence it has disappeared. The jeep trail coming in from the two-lane highway has been widened and paved, a luxurious campground and visitor's center have been developed, and what the Park Service calls "visitations" have increased twentyfold since Abbey's day. Moab itself, after nearly drying up and blowing away when the uranium boom busted in the 1960s, was transformed in the 1990s by a gaudy efflorescence of the industrial tourism Abbey despised. Even so, the rosy and sunburnt stillness of the vast and empty desert still surrounds the breaking snow-covered peaks of the La Sal Mountains with which it merges by seven or eight climatic zones: up from the muddy Colorado River through sagebrush plateaus to the piñon-juniper breaks on the slickrock benches above the town, on toward the lime-green aspen forests, and into the black timber edging the snowy talus slopes pointing at an ultraviolet sky. "This is the most beautiful place on earth," Abbey writes in the first line of his book.

Edward Abbey spent a career refining the style and persona that sprang, fully formed in its essentials, from the writer's mind onto the blank page before him at the outset of his writing life. The evocative prose is matched by the provocative persona, both of them the creations of a born poet who was a naturally shy man. The shy man was also a deeply angry man (Joseph Wood Krutch called *Desert Solitaire* "a hymn of hate"), who learned to control and direct his anger by a savage humor as well earned as it is uniquely American in its homespun comic irony. Here, Abbey describes the intrusion of Progress on his solitary communion with nature:

> I was sitting out back on my 33,000-acre terrace, shoeless and shirtless, scratching my toes in the sand and sipping on a tall iced drink, watching the flow of evening over the desert. Prime time: the sun very low in the west, the birds coming back to life, the shadows rolling for miles over rock and sand to the very base of the brilliant mountains. I had a small fire going near the table—not for heat or light but for the fragrance of the juniper and the ritual appeal of the clear flames. For symbolic reasons. For ceremony.

The silence is broken by the grind of an engine off among the rocks, and presently a jeep appears out of the twilight. Abbey is about to write the driver a ticket when he recognizes the jeep as a government vehicle, with three men and a pile of surveying equipment inside. The men are thirsty, and he invites them into the trailer where he serves them a pitcher of water. They are laying out a new road into the Arches, the survey crew explains.

> And when would the road be built? Nobody knew for sure. . . . The new road—to be paved, of course—would cost somewhere between half a million and one million dollars, depending on the bids, or more than fifty thousand dollars per linear mile. At

least enough to pay the salaries of ten park rangers for ten
years. Too much money, I suggested—they'll never go for it in
Washington.

The three men thought that was pretty funny. Don't worry,
they said, this road will be built. I'm worried, I said. Look, the
party chief explained, you *need* this road. He was a pleasant-
mannered, soft-spoken civil engineer with an unquestioning
dedication to his work. A very dangerous man. Who *needs* it, I
said; we get very few tourists in this park. That's why you need
it, the engineer explained patiently; look, he said, when this
road is built you'll get ten, twenty, thirty times as many tourists
in here as you get now. His men nodded solemn agreement,
waiting to see what possible answer I could have to that.

"Have some more water," I said. I had an answer all right but
I was saving it for later. I knew that I was dealing with a mad-
man.

Desert Solitaire is an eclectic book, anticipating and including
every theme, interest, and concern touched on or developed in
the works to come. As a writer, Edward Abbey brought to perfection the art of the personal narrative essay in which poetry, adventure, observation, speculation, meditation, commentary, diatribe,
dythyramb, anecdote, elegy, comedy, and farce are interwoven.
Wonderfully unconstrained, its structure is scenic rather than epi-
sodic, fractured like a slickrock wall by fissures from which brac-
ing-cold essays in miniature gush and offering a view of life as
whole and wholesome as the author's philosophy affords. There is
no trace here of what Chesterton calls "the huge and healthy sad-
ness" of paganism, except perhaps in the anger, which is huge and
healthy enough. Like the Beethoven symphonies Abbey loved,
Desert Solitaire alternates between moods of exalted joy and a fury
that is soon spent, overwhelmed by its own exaltation.

As his season unfolds, the sun moving up toward the North
Pole, then south across the equator again, Abbey herds cattle with
a local rancher; comes close to losing his life in Havasu Canyon (a
tributary of the Grand Canyon); searches for a spectral moon-
eyed horse; floats the Colorado River through the ineffable Glen

Canyon doomed by the great dam already building at Page, Arizona; summits Mt. Tukuhnikivats in the La Sal Mountains above Moab; explores the Maze cut into the Escalante Plateau west of the Colorado; helps retrieve the body of a tourist dead of thirst and sunstroke at Grandview Point above the river. Between adventures, he tends to his rangerly duties; respectfully puts on the more naïve of the tourists; goes on the town in Moab; admires rock; sits under a tree at noon, surrounded by a thousand square miles of empty desert; watches the birds in the sky; continues writing the letter that will never be finished; sits up all night with a visitor arguing the proposition that wilderness is necessary to civilization and defending himself against the charge that he is "against civilization, against science, against humanity" by explaining that "I was not opposed to mankind but only to man-centeredness, anthropocentricity, the opinion that the world exists solely for the sake of man; not to science, which means simply knowledge, but to science misapplied, to the worship of technique and technology, and to that perversion of science properly called scientism; and not to civilization but to culture."

And, of course, he *writes*. . . .

I feel myself sinking into the landscape, fixed in place like a stone, like a tree, a small motionless shape of vague outline, desert-colored, and with the wings of imagination look down at myself through the eyes of the bird, watching a human figure that becomes smaller, smaller in the receding landscape as the bird rises into the evening—a man at a table near a twinkling campfire, surrounded by a rolling wasteland of stone and dune and sandstone monuments, the wasteland surrounded by dark canyons and the course of rivers and mountain ranges on a vast plateau stretching across Colorado, Utah, New Mexico, and Arizona, and beyond this plateau more deserts and greater mountains, the Rockies in dusk, the Sierra Nevadas shining in their late afternoon, and farther and farther yet, the darkened East, the gleaming Pacific, the curving margins of the great earth itself, and beyond earth that ultimate world of sun and stars whose bounds we cannot discover.

Lastly, a word to the wise:

Do not jump into your automobile next June and rush out to the canyon country hoping to see some of that which I have attempted to evoke in these pages. In the first place you can't see *anything* from a car; you've got to get out of the goddamned contraption and walk, better yet crawl, on hands and knees, over the sandstone and through the thornbush and cactus. When traces of blood begin to mark your trail you'll see something, maybe. Probably not. In the second place most of what I write about in this book is already gone or going under fast. This is not a travel guide but an elegy. A memorial. You're holding a tombstone in your hands. A bloody rock. Don't drop it on your foot—throw it at something big and glassy. What do you have to lose?

41

THE HABIT OF BEING: THE LETTERS OF FLANNERY O'CONNOR

selected and edited by Sally Fitzgerald

1979

The two greatest collections of letters by American novelists are *Selected Letters of Raymond Chandler,* edited by Frank MacShane, and Flannery O'Connor's *The Habit of Being.* Both authors had, as it were, half-careers. (Chandler, a native Englishman and former California oil executive, began to write for a living only in his mid-forties; O'Connor died at the age of thirty-nine.) Both were intensely private figures who restricted their publications to works of fiction and forbore to pontificate on politics, society, and "ideas" in the major journals of opinion and erudite literary watering holes frequented by other artists and public intellectuals. Their letters are the closest thing (excepting O'Connor's lectures on writing, published posthumously as *Mystery and Manners*) we have to the essays they never wrote stating directly what they were demonstrating indirectly, through the medium of their art.

Flannery O'Connor (1925–1964) was born in Savannah, Georgia. The family moved to Milledgeville when she was twelve, three years before her father's death from lupus erythematosus. After

graduating from Georgia State College for Women in Milledgeville, she attended the school for writers at Iowa State University
and in 1949 accepted a place at Yaddo, the artists' retreat in Sara-
toga Springs, New York. O'Connor spent several weeks in New
York City that summer before visiting Milledgeville, but came
north again in the fall to live with Robert and Sally Fitzgerald
(the Harvard classicist and his wife) at their home in Ridgefield,
Connecticut. Two years later, while still living with the Fitzgeralds,
O'Connor became ill and returned to Milledgeville, where she received her diagnosis of lupus. From that time on, Flannery O'Connor lived with her mother, Regina, at Andalusia, a dairy farm not
many miles from town. Except for brief occasional trips to give
readings and lectures, she never left home again.

Though local and out-of-town company (including Katherine
Anne Porter and Elizabeth Fenwick Way) visited occasionally,
O'Connor's social life was largely epistolary, laying on her personal
and literary correspondence an untoward burden. Fortunately,
O'Connor was up to the challenge. Certain of her ardent admir-
ers have actually concluded that, great as are her two novels (*Wise
Blood* and *The Violent Bear It Away*) and the still better-known sto-
ries ("A Good Man Is Hard to Find," "The Life You Save May Be
Your Own"), *The Habit of Being* is really her finest book.

It is also the work by which her literary reputation has been
reevaluated and revised over the past twenty years. America and
the South, literature, publishing, the academy, and social relations between men and women as well as between whites and
blacks are all greatly changed since Flannery O'Connor's day. So
is the dominant approach to reading (as well as writing) literature.
The New Criticism, which considered the printed text alone and
almost in a vacuum, has been replaced by Deconstructionism
and political correctness, both of which insist on not only the importance of the author behind the text, but the political accept-
ability of the person behind the author.

In the case of Miss O'Connor, the revisonists have made two
separate approaches. The first has been to claim the woman as
well as her work for the progressive Left, by identifying O'Connor
as a closet lesbian and discovering in her writings a repressed

feminist rage; the other to take the letters, novels, and stories at their word, denigrate the writer as an unreconstructed white Southern gentlewoman and pre-Vatican II Catholic, and revise the reputation of her literary production downward. The artist who wrote "The Artificial Nigger"—a story whose theme is "the redemptive quality of the Negro's suffering for us all"—also refused to meet James Baldwin in Milledgeville ("I observe the traditions of the society I feed on") and declared a plague on both sides of the civil rights movement. While so much critical reevaluation amounts to a cottage industry, the damage done her reputation has not prevented O'Connor's inclusion in the Library of America series, where she keeps company with such literary immortals as Nathaniel Hawthorne, Edgar Allen Poe, Mark Twain, and Edith Wharton.

The obsessive theme in O'Connor's fiction is modern man's blindness to, or defiance of, supernatural reality, from which (in the stories) he is rescued by an "action of grace," typically of a violent nature. While the objective scope of the letters is naturally broader, the extent to which the author's concerns as a correspondent cohere with her focused subject as a novelist is remarkable. O'Connor, an invalid and a spinster, was humanly and intellectually of a piece, the more concentratedly as illness advanced unremittingly and the time ahead shortened inexorably. From reading *Art and Scholasticism,* she was familiar with Jacques Maritain's concept of the habit of art as a virtue: "that is to say a quality which, triumphing over the original indetermination of the intellective faculty, raises it in respect of a definite object to a maximum of perfection, and so of operative efficiency." Sally Fitzgerald argues that O'Connor, in acquiring this habit of art, acquired with it "the habit of being," described as "an excellence not only of action but of interior disposition and activity that increasingly reflected the object, the being, which specified it, and was itself reflected in what she did and said."

Flannery O'Connor, had she been asked to do so, probably would have identified herself as a Catholic and a Southerner, in that order. (And given you a steely look as if to say, "I know some folks that don't mind their own bidnis.") "To be conservative,"

Michael Oakeshott writes, "is to prefer the familiar to the unknown, to prefer the tried to the untried, fact to mystery, the actual to the possible, the limited to the unbounded, the near to the distant, the sufficient to the superabundant, the convenient to the perfect, present laughter to utopian bliss." With the possible exception of the opposition of "fact" and "mystery" (though by the second term Oakeshott appears to intend something other than the Christian mystery that would have leaped immediately to O'Connor's mind), that is a description that reasonably applies to O'Connor's habit of being.

Her letters amount to an epistolary autobiography by a literary genius who once remarked that she had "never been anywhere but sick"; compelled by circumstance to lead a life that, though cripplingly restrictive for most people, in some ways is ideally suited to the purpose and practice of a serious literary artist. Dependent as she was on her mother at Andalusia, O'Connor was never tempted to stay up late drinking at the Algonquin Hotel, have affairs with best-selling authors, go to literary dinners and awards parties, work for the studios in Hollywood, become a Left Bank expatriate, or do any of the other things modern writers do. Faulkner had a choice, whether to accept or not Sherwood Anderson's advice to stay home and write about his "postage-stamp" sized corner of Mississippi. O'Connor had no choice but to take rural Georgia for her subject as well as her home and make the most of it. And so she did; "devoted," as J. O. Tate writes, "not so much to her work as to the cultivation of her vision." There is all of life in the *Letters* because O'Connor's was a life accepted—not just patiently and cheerfully but gratefully—in its imposed restrictiveness and simplicity.

In the degree that her daily experience is restricted, her depiction of that experience is particular and specific—qualities as essential to a good letter as to a work of fiction. Many of the elements of the fiction in progress are there, but never as rehearsals, not even as raw material (though for one who has read the formal work, many passages ring a bell or turn on a light); simply, rather, as fragments of life perceived, relished, and casually passed on for relishing—exactly as one does in conversation. Flannery O'Connor wrote to chat, not just communicate: a typical letter touches on a variety of unrelated topics, approached in a succession of moods and assuming several voices, most often and amusingly a white-cracker persona adopted by the author, as if she were a character in one of her own books.

On the homely level, O'Connor writes of her bird collection— her chickens, ducks, turkeys, and trademark peafowl—of Regina's tribulations as a dairy farmer and her problems with the primitive (in the 1950s and early 1960s) black help, and of Regina herself. ("Regina is getting very literary. 'Who is this Kafka?' she says. 'People ask me.' A German Jew, I says, I think. He wrote a book about a man that turns into a roach. 'Well, I can't tell people *that*,' she says. 'Who is this Evalin Wow?' ") In her treatment of friends and acquaintances, she usually resorts to anecdote, of which she was a master. ("[Russell Kirk] is nonconversational and so am I, and the time we were left alone together our attempts to make talk were like the efforts of two midgets to cut down a California redwood. However, at one point we burst forth in the following spurt of successful uncharitable conversation: ME: I read old William Heard Kilpatrick died recently. John Dewey's dead too, isn't he? KIRK: Yes, thank God. Gone to his reward. Ha. Ha. ME: I hope there're children crawling all over him. KIRK: Yes, I hope he's with the unbaptized enfants. ME: No, they would be too innocent. KIRK: Yes. Ha. Ha. With the baptized enfants. ME: Yes. CURTAIN.")

At the professional level, she addresses the craft of writing with an insight that few if any other writers of her caliber have managed, or even attempted, to articulate—perhaps because she is the only writer of the first rank to have attended writing school, where she studied under Andrew Lytle. ("I believe that the fiction writer's moral sense must coincide with his dramatic sense.") At the literary level, she handles fellow writers and their works with dispatch and aplomb. ("What [Graham Greene] does, I think, is try to make religion respectable to the modern unbeliever by making it seedy. He succeeds so well in making it seedy that then he has to save it by a miracle.") Finally, as a Catholic apologist and lay theologian, she is superb: In fact, it is possible to obtain the basis of a Catholic education from this book. ("I write the way I do because and only because I am a Catholic. I feel that if I were not a Catholic, I would have no reason to write, no reason to see, no reason to feel horrified or even to enjoy anything. . . . I have never had the sense that being a Catholic is a limit to the freedom of the writer, but just the reverse. . . . I feel myself that being a Catholic has saved me a couple of thousand years in learning to write.")

There is a clairvoyant quality to this book, uncanny in the way that the famous optometrist's sign, emblazoned with an enormous pair of bespectacled eyes, in *The Great Gatsby* is uncanny. Here again, we seem to confront the shocking binocular stare. With *The Habit of Being,* however, one of the eyes belongs to penetrating human genius while the other represents the divine gaze, intense and depthless as the eyes in a peacock's spread fan.

42

THE CAMP OF THE SAINTS

by Jean Raspail

1973

Jean Raspail (1925–), a self-described "man of the right," has succeeded nevertheless in making not just a career but a name for himself in his native France, whose intellectual and literary establishments have been predominantly leftwing since the eighteenth century. (A regular contributor to *Le Figaro*, he was also the recipient, in 1970, of the Académie Française's Jean-Walther Prize.) His success as a conservative writer in a liberal culture, which in some sense seems nearly miraculous, is partly owing to strength of character and mind, coupled with charm and enormous talent.

The Camp of the Saints—one of the most uncompromising works of literary reaction in the twentieth century—would have sunk most literary reputations. Instead, Raspail has continued in the thirty years since the novel's publication to publish more books and garner further honors and awards, including (in 1998) the prestigious T. S. Eliot Award sponsored by the Ingersoll Foundation in Rockford, Illinois.

Raspail makes no pretensions in his book to elaboration of plot, depth and subtlety of character development, brilliance in dialogue, or stylistic innovation. For plot, he substitutes linear narrative, almost journalistic in its single dimensionality; for individual character, social psychology; for crafted dialogue, impassioned monologue that barely strives for realism; for style, a mordant, informal narrative that seems hardly to hear its own voice, let alone rewrite, correct, and polish it. The narrator, who assumes by turns the role of bard (or rather antibard, reciting his "antiepic"), historian, journalist, commentator, satirist, diatribist, and prophet, is alternately distant and impassioned, philosophic and emotional, bitter and sardonic, despairing and amused, loving as he does his decadent and decrepit civilization for what it once was while despising it for what it has become; aware that it deserves its fate, perhaps, but also that its barbarian enemies and despoilers do not deserve to inherit so much as the rotting remnant. Jean Raspail's *Camp of the Saints* has no *living* heroes. Or almost none. Twenty men, to be exact, making up in their numbers the sole remainder of what was once the conquering, dominant, and resplendent Western world: more straightforwardly the *white* world, whose end at the hands of what once were called the colored races the book prophesizes and attempts to explain.

Raspail sets his novel at the end of the twentieth century or the beginning of the twenty-first—around the present time, in fact. In Calcutta, a crowd of people has gathered outside the Belgian consulate to press their children forward for inclusion in an adoption program that would rescue them from a life of poverty by relocating them with families in Belgium. When the consul declares the program ended, a giant bearing on his shoulders a deformed monster with lidless eyes, a flap of skin for a mouth, and stumps for arms harangues the swelling crowd by reciting for them a parable in which the Hindu gods take the "little Christian god" down from his cross and exact his kingdom from him, in return for his life. "Now the thousand years are ended," the little god concedes, quoting almost verbatim from the Book of the Apocalypse (a text one assumes the giant, whose trade is gathering human feces and patting it into bricquets for cookfires, has never read). "The nations are rising from the four corners of the earth, and their number is like the sand of the sea. They will march up over the broad earth and surround the camp of the saints and the beloved city." Inspired by the charismatic turd gatherer, the crowd presses on to the docks and commandeers a sixty-year-old four-stack liner, the *India Star*, and (with the blessing of the prefect apostolic to the Ganges region) another big ship, the *Calcutta Star*. In no time, the popular example has been imitated up and down the Ganges until a fleet of ninety-nine ships, carrying a total of a million people, sails for Europe, the land flowing with milk and honey.

Very soon, the West learns of the fleet's departure and its intended destination. The governments of Europe are unsettled by the thought of a million impoverished Third World refugees landing on their shores, but "the beast" or "monster" that has been subverting the West for the past several centuries is eager to accept this latest Trojan horse and exploit its possibilities for further subversion and destruction. The media, the churches (including the Catholic Church, headed by a Brazilian Pope), the educational and cultural establishments, the trade unions, most of government itself—all are united in their determination to welcome what the revengeful Ben Saud (an Algerian immigrant and grandson of a black slave, now enjoying an immensely lucrative career as a left-wing journalist under the name of Clément Dio) dubs the "Last Chance Armada" in the name of the Brotherhood of Man and of Christian charity and love.

The president of the French Republic, himself secretly a contributor to *La Pensée Nationale* (a right-wing paper with a paid subscription of four thousand readers), dares not set his government forthrightly against the armada. As the Ganges fleet approaches closer to Europe, the propaganda campaign on its behalf swells (concurrent with a mass migration of Frenchmen from the southern coastal region to the north of France). The welcomers make two attempts to provision the ships (one from South Africa, the other from France), to which the refugees respond by throwing the proferred supplies overboard, along with the fresh-killed body of one of the few white passengers. And then, "At midnight, as Saturday passed into Sunday, the first minute of Easter, the day of the Resurrection, a great noise was heard along the coast,

somewhere between Nice and Saint-Tropez. The prows of ninety-
nine ships plunged headlong onto the beaches and between the
rocks, as the monster child, waking from his cataleptic sleep, let
out a triumphant cry."

As the president begins an address to the nation, he is resolved
to announce his decision to order the French army to destroy the
debarking hordes, now amounting to eight million people.
Instead, he ends by departing from his script to exhort the troops
to follow their individual consciences. As thousands of hippies,
left-wing priests, and other sympathizers race southward to welcome the Ganges immigrants to France, the colored ghettos in
Paris and other major cities rise up, most of the army defects to
marauding gangs of radical students and other youths, prison
guards free their prisoners, and the unions revolt, all in the name
of creating a new world. The government of Paris collapses and is
replaced by a "multiracial" coalition in which whites enjoy token
representation; the most celebrated of the friends of the Last
Chance Armada (Clément Dio and two left-wing radio hosts
among them) are brutally murdered by the people whose cause
they had championed; white women are kidnapped and sent to
brothels patronized by colored patrons.

The narrator (who, we learn, is writing some time after the cataclysm in an epoch in which history has been rewritten to standards of political correctness) explains that "[w]ith France the
Enlightened," inventor of the Rights of Man, "glad to grovel on
her knees, no [Western] government [had dared] sign its name to
the genocidal deed" of self-defense in the face of racial incursions
across Europe and in the United States. Africans swarmed unop-
posed across the Limpopo River to attack South Africa. The
Chinese invaded the Soviet Union beyond the Amur. In England,
colored immigrants from the Commonwealth countries converged (with British politeness) on London, to demand that the
royal family engage in a genetic exchange with the Pakistani community; in America, New York was taken over by revolutionary
blacks.

The collapse of the Western world occurred, the narrator explains, with the French air force's destruction of a seventeenth-

century villa overlooking the beach where the Last Chance Armada had landed, killing the owner of the house—one Monsieur Calguès, a retired professor of literature—and nineteen other resisters. These included a former undersecretary for foreign affairs, an ex-deputy for Pondicherry, a tank commander, a duke and two of his servants, and the owner of an elegant brothel, who together had succeeded in reclaiming and holding a Free French, whites-only zone by means of a sniper war waged against the marauding Ganges immigrants and their French collaborators. "Just a victory Western style, as complete as it was absurd and useless," like M. Calguès's shooting of the hippy barbarian who had broken into his home at the start of the invasion—but achieved with panache and a sense of humor totally alien to Leftists and to Leftism.

Thirty years after its publication in 1973, *The Camp of the Saints* has shown itself to have been prophetic, as western Europe, North America, and Australia suffer invasion by scores of millions of immigrants from beyond the borders of the white world. Prophetic powers were not, of course, required to foresee the danger posed by global demographic trends compounded by the pusillanimity of Western governments "morally disarmed" (as James Burnham would say) by Third World suffering. Where Raspail demonstrates truly visionary powers is in his understanding of the process by which key left-wing elements in Western society, from their varying but related motives, combine naturally with aggressive external forces to cooperate in the destruction of the Western world. The death of the West, it seems, is even more a Western project than it is a Third World dream. Certainly, it could not be accomplished by a hundred Last Chance Armadas alone, so long as the West retained intact a sense of its own identity, its nerve, and its self-confidence. "In this curious war taking shape, those who loved themselves best were the ones who would triumph": Those, that is, who feel "[t]hat scorn of a people for other races, the knowledge that one's own is best, the triumphant joy at feeling oneself to be part of humanity's finest."

The West's paramount enemy is hate in its social, ethnic, metaphysical, and theological forms: hatred of quality, hatred of racial differences, hatred of intelligence, hatred of truth. Because all conflict is at bottom theological, this hate must be understood as satanic in its nature and origin. Its totem and figurehead is the turd gatherer's monster child from the Ganges, a deformed counter to the Christ Child in Whose name Western civilization assumed its form and development. And so it is not, Jean Raspail tells us, the West itself, but rather this same Child Who represents, finally, the object of attack from within and without what once was called Christendom.

Magnificent as Raspail's thunder is, perhaps the most moving scene in *The Camp of the Saints* is also its quietest and most elegiac. Coming at the beginning of the novel (in chapter 3), it describes Professor Calguès at his solitary supper after having spent the day observing the ninety-nine rusted ships beached along the coast below his veranda. Having drunk a glass of wine and poured another, sliced a ham into fine slices and arranged them on a pewter plate, set out some olives, laid the cheese on a bed of grape leaves, and filled a basket with bread, he sits down to his meal with a contented smile:

> He was in love. And like any successful suitor, he found himself face to face now with the one he loved, alone. Yet tonight that one was no woman, no living creature at all, but a myriad kindred images formed into a kind of projection of his own inner being. Like that silver fork, for example, with the well-worn prongs, and some maternal ancestor's initials, now rubbed almost smooth. A curious object, really, when you think that the Western World invented it for propriety's sake, though a third of the human race still grubs up its food with its fingers. And the crystal, always set out in a row of four, so utterly useless. Well, why not? Why do without glasses, like boors? Why stop setting them out, simply because the Brazilian backwoods was dying of thirst, or because India was gulping down typhus with every swallow of muck from its dried-up wells? Let the cuckolds come pound on the door with their threates of revenge. There's no sharing in love. The rest of the world can go hang. They don't even exist.

Part VI
THE PRESENT DAY

43

ALIEN NATION: COMMON SENSE ABOUT AMERICA'S IMMIGRATION DISASTER

by Peter Brimelow

1995

If a litmus test or touchstone of conservatism exists, in the context of the political realities of the modern world, the immigration issue must be it. It is really impossible to imagine a genuine conservative, in this day and age, who does not take a restrictionist position in respect of the transformative mass immigration to the West by tens and scores of millions of people from the Third World.

The Second Great Wave of immigrants to the United States began in the 1970s, less than ten years after the passage of the 1965 Immigration Act—one of the most revolutionary pieces of legislation ever passed by a U.S. Congress. A by-product of the postwar revulsion toward Adolf Hitler's genocidal policies and of an egalitarian enthusiasm produced by the American civil rights movement, the Immigration Act was designed to counter charges of "discrimation" against would-be immigrants from non-European countries by including a set of provisions that effectively disfavored immigrants from the European countries, while favoring those from the Western Hemisphere and Asia. Sponsors of the bill insisted that the change from the old national-origins quota system was merely symbolic and that "reform" did not mean an increase in the number of immigrants accepted annually by the United States. Yet, within a decade, the Immigration Act proved the first in a series of increasingly lenient, loose, and irresponsible legislation whose effect has been a vast increase in immigration, legal and illegal, to the United States; almost half of it from Mexico and nearly all of it from Third World societies.

By the early 1980s, the transformative potential of America's immigration phenomemon was plain to those who encouraged, as well those who deplored, it. Yet, the "debate" on immigration policy, so far as it existed at all, was never more than the sound of one hand clapping. Nobody, whether liberal or conservative, wished to discuss immigration, except to celebrate its multitudinous benefits and to felicitate the immigrants themselves. And the few brave souls who dared dissent from the happy-talk surrounding the subject had a bad habit of losing their jobs and their livelihood and slipping into nonpersonhood so far as the realm of public debate was concerned. Following dissent by its editors from the prevailing orthodoxy, the paleoconservative journal *Chronicles: A Magazine of American Culture* and its publisher, the Rockford Institute, were defunded and nearly destroyed by the "conservative" donors who had previously supported them. Nevertheless, the magazine survived and continues to press its arguments, in company with a handful of mostly paleoconservative columnists (most prominently Patrick Buchanan and Samuel Francis), pamphleteers, and Web site writers. Paralleling the effort by paleoconservatives, a small group of academics (George Borjas, Nathan Glazer, and Samuel Huntington) in Cambridge, Massachusetts, developed the scholarly case against immigration; Buchanan gave the restrictionist cause a political boost in 1992 when he made his first run for the presidency. Three years later, the author of *Alien Nation: Common Sense About America's Immigration Disaster*—the first and most famous of a series of for-the-trade titles urging immigration reform—felt confident in claiming that, though the political cause remained precarious, the intellectual case for restriction was already won.

In 1995, Peter Brimelow (1947–), a highly respected financial journalist, was a senior editor at both *Forbes* and *National Review.* Himself an immigrant from the north of England and married to a Canadian wife, Brimelow became enthralled by the spectacle of the U.S. government dissolving a people and electing a new one (to paraphrase Bertolt Brecht). After mulling the subject of immigration for years, and with the encouragement of *National Review*'s then editor, John O'Sullivan, Brimelow in 1992 wrote a lengthy cover story for the magazine entitled "Time to Rethink Immigration?" from which *Alien Nation* followed three years later. "And why," Brimelow asks in the introduction to his book, "do I, an immigrant, care? For one reason, there is my immigrant toddler, Alexander. He seems to like it here. A second reason: just as Thomas Jefferson said . . . that every man has two countries, his own and France, so in this century no civilized person can be indifferent to the fate of America."

Thus, a naturalized Englishman rushed in where most native-born Americans feared to tread. The response (described by the author in the afterword to the paperback edition) was immediate and intended to be devastating. Though in terms of sales never more than a midlist title, *Alien Nation* remained fixed in the eye of a hurricane of media attention—nearly all of it hostile and much of it hysterical—that lasted for months. (Reviewers and radio show hosts were particularly apt to point out that Peter Brimelow is an immigrant himself; also that father and son, as pictured on the bookjacket, share a distinctly Aryan, and therefore unpleasing, appearance.) That he had presumed to address a major—perhaps *the* major—national issue from the officially disapproved angle was very insensitive of Peter Brimelow. That he had questioned the underlying assumptions of the official version and exploded its myths was offensive of him. But that he had proceeded to question the motives of the people he described as "immigration enthusiasts" was intolerable. An immigrant with a British education, a fine critical mind, and a lucid, informal prose style was—it seemed—the one kind of immigrant America at the end of the twentieth century did *not* need (even if Americans could not be found to do his sort of work).

The American public, as poll after poll over the past three decades at least have shown, believes that, where immigration is concerned, enough is simply enough. "This is not," Brimelow argues, "an unreasonable position. Unfortunately, and greatly to the discredit of the American political elite, there is no longer a respectable language in which to express it. I like to think of this book as a sort of toolkit of arguments for ordinary Americans. Some immigration enthusiasts will resent having their tranquility disturbed. But their choice is to hear arguments for reform now, or for total restriction later." This is because, as Brimelow argues in the body of his book, immigration resulting from current American policy is more numerous, less skilled, and less compatible with the American majority than had supposedly been intended; that it brings few economic benefits; that it entails negative consequences across a wide spectrum, ranging from environmental damage to the undermining of American political institutions; and that it is transforming America ethnically and racially to a degree unheard of in world history. Mass immigration to the United States, in short, is "an astonishing social experiment launched with no particular reason to expect success."

Although the knockout argument from the immigrationist corner is widely imagined to be the economic one (i.e., the American economy would simply implode if immigration were halted or even significantly curtailed), Brimelow dissents from this orthodoxy. Immigration today, he insists, is not an economic policy; rather, it is a political one. "Race and identity are destiny in American politics. The racial and ethnic balance of America is being radically altered through public policy. This can only have the most profound effects. *Is this what Americans want?*"

Alien Nation owes its shock effect on American policy making and journalistic circles to three factors. The first is that Peter Brimelow is that rare thing, a financial writer for whom finance is an aspect of civilization, rather than the reverse. The second is that he persists in the traditional view of the nation-state as the West has understood it since the nation-building era that began in the fourteenth and fifteenth centuries, and in an understanding of human society (compare St. Augustine's *City of God*) already in existence for centuries before that. Today, the concept of the nation-state is being challenged, renovated, and discarded by intellectual and policy elites who profess to believe (with a recently deceased editor of the *Wall Street Journal*) that "the nation-state is finished." Advocates on both sides of the immigration "debate" insist that immigration is essentially a moral, not an economic, issue; enthusiasts stretching the individualist argument nearly to the point of claiming that immigration amounts to a civil right America cannot refuse anyone who asks for it. Countering *Time* magazine's argument that "for the first time in its history, the U.S. has an immigration policy that, for better or worse, is truly democratic," Brimelow observes that "[*Times*'s] notion of democracy . . . has degenerated to the point where it is assumed to require invalidating the right to an independent existence of the very *demos*, people, community, that is supposed to be taking decisions on its own behalf. Democracy becomes self-liquidating." And so do nations.

The third reason for *Alien Nation*'s shock power is Brimelow's refusal to be intimidated by the great American taboo regarding issues of race and ethnicity, none of which he neglects in his treatment of the immigration problem. From his earliest days in America, Brimelow understood that *"anyone who says anything critical of immigration is going to be accused of racism"*—and of anti-Semitism to boot. For Brimelow, America's having been created by whites is, like its continuing white majority, no scandal but simply historical fact. The United States was founded as an extension of Western civilization, and its present-day majority has the right—in fact, it has the duty—to maintain its historical makeup and character. Additionally, such racism as white Americans have expressed is reciprocated in kind by its nonwhite citizens, many of whom regard nonwhite immigration as a means of racial and ethnic displacement—and revenge. ("[T]he double standards," Brimelow notes, "are irritating. Anyone who has got into an immigration debate with, for example, Hispanic activists must be instantly aware that some of them really are consumed by the most intense racial animosity—directed against whites.") As for the Jews, it is more or less an open secret these days that Jewish organizations have sought for decades to ensure that "it can't happen here" by advocating an immigration policy that would swamp or dilute the Aryan majority with tens of millions of nonwhite immigrants from the Third World.

"The disappearance of nations," Aleksandr Solzhenitsyn said in accepting the Nobel Prize, "would impoverish us no less than if all peoples were made alike, with one character, one face. Nations are the wealth of mankind, they are its generalized personalities: the smallest of them has its own particular colors, and embodies a particular facet of God's design." Brimelow blends Solzhenitsyn's idea with a doctrine of Thomas Aquinas that holds men's responsibilities to be compelling in the degree to which the object of responsibility is near to them. Thus, he writes of the nation-state, "Like the family, it is one of those happy inventions through which human beings are enabled to experience the world. It is a foundation upon which a more general approach to the world might perhaps be built. But it is not something for which a more general approach to the world can be substituted. Respect for the nation-state, perhaps, is the ultimate family value."

The United States cannot solve the world's problems, Brimelow argues, alleviate the global population crisis, or minister effectively (as liberal and left-wing religionists argue it should do) to all those foreigners who wish to come here—not even those who succeed in coming here. Yet, mass immigration at today's level poses a dire ecological threat to America and a substantial risk to the integrity and stability of the American political and social systems. Half a century from now, this country could discover itself utterly transformed—"for nothing." Unlike immigration enthusiasts, Brimelow insists on setting the welfare of his own country and his own people above those of other peoples and other countries. In the minds of immigrationists, this insistence marks him as a "nativist" or a "restrictionist." Peter Brimelow suggests another word to identify his sort. "They should call themselves—patriots."

44

THE DEATH OF THE WEST: HOW DYING POPULATIONS AND IMMIGRANT INVASIONS IMPERIL OUR COUNTRY AND CIVILIZATION

by Patrick J. Buchanan

2002

Patrick Buchanan (1939–), like William F. Buckley Jr., is a multi-media conservative and politician often seen (also like Buckley) as a flesh-and-blood synecdoche for conservativism as a whole. In fact, the two men represent different schools, or factions, within the American conservative movement. Buchanan is the best-known representative of what since the late 1980s has been known as paleoconservatism, Buckley the founder and leading exponent of the mainline conservatism that was the chief force in the anti-communist movement in the 1950s, 1960s, and 1970s.

A professional Black Irishman who plays the role to the hilt, Buchanan has never shrunk from association with persons, ideas, and positions as unpalatable—or even more so—to establishment conservatives and neoconservatives as they are to conventional liberals and the social-democratic Left. Buchanan has been a senior advisor to three Republican presidents, starting with Richard M. Nixon on whom conservatives have never been able to agree. After breaking with the Republican Party, whose nomination for president he sought without success in 1992 and 1996,

Buchanan ran as the presidential candidate of the Reform Party in 2000, heedless of the fury of the George W. Bush Republicans, who feared the possibility of his throwing the election to Al Gore. Buchanan's syndicated column, save only for those of Samuel Francis and Paul Craig Roberts, is the most uncompromising in the business; his presence on NBC's *The McLaughlin Group* and CNN's *Crossfire* and *The Capital Gang* were always equally hard-nosed. Having been a loyal Republican all his life, Buchanan split with the GOP in recognition of irreconcilable differences regarding globalism, imperialism, free trade, mass immigration, multiculturalism versus a recognizable American identity, secularization, and an uncritical and unlimited support for the state of Israel at the expense of an intelligent and responsible foreign policy in the Middle East. Developed over a period of years by a fertile exchange of ideas with the editors of the paleoconservative journal *Chronicles: A Magazine of American Culture* and the conservative-libertarian von Mises Institute at Auburn State University, Buchananism is paleoconservatism at the popular level, raised to a household concept if not a household word.

Patrick Buchanan's brand of conservatism is at loggerheads with the neoconservative program to realize "national greatness" by establishing American hegemony in world affairs; export democratic politics and capitalist economics abroad; create the "first universal nation," dedicated to abstract propositions of "freedom" and "equality" at home; and reconceptualize the United States as essentially an economic engine, fueled by consumerism and geared to the production of more and more consumer goods. Its concern is with what Buchanan in *The Death of the West* describes as the "[the] struggle to preserve the old creeds, cultures, and countries of the West. . . . This is the cause of the twenty-first century and the agenda of conservatism for the remainder of our lives."

The Death of the West is an extended essay on the impending fall of the greatest civilization the world has yet seen, engineered by enemies internal as well as external and facilitated by the acquiescence of faithless, negligent, and corrupt masses of its own people. Buchanan, an outspoken Catholic in a militantly pagan and anti-Christian culture, never hesitates to identify the crisis of the West with the crisis of the Christian faith that (as Hilaire Belloc devoted a lifetime to arguing) created and sustained it. "All culture," Russell Kirk writes, "arises out of religion. When religious faith decays, culture must decline, though often seeming to flourish for a space after the religion which has nourished it has sunk into disbelief." To which T. S. Eliot adds, "A people without religion will in the end find that it has nothing to live for."

People who have nothing to live for have no future, and people who have no future leave no children to populate a nonexistent chronological dimension. In America and in Europe, birth rates are either stagnant or falling; with the Third World projected to account for an increase of 50 percent in the global population between 2000 and 2050, Westerners must expect to become an endangered species. Declining populations in the West are being supplanted by invaders from non-Western countries, who stand to displace the aboriginal inhabitants. The population crisis, Buchanan argues, is a direct result of the weakening of marriage both as a religious sacrament and a social institution: an aspect of what a Belgian demographer has described as a "shift in the Western ideational system" away from the Christian values of sacrifice, altruism, and commitment, toward the aggressive "secular individualism" dubbed by Tom Wolfe in the 1970s "the Me Generation." The devaluation of marriage is accompanied by divorce, unbridled sexual promiscuity, and the moral acceptance and even idealization of homosexuality, abortion, and euthanasia. "The America many of us grew up in," Buchanan writes, "is gone. The cultural revolution has triumphed in the minds of millions and is beyond the power of politicians to overturn, even if they had the courage to try. Half the nation has converted." Also, it appears, more than half of Europe. "Irony of ironies," he concludes. "Today, an aging, dying Christian West is pressing the Third World and the Islamic world to accept contraception, abortion, and sterilization as the West has done. But why should they enter a suicide pact with us when they stand to inherit the earth when we are gone?"

The cultural revolution that exploded in the 1960s and continues to expand throughout the West like the universe following the Big Bang, is itself the product of centuries going back at least to the sixteenth century, and perhaps as early as the thirteenth. More immediately, it is traceable to World War I, when Marxists, disillusioned and disheartened by the readiness of the European proletariat to refuse class warfare and fight in the armies of their capitalist masters, concluded that the traditional Christian society—not capitalism—was the primary obstacle to revolution in the West. Georg Lukacs, a Hungarian agent of the Comintern and deputy commissar for culture in Bela Kun's government, writes, "I saw the revolutionary destruction of society as the one and only solution. A worldwide overturning of values cannot take place without the annihilation of old values and the creation of new ones by the revolutionaries." Antonio Gramsci, an Italian communist who escaped to Russia after Benito Mussolini came to power in 1922, having observed the Soviet Union at firsthand, recognized that the future did *not* work. "The civilized world had been thoroughly saturated with Christianity for 2000 years," he laments. Western Marxists must therefore work to destroy the culture by a process of what Gramsci calls a "long march through the institutions," after which the governments, and with them the economic structure of the West, would fall to the ground.

Lukacs, with the help of the German Communist Party, in 1923 established at Frankfurt University the Institute for Marxism, later called the Frankfurt School. When the Nazis came to power, the Frankfurt School, all of whose principal members—Max Horkeimer, Theodor Adorno, Erich Fromm, Wilhelm Reich, and Herbert Marcuse—were Jewish Marxists, moved to New York City, where they developed what came to be known as Critical Theory, described by one critic as "essentially destructive criticism of all the main elements of Western culture, including Christianity, capitalism, authority, the family, patriarchy, hierarchy, morality, tradition, sexual restraint, loyalty, patriotism, nationality, heredity, ethnocentrism, convention and conservatism." "Where Marx criminalized the capitalist class," Buchanan aptly summarizes, "the Frankfurt School criminalized the middle class." The School's work was enormously facilitated by the self-critical spirit of liberalism that, encouraged by Frankfurt and similar influences, easily transformed itself into a self-destructive one. Marcuse, who became in the 1960s a New Left guru, advocated the creation of a "polymorphous[ly] pervers[e]" world by a strategy of "repressive tolerance," which he defined as one of "intolerance against movements from the right, and toleration of movements from the left."

The most efficient means to weaken and destroy the character of a people is to reassure them endlessly that something is deserved by or owed to them, or simply that there is no reason why they should not possess that thing (or *any* thing). It is the genius of the Left to have grasped this fact, to which the cultural revolution owes its success. The political revolution is only the direct result of the cultural one, after it had subverted and weakened the piety, morality, intellect, self-identity, self-assurance, self-respect, and finally the nerve of Western societies. Revolution has destroyed, in other words, the natural defenses of the West, leaving it vulnerable to political correctness in the form of blatantly racialist, anti-Western politics at home and a suicidal immigration program amounting to a kind of foreign policy. With England mobbed by immigrants from Central and East Africa, France by North Africans, Germany by "economic refugees" from Turkey, Canada by Asians, and the southwestern United States by Mexicans threatening *reconquista,* Buchanan asks, "Is our era of the equality of nations really the end of history or a temporary truce, a phony peace, an armistice, a time of transition from a day of Western dominance to a day when the West pays tribute?" The Western world does not lack the *power* to turn its challengers back upon themselves; what is absent is the *will* to prevail against them. "Needed for victory is not only a conservative spirit, to defend what is right about America and the West, but a counterrevolutionary spirit to recapture lost ground. To preserve their rights, and the right to live as they wished, the Founding Fathers had to become rebels. So shall we."

Because the Third World is manifestly incapable of governing anything (including itself), the sole alternative to the primacy of the West is (1) global chaos or (2) global government presiding over the "world community" long dreamt of by Western visionaries. Typical of these is Strobe Talbott, Bill Clinton's Oxford roommate who served as undersecretary of state in the Clinton administration after the president drafted him from his job at *Time*. "All countries," Talbott writes, "are basically social arrangements. . . . No matter how permanent and even sacred they may seem at any one time, in fact they are all artificial and temporary. . . . Within the next hundred years . . . nationhood as we know it will be obsolete; all states will recognize a single global authority. A phrase briefly fashionable in the mid-20th century—'citizen of the world'—will have assumed real meaning by the end of the 21st."

World government and the end of the international system are not only unfeasible, they are in fact an impossibility. Also, they amount, as Patrick Buchanan knows, to Christian heresy, as St. Augustine in *City of God* suggests in speaking of "differences in laws, customs, and institutions, by which earthly peace is achieved" and maintained by Providence to that end. It is possible to dismiss Christianity as superstition (many great Western minds have done exactly that) and Augustine himself as a bishop and saint in Christianity's church. What cannot be honestly maintained, or rationally argued, is that the West and Christianity are historically separable. While Christianity will not fall with Western civilization, Western civilization must nevertheless perish without Christianity, if only by becoming something other than itself. For conservatives of all faiths, and even of none, that is a fact to hold in mind, no matter the temptation to believe otherwise.

45

FROM UNION TO EMPIRE: ESSAYS IN THE JEFFERSONIAN TRADITION

by Clyde N. Wilson

2003

Clyde N. Wilson (1941–), the eminent American historian and editor of the John C. Calhoun Papers at the University of South Carolina, was a leading theoretician of the New Right in the 1970s and early 1980s, before that hopeful attempt at reviving a genuinely conservative political movement came to grief when the Reagan presidency betrayed it to the better funded and better connected neoconservatives. (Wilson's initial enthusiasm for the so-called Reagan Revolution and his progressive disillusionment with the ensuing Devolution are strongly apparent in this book.) Following the debacle, Wilson rapidly emerged as an architect of the paleoconservative movement—highbrow and traditionalist successor to the New Right—whose antecedents are discoverable in Wilson's and Thomas Fleming's *Southern Partisan Quarterly Review,* founded in 1979.

The collapse of the Union of Soviet Socialist Republics in 1989 and the end of the Cold War might have been expected to produce a reorientation of American foreign policy, away from multiple diplomatic missions and military commitments overseas toward a reassertion of its historical skepticism of foreign entanglements that had prevailed from the presidency of George Washington down to the Spanish-American War. In fact, the passing of America's archenemy from the historical stage had precisely the opposite result. Four presidential administrations in succession have now sought to consolidate and exploit the United States' position as sole superpower, promote its identity as the world's "first universal nation," and force a global economy and global democracy in the American style on the international community. (Since 1989, the United States has waged war—always undeclared—in Kuwait, Panama, Somalia, Bosnia, Afghanistan, and Iraq.) This new imperial America is chiefly the creation of neoconservatism, which has succeeded in committing both the Republican Party and the "conservative" movement to the project of realizing what neoconservatives call "National Greatness Conservatism"—a concept that, to Clyde Wilson's mind, has nothing that is great, conservative, or American about it.

Wilson's reading of American history differs not only from the standard liberal interpretation, but from the accepted conservative one as well. A staunch antifederalist, he defends Jefferson against the federalist and "conservative" charge of radicalism and the Articles of Confederation against the U.S. Constitution that, he argues, by "balancing" the executive and judicial branches against the legislative one ensured the eventual replacement of republican government by the aristocratical variety. Jacksonian Democracy, Wilson insists, was not the forerunner of the New Deal and of twentieth-century liberalism that Arthur Schlesinger Jr. has made it out to have been. Rather, it was a fundamentally conservative movement that opposed oligarchy, monopoly, and special economic privilege, while defending free economic enterprise and private property. Similarly, the Populist movement of the late nineteenth and early twentieth century was essentially conservative, not radical, in its nature. ("Direct democracy in the Populist program was radical in method but conservative in instinct in that it aimed nostalgically to restore a more honorable relationship between people and representative.")

The War Between the States resulted in the destruction of the

Old Republic and of the Constitution on which it rested. After 1865, the federalist principle, by which the Union had been understood as the creation of the consenting states that comprised it, became a dead letter, and a new Leviathan was in the making. Henceforth, the attempt to understand and to "conserve the structure and society and government that is the most organic, legitimate, and just for the American nation, i.e., the federal republic bequeathed to us by that unique event, the American Revolution, a 'revolution' which was prudential rather than revolutionary, preservative rather than innovative, legalistic rather than speculative," was abandoned. In the half-century between the so-called Civil War and World War I, a new form of American nationalism established hegemony. "The settlement that emerged," Wilson writes, "was part and parcel of the Progressive era. Progressivism was not simply the clearcut reform movement of the history textbooks—it was a seachange in consciousness, the completion of a stage of mental modernization with vast and sometimes ambivalent and contradictory implications with which we are still living and which historians have barely begun to describe accurately."

Progressivism achieved its aim, which was the creation of the nationalized society that was also a mobilized society and the re-creation of America as a vast machine dedicated to the identification of social "problems" and their "solution." The mobilizers, of course, were the American "elite," the mobilized, ordinary American citizens whose existence was justified—or not—by their willingness to be dragooned by their betters in a succession of grandiose national and international enterprises. "Where there is no solution," James Burnham liked to say, "there is no problem." For the Progressive mind, there are *always* solutions—hence perennial problems, unlimited in scope and affording the nation's "leaders" the mandate first, and next the powers, to solve those problems. The instauration of Progressivism as the national ideology bore final fruit during World War II in "a plan for the post-war world," which became itself a step toward global revolution. "The defeat of the fascist powers," Wilson argues, "was only the first goal in an ongoing transformation of the world. While many or most Americans thought in terms of defeating their enemies, reestablishing a degree of order and decency in the world, and going back to peaceful pursuits, by this view the end of the war would be but a beginning. For the first time America had become [in the mind of the American elite] not an end but a means, expendable material for the construction of a new world order (although the new order often curiously resembled America writ large)."

This alone would be insufficient grounds, Wilson cautions, from which to conclude that the republican form of government in America has been replaced by the imperialist kind. "An empire is not to be distinguished from a republic by the extent of its overseas commitments or the possession of foreign colonies or the size of its military forces. It is possible, though not necessarily easy, for a people to remain republican while engaging in extensive trade, military campaigning, and even colonization overseas. An empire is differentiated from a republic by the nature of its domestic society and by the purposes which inform its official and public activities."

Even so, Wilson's criterion for empire is hardly a reassuring one:

The republic passes over into empire when political activity is no longer directed toward enhancement of the well-being of a particular people, but has become a mechanism for managing them for the benefit of their rulers. That is to say, an empire's political behavior reflects management needs, reflects the interests of maintaining government itself, reflects the desires of those who happen to be in control of its machinery of administration, rather than the personality and the will of the nation being governed. The government of an empire is abstract, manipulative, a government of, by, and for the government, not of, by, and for the people. Power flows downward rather than upward.

For Wilson, the conclusion is inescapable: America is no longer a republic and has not been for 50 years at least, and perhaps as much as one hundred and fifty.

Not the Union, Wilson insists, but the consent of the governed ("to which the Union might or might not be of assistance") was sacred to the founders of the old republic. With the loss of that republic has occurred the loss of self-government as well. How might both be restored—at this date so late in the history of the American nation that it is questionable whether or not the American community can continue to exist in any other than imperial form?

The answer, Wilson believes, is a simple one—simple in the sense that all great issues are simple. It consists in the rediscovery of the true federalist principle, which is that of states' rights. Federalism, however misunderstood it may be today, is nevertheless the most practical of all political forms. Far from being unsound in principle, it has been overridden by the will to consolidated power against which the founders warned. If federalist principles appear inapplicable today, that is owing rather to an absence of political will than to the impracticability of the principles themselves.

"It would be a shame," Wilson concludes,

if in this world-historical time of devolution, Americans did not look back to an ancient and honourable tradition that lies readily at hand. To check power, to return the American empire to republicanism, we do not need to resort to the drastic right of revolution nor to the destructive goal of anarchic individualism. We have in the states ready-made instruments. All that is lacking is the will. Our goal should be the restoration of the real American Union of sovereign states in place of the upstart empire under which we live.

As the United States grows increasingly polarized politically and—once again, sectionally—a Second Constitutional Convention seems hardly inconceivable, even in the context of the imperial deadlock against which Clyde Wilson warns.

46

REVOLUTION FROM THE MIDDLE

by Samuel Francis

1997

Samuel Francis (1947–)—author, columnist, editor, newspaper-man, and public speaker—is widely regarded as the chief political theorist for what has become known as paleoconservatism: a re-tooling, extension, and deepening of Old Right doctrine and principle to counter neoconservatism and the new Old Right (Francis calls it "progressive conservatism") itself. A careful stu-dent of James Burnham on whom he has written a monograph (*James Burnham*), Francis has done much to elucidate, update, and, to some degree, expand Burnham's understanding of the managerial revolution. Also, he has reconsidered the great anti-Western revolutionists of the twentieth century whom Burnham, in his book of the same name, calls "the Machiavellians" (Gae-tano Mosca, Vilfredo Pareto, and Roberto Michels), who, in the course of their "long march through the institutions" of Western culture and society, have pretty well succeeded in bringing both to their knees.

As Samuel Francis understands the present-day American and western European political systems, the word "conservative" is misapplied to every type of "conservatism" *but* paleoconservatism and what he terms "middle American radicalism." "For years," Francis noted recently in an open letter to certain of his friends and colleagues,

> I have written that liberalism is essentially an ideology or political formula that rationalizes elite power. . . . [L]iberalism is not for the most part irrational or insane, but rationally directed to achieve a certain goal—to support the power of those who gain from it. Indeed, in my view that is the only thing that can explain its persistence after being discredited in both fact and logic. Because liberalism is an ideology or formula that has other purposes than explaining reality (its other purposes being, namely, the justification of the power of certain groups), it does not respond to refutation or criticisms, any more than Soviet Communism did. This is why the conservative mantra "Ideas Have Consequences" is irrelevant. . . . Ideas have consequences mainly when certain groups (social, political, economic, racial, religious, etc.) attach themselves to them and push them as ideologies. . . . People manage to convince themselves of those ideas that tend to support and advance their own interests and what they would like to believe. Those who argue that liberals can't possibly believe in their own ideology because it leads to national and civilizational suicide misunderstand that liberals do not regard themselves as part of the nation or civilization. Their loyalties are to the fictitious nation or civilization they've constructed in their imaginations . . . and they have "disengaged" from the existing or traditional ones and wish to see them destroyed (or "overcome" or "liberated" or "transcended," euphemisms that all mean destruction). Suicide of the nation, race, and civilization is exactly what they want to induce in the old civilization, etc., and that's what liberals help do. But at the same time it also enhances their own power and the structures that keep them in power and is supposed to be building the "New Civilization" liberals like to babble about.

That is a broad indictment; yet, the social class comprised by liberals is wider still. Indeed, since World War II that class has expanded to include, not everyone to be sure, but *everyone who "matters"* in America and in the Western world; even as the managerial revolution has expanded in nearly every direction and conquered on almost every hand. The managerial class, not the business and manufacturing class, is the New Establishment, to which much or most of the Old Establishment—including the Old Right—has thrown its support and pledged its allegiance. Because that, of course, is how establishments behave, since, in politics, ideas always follow power. (Or, in John Lukacs's formulation, what men do with ideas is always of greater interest than what ideas do with men.)

"The changes in thought and rhetoric that distinguish . . . 'progressive conservatism' . . . from its predecessors of the Old Right reflect a significant social and demographic transformation of American political culture," Francis argues in *Revolution from the Middle.* (The book's thirty chapters correspond with thirty installments of "Powers and Principalities," his monthly column in *Chronicles: A Magazine of American Culture.*) "Whereas Old Right conservatism was by and large the expression of the interests, values, and aspirations of the American bourgeois elite, [progressive conservatism] express[es] those of a relatively new elite of urbanized, technocratic professionals who make their living and gain power and status in mass organizations." Thus, established conservatism merges with a managerial elite of longer standing whose ideology was exhausted and discredited in the 1960s and 1970s.

"This is where 'progressive conservatism' comes in," Francis explains. The yuppies of the managerial elite in the 1980s, though they opposed the liberalism of the New Deal and the Great Society, nevertheless were at bottom cultural cosmopolitans and philosophical liberals who, being comfortable with Big Government in theory, sought to restrict its reach into their own pockets and those of their friends, while acknowledging its role in creating "openness," "opportunity," and "democracy" for the masses—as well as for the minorities. Also, they evinced an enthusiasm for the technological approach (always beloved by liberals) to social "problems," regularly discovering new techniques they imagined would make an end to war, poverty, theocracy, autocracy, and for global unification in political and cultural, as well as in economic, terms. This, for progressive conservatives, would be Heaven on Earth (Francis Fukuyama's end of history) that for centuries has been the central historic vision of the Left—not the Right. "What is called the 'right' in American politics today seems to invoke and take seriously all the slogans and clichés that derive from Liberty, Equality, and Fraternity and which would ordinarily locate their exponents on the Left." And so, "the union of the Republican Party [the "Stupid Party," Francis calls it] with the managerial elite and its apparatus in the government means the end of an era in American political culture" and the advent of a time when the GOP has no other use for "plain old Middle Americans" than captive electoral fodder for winning elections.

It is possible that the term "Middle American," and thus the concept "Revolution from the Middle," need to be interpreted more broadly than Francis often does. The acronym MARs (Middle American Radicals), borrowed from the late Donald Warren and a favorite of Francis's, indicates rather specifically angry blue-collar males (and females), often of ethnic origin. Francis, however, uses "middle class" in another sense, to differentiate it from the old American bourgeoisie—an urbane, interior, independent, and self-possessed class whose heyday lasted from the demise of the Old American Republic to the end of World War II, when its self-destructive, liberal-genteel tendencies were exploited by the rising managerial elite to undermine and wreck it. Unlike the bourgeoisie, the new middle class in America is defined by economic standing rather than in terms of social class (birth, gentility, manners, education, self-assurance, independence, and republican virtue). Unlike the secure, self-assured, and nearly invulnerable bourgeois of the past, the middle class man in the present day is highly vulnerable and insecure, being salaried, in real terms propertyless, and dependent on the mass organizations run by the managerial elite, which regard him as interchangeable—and dispensable. The new American middle class, in short, has left the old middle class to become a proletariat in its own right.

In the circumstances of economic giantism and political centralism, middle-class financial insecurity and electoral impotence are in some degree inevitable. They are, however, vastly aggravated and intensified by the three principal obsessive agenda of the national bipartisan managerial elite: economic globalism, political globalism, and mass immigration to the United States. Destructive as these programs are to most of the country (excepting only the exploitive minority that pushes them), it is Middle Americans who feel the full brunt, suffering the worst, and losing the most. Thus, it is to Middle Americans that Samuel Francis has appealed for most of his perilous career and on whom he has based much of the strategic thinking further developed by Patrick Buchanan, whom Francis has served for many years as an informal advisor. "It is hardly an accident," he notes, "that the decomposition of the American nation and its culture is paralleled by the decomposition of the American middle class."

"The 'global economy,'" Sam Francis writes,

> and political one-worldism jeopardise the historic character, independence, and the very sovereignty of the United States. The third threat, the mass immigration that this country has endured for the last [thirty years or so], is no less a danger to the cultural norms by which American civilization has identified itself throughout most of its history. Nevertheless, like the internationalization of our economy and government, the internationalization of our population is consistent with the interests of the elite that welcome and encourage it.

The elite may well (indeed, it probably will) end up by losing more than it bargained for, in proportion to the advantage it realizes from its grandiose schemes. And yet, the country as a whole—the abstract, half-imaginary reality we call Middle America—has obviously the most to lose:

> Americans . . . will cease to be Americans at all and find themselves reduced to "resources," stripped of the distinctive set of norms that unite and identify them as a people and dispossessed even of the memory of how to make themselves one. As resources, they will become interchangeable parts in the global economic mechanism, and their functions in it can be performed

just as easily (or better) by workers from Latin America, managers from Asia, or investors from Japan or Europe. If what remains of the Middle American core of the American nation and its civilization is to preserve itself from the dispersion and dispossession that the new global economy promises, it will have to assert its national identity and interests in economic no less than in cultural and political terms.

In order to survive—let alone prevail—Francis believes, the postbourgeois middle class must develop self-consciousness as a class lying somewhere between the nearly extinct bourgeoisie and the technobureaucracy of global managerialism. It must then abandon the defensive strategy historically employed by the Right to resist Leviathan and adopt an offensive one, for the purpose of gaining power for itself. In the attempt, Francis cautions, the means employed should be political, constitutional, and peaceful, eschewing the extrapolitical violence practiced by resisters like Timothy McVeigh and associated by the ruling class with the lumpenproletariat. "Once the sociology of liberty is destroyed [as the elite itself is bent on doing]," he warns, "it cannot be restored. Once the institutions and habits of independent discipline have withered, they do not naturally blossom again." In the present circumstances, the question is: "Who, in the wrecked vessel of the American Republic, is to be master?"

In recent years, Samuel Francis has admitted that the prospects for organized (or even disorganized) resistance to the New Order appear dim, in a country whose fat, contented, and suborned populace refuses to pay attention to (and seems hardly to care about) what its masters are up to. The fact in no way compromises the acuteness of Francis's political understanding, as it is at least conceivable that the present situation will need to deteriorate, rather than improve, before popular opposition to it takes form at last.

47

THE MORALITY OF EVERYDAY LIFE: A CLASSICAL ALTERNATIVE TO THE LIBERAL TRADITION

by Thomas Fleming

2004

Thomas Fleming (1945–), as cofounder of *Southern Partisan Quarterly Review,* is a founder as well of paleoconservative journalism. A classicist trained at the University of North Carolina, where he first made the acquaintance of his future comrades-in-arms Clyde N. Wilson and Samuel Francis, Fleming had a brief academic career before being elevated in 1985 to the editorship of the Rockford Institute's flagship publication *Chronicles: A Magazine of American Culture,* following the sudden demise of its founding editor, Leopold Tyrmand. Fleming's combination of scholarly erudition with journalistic flare made him in almost no time a force to be reckoned with on the American Right, which the wedge of his original and aggressive editorship helped to split between paleoconservatism (on the right) and neoconservatism (on the left). With Paul Gottfried, Fleming coauthored *The Conservative Movement* in 1988. In another work, *The Politics of Human Nature* (published the same year), he argues that the stages of human social evolution are recapitulated in the social life of individuals and that human development is reflected in a federal system, violations of which account for most social and political problems.

The Morality of Everyday Life: A Classical Alternative to the Liberal Tradition may be read both as an extended elaboration and an illustration of Michael Oakeshott's great essay "The Tower of Babel" (in *Rationalism and Politics, and Other Essays*). Here, Oakeshott suggests that the moral life assumes two forms, or habits: the "habit of affection and behavior" and the "habit of reflective thought." The first is essentially what Thomas Fleming calls the morality of everyday life; the second, what he condemns as the rationalist (meaning abstracted and universalized) morality insisted on by modern-day philosophers and politicians. "Where René Descartes or John Locke," Fleming explains,

> looked out at the everyday world and saw nothing but a few universal rules reducible to a mathematical formula, Aristotle and the writers of the Old Testament discerned an intricate network of peculiar obligations arising from specific circumstances and experiences. Where modern philosophers (from Kant to Kohlberg) regard a mother's self-sacrificing love for her children as beneath the level of morality, folk wisdom tells us it is nearly the highest morality, taking precedence over the duties of citizenship or the claims of humanity. In the modern theories, moral conflicts can almost always be resolved into a choice between right and wrong, between human rights and oppression. The older tradition was more complex.

Aristotle understood laws as universal statements that cannot anticipate every contingency to which they must needs be applied. "Justice," Fleming continues, "cannot be reduced to simple universals, because different kinds of virtue are required of different people. One cannot be just to one's children, for example, because they are so much a part of oneself."

The discipline whose aim is to determine, on a case-by-case basis and with scrupulous accuracy, the type of virtue appropriate to any given moral dilemma and to calibrate the application of that type as precisely as is humanly possible, is called casuistry.

Casuistry (as it has been known since the Middle Ages) has suffered a bad name in modern times, which have insisted on making the word synonymous with Jesuitism, moral evasion, and hypocrisy. The tradition, nevertheless, greatly predates the medieval Church and St. Thomas Aquinas, whose casuitical labors were preceded by those of Aristotle and Cicero. As Fleming describes it, "A genuine casuistry is based on two principles: first, that there are general and universally applicable moral laws governing human conduct; second, that these laws may not be applied simplistically and uniformly to the great variety of human circumstances and situations." In the eighteenth century, St. Alphonsus de Liguori developed a position midway between the supposed laxity of the Jesuits and the severity of the Jansenists that became known as "probabilism," and rejected moral absolutism for imposing on human beings a standard of morality that frail human nature can never approach. Already, however, the Protestant world was enthralled by the absolutist abstractions propounded by Francis Bacon, John Locke, and Gottfried Leibniz that became an incentive to moral evasion at the private level of society and universalism on the public one.

The humane and humble morality of the ancient world, merged with the peasant morality of Europe, lies beneath the thin-stretched abstracted and universalized morality of modernity. "In fact, Aristotle and Aquinas (to say nothing of Moses and St. Paul) are far closer in spirit and outlook to the common sense of ordinary people than they are to the thought of most modern philosophers." In its political expression, modern morality is the equivalent of liberalism: the commitment to "universality, rationality, individualism, objectivity, and abstract idealism." Again, Oakeshott, in *Rationalism in Politics*, observes that the rationalist ideology has claimed even liberalism's institutional rival: the supposed "conservative" opposition. Fleming concurs with this insight. "There is a strange convergence," he notes,

> . . . in the style of reasoning employed by international philanthropists, liberal "do-gooders," and right-to-life activists. Our obligation to do right, they will tell us, does not come out of the

peculiar circumstances of being a mother or being a Jew, but from a philosophical or theological commitment to a global responsibility that is determined by a rational individual who considers the matter objectively as it relates to the entire world and keeps his attention, not on things as they are, but on how they ought to be in an ideal world.

The problem with this kind of moral idealism (amounting in the post-Christian era to a successor religion of humanity) is, Fleming insists, its tendency to create an indifference to—and, finally, contempt of—everyday life.

The Morality of Everyday Life, having considered the obligations we have toward one another (family members, friends; fellow members of our community, our nation, and our world) concludes with St. Augustine that "[s]ince one cannot help everyone, one has to be concerned with those who by reason of place, time, or circumstance, are by some chance more tightly bound to you," and with Aquinas that charity is owed to God first, next to those who are closest to us by nature. It upholds national attachments and loyalties, on the orthodox Christian presumption that individual kingdoms are a part of the natural order ordained by God, while denegrating nationalism for its ideological, arrogant, and aggressive tendencies—all incompatible with old-fashioned patriotism, which indicates simply love of, and predilection for, one's own country. It praises a hierarchy of loyalties and condemns the notion of the global village, "the pornography of compassion," "telescopic philanthropy" (which might conceivably be called a form of "social justice," but certainly not "charity"), and "the global philanthropy racket"—all of them artificial in proportion to their level of abstraction and absurd in relation to the degree that they *are* abstract. (Fleming quotes T. S. Eliot's *Four Quartets*—"Human kind / Cannot bear very much reality"—to comment, "How much is very much will vary with time, from human to human, but this much is certain: Without the aid of those we love, we cannot bear the weight of the entire world.")

The book considers the limits of objectivity and impartiality, insofar as these qualities are possible and insofar also as they are desirable. (A liberal, it has been said, is someone who declines to take his own side in an argument.) William Godwin, the nineteenth-century British philosopher, claims in the influential work *Political Justice* that "[t]he soundest criterion of virtue is to put ourselves in the place of an impartial spectator, of an angelic nature, suppose, beholding us from an elevated station, and uninfluenced by our prejudices, conceiving what would be his estimate of the intrinsic circumstances of our neighbor, and acting accordingly." Here, as so often happens, idealism takes a fatal step up to angelism and falls to Earth with a crash—under the skeptical eye, one assumes, of genuine angels. (The noble "impartial spectator" who wrote these lines fathered a daughter, Mary, out of wedlock with Mary Woolstonecraft, and for many years played the role of extortionist in shaking down Percy Bysshe Shelley, her poetic seducer.)

Fleming's conclusion is that attempts to substitute rational systems of objective value for natural love can only turn us into monsters who kill strangers (and others) for the sake of a "higher" cause and from a safe distance (the six thousand miles, say, that separate Washington, D.C., and Baghdad, or the forty thousand feet between the streets of Belgrade and the bombers overhead). Here is the connection, as drawn by Fleming: "Rational, universal, objective ethics, culminating in the doctrine of international rights, represents a more profound threat to the human future even than the environmental havoc (nuclear waste, industrial pollution, devastated farmlands and wilderness) that is also the residue of Western liberalism. Serious resistance, supposing there is to be resistance to the global regime, will only begin when intelligent people have understood the theoretical justifications of this Fourth Rome and rejected them."

Not charity alone, but moral sanity itself begins at home. Firmly rooted in the morality of everyday life, it rises from ground level to effect a natural application to the morality of communal and of public life at the middling height, and from there—by a stretch wholly natural—to the upper reaches of the international sphere, without suffering rarification in the process. In his book, Thomas Fleming demonstrates why this amounts to a law of human nature and lays out a curriculum by which we may observe that law.

48

REVOLT FROM THE HEARTLAND: THE STRUGGLE FOR AN AUTHENTIC CONSERVATISM

by Joseph Scotchie

2002

Half a century ago, it was a matter for serious intellectual, historical, and political debate in America whether conservatives could lay claim to anything properly describable as a conservative tradition in America. Today, as the twenty-first century gets under way, the question of which of a variety of self-proclaimed conservative movements—Old Right, New Right, Beltway Right, neoconservative, paleoconservative—most accurately represents an historically verifiable cultural and political tradition that all but the neoconservatives take for granted is the passionately contested issue. Joseph Scotchie (1956–) is a Brooklyn newspaper man and author whose previous books include *Barbarians in the Saddle: An Intellectual Biography of Richard M. Weaver,* biographies of Patrick Buchanan and Thomas Wolfe, and the edited collection *The Paleoconservatives: New Voices of the Old Right.* Unequivocally, Scotchie identifies the smallest, least-funded, and most contemned of them all—the paleoconservatives—as the true inheritors of a uniquely American conservatism, to which they have added something of their own and to which their rivals are only pretenders.

The Beltway, or Mainstream, Right is the Republican Right, the Careerist Right, the Placeholders' Right, the Jobbers' Right, with which the neoconservative Right—the Right as it was reimagined, re-created, and reintroduced in the 1970s and 1980s by prudent renegades from the Old Left—is interlocked. The New Right, also dating from the 1970s, is the Populist Right, the Country and Western Socialist Right, which, after having enjoyed a certain success in the early 1980s, was steamrollered by the better organized and far better funded neoconservatives and barely exists today (though echoes of its voice emanate at times from the so-called Christian Right). Arguably, the Old Right had its beginnings in the anti-Federalism of Patrick Henry (who opposed ratification of the U.S. Constitution), John Dickinson, John Randolph, and the Jeffersonian Republicans, and went on to develop the case for regional autonomy and, eventually, secession in the antebellum period.

Around the turn of the twentieth century, the Old Right opposed American imperialism, which it considered destructive of republican institutions; two decades later, it resisted the interventionist impulse that took the United States into World War I and, following the war, the internationalist temptation, represented by the League of Nations. This political tendency, or movement, Scotchie terms the First Old Right; precursor to the Old Right that had its beginnings in the anticommunist Dies Committee (later infamous as the House Un-American Activities Committee), the Liberty League organized to fight the New Deal, and the America First Committee, which before Pearl Harbor opposed America's entry into World War II. During the postwar era, the Old Right advocated containment—or, better yet, rollback—of the Soviet empire and extirpation of communist subversives at home. In the 1950s, it battled the civil rights movement as an enemy of states' rights, property rights, and local custom; in the late 1960s and 1970s, it defended religion, traditional values, and Western culture against the irreligion, amoralism, and nihilism of the New Left and the age of Aquarius.

At that point, the neoconservatives—in those days, mostly former socialist academics alarmed by black racialism and the New

Left's hostility to Israel—converged on the Old Right from the Old Left. With the mingling of the two camps, the Old Right began to accommodate its positions to the "responsible" and "realistic" politics of the newcomers, who accepted as axiomatic the propositions that the welfare state created by the New Deal was forever; that the days of the old European America were over (thank God!); and that the United States of America is not a true nation but a "proposition country," taking its character from an ideology of universal freedom and equality rather than from the nature of a particular people and the quality of their historic civilization. As a response to the hijacking of the Old Right by neoconservatism, what Joseph Scotchie calls the New Old Right (or paleoconservatism), early in the 1980s, began to take form.

Scotchie is among the few observers who recognize that paleoconservatism is more than a rescue version, a last-ditch recreation of the Old Right: that, in reacting against the peculiar historical situation in which it finds itself, it has rather added something of its own. To begin with, there is its identification of mass immigration from the Third World as the preeminent threat in our time to American security and identity. "In many respects," Scotchie suggests, "immigration [is] to the [New] Old Right what anticommunism was to the Buckleyites [of the Old Right]." The accuracy of this judgment is demonstrated by the fact that the paleoconservatives' allegedly "racist" stand against immigration amounts to the opposition's Exhibit A against paleoconservatism, as "hysterical" anticommunism was the preferred charge against the Old Right from the 1930s up until Richard M. Nixon's and Henry Kissinger's policy of détente with the Soviet Union in the 1970s.

The internecine Cold War over immigration escalated overnight to a battle royal in 1989, when *Chronicles: A Magazine of American Culture* presented the restrictionist case in its March number, described by an observer as "one of the most controversial issues . . . in the history of American conservative journalism." In response, the Beltway Right threatened the Rockford Institute, *Chronicles'* publisher, with the economic and political equivalent of nuclear annihilation, and contributing foundations on the neoconservative Right cut Rockford off without a penny. Well before 1989, however, paleoconservatism was up and running—and with more horses than immigration in their race.

The paleoconservative movement grew directly from what the novelist Walker Percy once jokingly referred to as the Chapel Hill Conspiracy; three of its intellectual leaders—Thomas Fleming, Clyde N. Wilson, and Samuel Francis—having attended the University of North Carolina together in the 1970s. In 1979, Wilson and Fleming founded *Southern Partisan Quarterly Review*. Although the magazine ceased publication after only two numbers and passed soon after from the founding editors' hands, *Southern Partisan* did help to establish regionalism, decentralization, and local control as signature themes of the paleoconservative critique of mass culture and the centralized American superstate. Other themes (in addition to immigration) developed by paleoconservative writers over the past two decades include an emphasis on the American civilization's classical, Christian, and west European antecedents; the necessity for reform of the educational system and curriculum and, short of that, the need to encourage alternative means of education, including home schooling; the virtues of America's protectionist history, wholly at odds with the Mainstream Right's idolization of free trade; and the associated evils of corporate capitalism, crusading democratism, globalism, and empire. Lastly, there is the insistence that what passes today for "conservatism," or "the Right," is no more than a cynical capitulation to postmodern liberalism, disguised as phony oppositionism.

Paleoconservatives have suffered the consequences naturally entailed by their opposition to the philosophy and agenda of the Establishment, Left and Right. Treated as pariahs and dismissed as reactionary cranks when not ignored as nonpersons, they have paid for their independence in place, preferment, and exposure. Their political figurehead and three-time presidential candidate, Patrick Buchanan, while somehow maintaining his journalistic career intact, has been subjected to political attacks unprecedented in American politics for their vehemence and viciousness during the course of his campaigns. So it is with reason that Joseph Scotchie predicts "the Old Right faces a long road ahead." "Every day," he concludes,

> is Monday. Pessimism aside, the rejuvenated Old Right and its worldview provides [sic] enormous benefits to those Americans willing to listen. Paleoconservatism amounts to a thorough education in Western and American history: where America came from, what the nation was intended to become, what it has disintegrated into, and how Americans might find their way back. American "exceptionalism" does not mean abstractions like democratic capitalism, but simply republican living. A republic means self-reliant citizens, like those early Americans "too proud and too poor" to live under a monarchy. It also means citizens who are active in the lives of their community and nation. The Old Right hopes to stir up the defiance of those "insubordinate Americans" who nourish the tree of liberty with their occasional rebellions. Paleos know that only a minority of peoples (not a "silent" majority) ever makes a true revolution. The road back to a republic is a hard one. Still, it is an American heritage most worth saving.

No cause is ever lost, because none is ever won, said T. S. Eliot.

49

THE POWER OF THE POSITIVE WOMAN

by Phyllis Schlafly

1977

A grande dame of the Old Right, Phyllis Schlafly (1924–) was despised as Public Enemy Number One in the 1970s and 1980s by the women's liberation movement, which has always cultivated hatred as if it were a black orchid. In the eyes of the "libbers" (as feminists were then called), Schlafly was a traitor to her sex: The person most singly responsible for the defeat of the Equal Rights Amendment, which thanks to her is today as obscure as the Volstead Act. An attorney and the mother of six children as well as a writer, Schlafly is the best-selling author of *A Choice Not an Echo,* among other books, and a journalist whose syndicated political column continues in existence after many years. Unlike so many successful conservative writers and activists of her generation, she has steadfastly resisted the temptation to sign on with the modern pseudo-conservative movement, declare victory, and announce that all is now for the best in the best of all possible worlds. Only recently, indeed, Schlafly observed to the *Washington Times* that "[w]e won the battle against communism, but we've largely lost the battle against big government and we've lost lots of our liberties." Stonewall Schlafly has never yielded ground to anyone, left or right.

The Power of the Positive Woman was published in 1977, when "Women's Lib" and the Equal Rights Amendment (ERA) were Very Big Things. While the subject of the book is not the ERA itself, *Positive Woman* was written under the threat of that imminent assault on the Constitution, and so it is with this threat in mind that the reader should approach the book today, nearly thirty years later. If some of Schlafly's material—and her response to it—seem dated, we need to remember that the libbers, having failed to counter her rebuttals with fit rejoinders of their own, have simply moved on, advancing the argument to levels of increased abstraction at which they hope its plausibility will seem enhanced. Ironically, the movement has treated itself to a facelift by reverting to the terminology of a century and more ago: Women's libbers call themselves "feminists" now. Schlafly, for her part, is usually careful to attack "libbers," not feminists, while implying that an older generation of feminists—for example, the suffragettes—properly took feminism as far as feminism should go, and no further. Here, perhaps, she can be faulted for conceding too much to the opposition. (A strong argument against female suffrage holds that families, not individuals, should be represented at the polls, by a vote of *one*.) The fact remains that modern-day feminism is among those toxic ideological "rights" movements, inspired by the civil rights crusades of the 1950s and 1960s and including homosexualism, environmentalism, disablism, animal rights, and all the rest. Feminists, like homosexualists, are working to realize a world that represents the moral, social, physical, and metaphysical inversion of human existence as it has existed from its African origins until the day before yesterday.

The broader theme of *The Power of the Positive Woman* is the personal ruin such an inversion offers women and the catastrophic prospect it implies for society; the narrower one the immediate danger presented by the ERA. As Phyllis Schlafly (with her legal mind) read the amendment, it would accomplish none of the good its more naïve proponents expected from it, and even

more evil than the "drastic reduction in the rights of the home-
maker" its destructive designers intended.

"The fundamental error of the Equal Rights Amendment,"
Schlafly argues, "is that it will mandate the gender-free, rigid, absolute equality of treatment of men and women under every federal and state law, bureaucratic regulation, and court decision,
and in every aspect of our lives that is touched directly or indirectly by public funding. This is what the militant women's liber-
ationists want and are working for with passionate and persistent
determination." Even its advocates admit, when pressed, that the
ERA would not give women any rights beyond those enumerated
in the Equal Employment Opportunity Act of 1972, which pro-
hibited discrimination on the basis of sex hiring, in pay, and in
promotion. As for what Schlafly calls the "tiresome litany of com-
plaints" that women lack the right to vote, are barred from serving on juries, and turned away from the professional schools, "All
those past discriminations were remedied years ago, or decades
ago, or even generations ago. They have no relevance to present-
day America."

Women naïve enough to believe the Orwellian slogan "Equal
Pay for Equal Work!" are, she insists, in for an unpleasant surprise. Because what the Equal Rights Amendment *would* do is
invalidate every state law requiring a husband to support his
wife and family, by making any law that would impose an obligation on one sex without imposing it equally upon the other unconstitutional. Readily admitting that it is impossible to predict
how the courts, the state legislature, and Congress will interpret
and enforce the notion of "equality," Schlafly suggests that this,
precisely, is the problem. Why should a legal determination not
be made that husband and wife must each contribute 50 percent of the family's income or that each should work for half of
every week, or half of each year, in alternation with the other?
The amendment's supporters, she reminds us, are frank in conceding that a woman, by accepting support from her husband, is
obliged to support him in turn. Thus, the ERA, so far from as-
suring women of greater "fairness" in marriage, would doubly

burden her, by adding financial obligation to the responsibilities of motherhood and housekeeping. One thing at least is clear, Schlafly insists: "Whichever of these alternative versions of equality might ultimately become the rule under ERA, it would bring a drastic reduction in the rights of the wife and a radical loosening of the legal bonds that tend to keep the family together. . . . The moral, social, and legal evil of ERA is that it provides as a constitutional mandate that the husband no longer has the primary duty to support his wife and children."

The most charitable explanation for the determination of a minority of women to impose hardship, unhappiness, and confusion upon the majority is that they hoped, or believed, that only from such travail could the New Woman finally emerge. This project, of course, is congruent with the Left's ambition to re-create mankind and reinvent reality itself. Schlafly, however, has no desire to be either re-created or reinvented, and she is convinced that the majority of women—including very much what she calls the Positive Woman—doesn't either.

The Positive Woman, for Phyllis Schlafly, is she who does not regard having been born female as a foul blow, her biological fertility as a fact of cosmic unfairness, differences between the sexes as illusory, and the division of the sex roles the result of historical conspiracy. Instead, "[t]he Positive Woman looks upon her femaleness and her fertility as part of her purpose, her potential, and her power. She rejoices that she has a capability for creativity that men can never have." In result, the Positive Woman, unlike her whining, self-pitying, and self-destructive sisters, has "found the road and possess[es] the map" that allows her to "[love] life as a woman and [live] love as a woman, whose credentials are from the school of practical experience and who has learned that fulfillment as a woman is a journey, not a destination."

Schlafly includes in her book a passage from Alexis de Toqueville's *Democracy in America* that does not receive nearly the attention it should. Tocqueville, after commenting unfavorably on an intellectual and social movement afoot in Europe that would make men and women "not only equal but alike," notes that nothing can result from this agenda but "weak men and disorderly women." He goes on to contrast with this madness the sane and wholesome view taken in respect of *la différence* by the Americans, who accept the sexes for what they are and refuse the attempt to make greatly dissimilar beings do nearly the same things. "The Americans," Tocqueville notes admiringly, "have applied to the sexes the great principle of political economy which governs the manufacturers of our age, by carefully dividing the duties of men from those of woman in order that the great work of society may be carried on."

"As for myself," this wisest of Frenchmen concludes,

I do not hesitate to avow that although the women of the United States are confined within the narrow circle of domestic life, and their situation is in some respects one of extreme dependence, I have nowhere seen a woman occupying a loftier position; and if I were asked, now that I am drawing to the close of this work, in which I have spoken of so many important things done by the Americans, to what the singular prosperity and growing strength of that people ought mainly to be attributed, I should reply: to the superiority of their women.

Their Positive Women, of course.

50

TREASON: LIBERAL TREACHERY FROM THE COLD WAR TO THE WAR ON TERRORISM

by Ann Coulter

2003

Liberals have a preternatural gift for striking a position on the side of treason. You could be talking about Scrabble and they would instantly leap to the anti-American position. Everyone says liberals love America, too. No they don't. Whenever the nation is under attack, from within or without, liberals side with the enemy. This is their essence. The left's obsession with the crimes of the West and their Rousseauian respect for Third World savages all flow from this subversive goal. If anyone has the gaucherie to point out the left's nearly unblemished record of rooting against America, liberals turn around and scream "McCarthyism!"

Liberals deserve every bad thing Ann Coulter (1961–), the entertaining columnist and television personality, has to say about them—and more, if so many kilobytes could be crowded into a single hard drive. And her forthright defense of Senator Joseph McCarthy, nearly half a century after his death, is as refreshing as it is well-founded and commendable. (There *were* communists in the State Department; McCarthy, as Joseph Sobran pointed out

311

years ago, did very few people, if anyone, significant damage; while it was Hollywood, not the government, who drew up and enforced the notorious blacklists.) Though Coulter's rhetoric is hyperbolic, her charges are not. Indeed, *Treason: Liberal Treachery from the Cold War to the War on Terrorism* is in an important sense an understatement, rather than an exaggeration, of the reality she describes. The state of American politics is worse, not better, than Coulter thinks, for the reason that the enemy is larger, more comprehensive, and more dangerous than she understands (or is willing to admit). Coulter's career is important by way of demonstrating how much forthright and courageous antiliberalism can accomplish in combating the Left. It suggests also that antiliberalism, of itself, is not enough.

Coulter is justifiably angry that liberals, having permitted communists to infiltrate the State Department in the 1930s, 1940s, and 1950s, defended them at the time—and still defend them. I suspect she would agree with James Burnham that liberals and communists are ideologically related, differing mainly in point of location along the same continuum. No one is better at attacking liberals than Coulter, unless it is the radio broadcaster Rush Limbaugh. Neither Limbaugh nor Coulter, however, is prepared to recognize that liberalism is no longer coterminous with the Democratic Party: that, since the 1980s, many liberals have become Republicans, that no small few of these Republicans are "neoconservatives," and that the neoconservatives are today's "mainline" conservatives. The problem with Coulter is that, as a mainline conservative herself, she is very much a team player in the seemingly endless (and essentially meaningless) rivalry between the Republican Reds and the Democratic Blues that amounts to the American political game today. She's won her red jersey and she isn't going to compromise it for anything—not even, apparently, for the purpose of writing books that are even more comprehensive, politically insightful, and creatively destructive than those she has already written. Which seems a pity.

"The fundamental difference," Coulter writes, "between liberals and conservatives is: Conservatives believe man was created in

God's image; liberals believe they *are* God. All their other behavioral tics proceed from this one irreducible minimum. Liberals believe they can murder the unborn because they are gods. They try to forcibly create 'equality' through affirmative action and wealth redistribution because they are gods. . . . They revere the U.N. and not the U.S. because they aren't Americans—they are gods."

Not a line of that paragraph is exceptionable; the enveloping indictment and the sentiment behind it alike are beyond reproach. But consider the kind of "conservative" Ann Coulter endorses and indeed represents. A fierce supporter of George W. Bush's War on Terror, she is an enthusiast as well for the Iraqi War because "we could beat [Saddam]." Vice President Richard Cheney, one of the chief architects and advocates of the war, had engraved on his Christmas card for 2003 a quotation from Benjamin Franklin: "And if a sparrow cannot fall to the ground without His notice, is it probable that an empire can rise without His aid?" As of early 2004, the Bush administration is proposing to legalize as many as fourteen million illegal aliens and to extend Social Security to the Republic of Mexico. A nation of gods, apparently, is entitled by its power to war against anyone it can beat, reconstruct the world politically in accordance with its own beliefs and institutions, admit one-half of the world and support the other half from its largesse—and be rewarded by the cooperative interference of the God above all gods! This attitude represents liberalism raised to the power of Jacobinism; but Coulter will not see it. Hating liberals as she does, she cannot perceive when a variety of liberal (the anti-imperial kind) is right—albeit for all the wrong reasons, or even by accident.

"Americans cannot comprehend how their fellow countrymen could not love their country. But the left's anti-Americanism is intrinsic to their entire worldview. Liberals promote the rights of Islamic fanatics for the same reason they promote the rights of adulterers, pornographers, abortionists, criminals, and Communists. They instinctively root for anarchy and against civilization. The inevitable logic of the liberal position is to be for treason."

Once again, the argument is correct—so far as it goes. Two

points, however, need to be made regarding it. The first is that liberals, so far from having a logic that is "inevitable," in fact have no logic at all. The second is that liberals are not, primarily or fundamentally, against civilization, they are against reality. And that goes for all liberals, whether they call themselves liberals—or "conservatives," "neo," or otherwise.

INDEX

ABOUT THE AUTHOR

Chilton Williamson, Jr., has been History Editor for St. Martin's Press, and Senior and Literary Editor for *National Review*. Currently, he is Senior Editor for Books at *Chronicles: A Magazine of American Culture* to which he contributes two regular columns, "The Hundredth Meridian" and "What's Wrong with the World." Additionally, he is the author of a number of works of fiction, nonfiction, and narrative nonfiction. Raised in New York City and Vermont, Williamson now lives in Laramie, Wyoming, with his wife, the former Maureen McCaffrey.